# Critical Incident Stress Debriefing
**An Operations Manual for CISD,
Defusing and Other Group Crisis Intervention Services**

*Third edition*

**Jeffrey T. Mitchell, Ph.D., CTS**
*University of Maryland*

**George S. Everly, Jr., Ph.D., CTS, F.A.P.M.**
*Johns Hopkins University
Loyola College in Maryland*

Chevron Publishing Corporation
5018 Dorsey Hall Drive
Suite 104
Ellicott City, MD 21042
(410) 740-0065

About the cover

A San Jose, California paramedic / firefighter comforts a police officer who risked his life attempting to rescue a child, but was beaten back by intense heat and smoke. The child died in the blaze.

Editorial / Production Supervision and Interior Design: Diane Gwin
Editorial Assistance: Kathlean Conneely and Peggy Johnson
Cover Design and Layout: Diane Gwin

Chevron Publishing Corporation, Ellicott City, Maryland

©1993, 1995, 1996, 1997 by Chevron Publishing Corporation
Published 1993.  Third edition 2001
Printed in the United States of America

Photo credits: cover – Angela Pancrazio
(courtesy San Jose Mercury News)

Library of Congress Card Catalogue Number
Application in process
ISBN 1-883581-19-2

Chevron Publishing Corporation
5018 Dorsey Hall Drive
Suite 104
Ellicott City, Maryland 21042
(410) 740-0065

*" ... but this I do know*
*you who will be truly happy*
*are those who will have sought for and found*
*a way to serve."*

- **Albert Schweitzer**

# DEDICATIONS

*To Shannon and Kyla who are my delight, my joy and my life.*

*Jeffrey T. Mitchell*

*To my children Marideth, George and Andrea, may you know only health, peace and happiness*

*George S. Everly, Jr.*

# ACKNOWLEDGEMENTS

The most dreaded part of writing any book is when it comes time to write the acknowledgements section. Every author knows that there are many people who supported the overall effort. The opportunity to acknowledge them is small, but the chance of inadvertently overlooking them in the final rush to meet publication deadlines is great.

Before we make feeble attempts to acknowledge a few individuals who have supported us and cared for us, we will first acknowledge that there are many thousands of unnamed people around the world who have contributed small bits and pieces to this work. Indeed, it is by their interest in the field of Critical Incident Stress Management and in this particular work that appropriate changes, additions and clarifications have been made. We are indebted to the thousands of people who serve on CISM teams in over seven hundred communities in twenty-eight countries. Their pooled experiences are reflected in the pages of this book. So, to all the unnamed, but much appreciated people who have given so much to us over these many years, we salute you. Naming each of you would be an impossible volume in itself. We thank each of you for all you have given.

Next, we turn our attention to our families who have tolerated our long hours away from them, but who continue to care for us and nurture us. They have always been there when we needed them the most. They have also contributed in many more ways than they know to this latest edition. We are humbled by their love for us and by their generous support of all our endeavors.

Diane Gwin and Kathlean Conneely of Chevron Publishing Corporation have been terrific throughout the entire publication process. So has Peggy Johnson who laid out the work and prepared it for production. They have worked countless hours on short deadlines trying to make this edition the very best. The pressure to put this book together in the midst of all their other duties was overwhelming. But their spirited support of the project made it a success.

Thank you to all of you who have believed in the work of Critical Incident Stress Management. But, most especially, thank you to all whom have believed in us personally and who have supported us with your loyalty, friendship and love. We are forever grateful.

Jeffrey T. Mitchell and George S. Everly, Jr.

# Contents

## Chapter 7
## DEMOBILIZATION

## Chapter 8
## CRISIS MANAGEMENT BRIEFING (CMB)

# TABLES

# FIGURES

**Appendix A**

# Chapter 1

# AN INTRODUCTION TO CRITICAL INCIDENT STRESS MANAGEMENT (CISM)

## INTRODUCTION

This book is designed to be an operational treatise on how to preserve and enhance the most important resource any organization or society possesses - the human resource. Preserving and enhancing human resources is a difficult enough task in the face of the normal stress and strain of living in the twenty first century. It becomes even more challenging when the human resources routinely face risks and working conditions well outside the usual realm of human endeavor. Having made that assertion, several professions immediately come to mind: emergency service personnel, public safety personnel, emergency communications personnel, military personnel, nurses, physicians and disaster workers. Few are likely to argue with the assertion that these individuals routinely find themselves in uniquely stressful, high risk and potentially traumatizing pursuits as part of their paid or volunteer careers. But the risk of traumatization is no longer limited to "high risk" professions. It seems as if we are all at some degree of risk. Terrorist bombings, airline disasters, school shootings, "road rage," workplace violence, "airline rage," traffic accidents, railroad disasters, and community violence are but some of the factors which contribute to a growing interest in emergency mental health initiatives, especially crisis intervention. Indeed, it has been estimated that 90% of American adults will be confronted by a traumatic event during the course of their lifetime.

While there have been substantial advances in the treatment of occupational stress and posttraumatic disorders in recent years (see Everly and Lating, 1995), there is a compelling logic that argues for efforts to be directed toward prevention of stress and posttraumatic syndromes. This is so espe-

*1*

cially among the high risk professions we have just enumerated (Butcher, 1980; Kentsmith, 1980; Yandrick, 1990; Mitchell and Bray, 1990). The Critical Incident Stress Management (CISM) program is specifically designed to mitigate and, if possible, prevent the development of dysfunctional and potentially disabling posttraumatic syndromes and stress disorders. We offer this text as a guide for understanding the most widely used crisis intervention system in the world, the Critical Incident Stress Management (CISM) approach to crisis intervention, while at the same time providing a step-by-step guide for the implementation of the most common group crisis intervention components of the CISM model: Critical Incident Stress Debriefing (CISD), defusing, the "crisis management briefing" (CMB) and demobilization.

## KEY TERMS AND CONCEPTS

One of the founding fathers of psychosomatic medicine, George Engel, noted that rational discourse is predicated upon the consistent use of terms. As da Vinci once said, "First study the science, then practice the art." In order to guide the reader through the subsequent chapters of this text, we will begin with a brief introduction to the terms which will recur and serve as an essential platform for understanding the principles of CISM and the group crisis interventions which will follow.

**STRESS** - Stress is a response characterized by physical and psychological arousal arising as a direct result of an exposure to any demand or pressure on a living organism. The more significant the demand, the more intense the stress reaction will be. Some stress is actually positive. Stress reactions which are moderate are actually helpful in that they motivate us to make positive changes, grow and achieve goals. When stress is helpful, it is called "eustress." When stress reactions are prolonged or excessive, they can cause harm. The destructive nature of stress is called "distress." Stress is perhaps best thought of as the sum total of "wear and tear" (Selye, 1956, 1974) and as such may be thought of as accelerating the aging process.

**STRESSOR** - A stressor is any event acting as a stimulus which places a demand upon a person, a group, or an organization. Mild stressors produce a mild stress reaction and severe stressors produce excessive stress reactions. More will be said about stress and stressors in Chapter 2, the Nature of Human Stress.

**TARGET ORGAN STRAIN** - Target organ strain is defined as the adverse effect of stress on the mind and/or the body. It is often described as the symptoms of wear and tear on the somatic and psychological systems. Target organ strain can result from excessively intense stress and/or excessively chronic stress (Everly, 1989).

**CRITICAL INCIDENT** – A critical incident is a stressor event (crisis event) which appears to cause, or be most associated with, a crisis response; an event which overwhelms a person's usual coping mechanisms (Everly & Mitchell, 1999). The most severe forms of critical incidents may be considered traumatic incidents.

**CRITICAL INCIDENT STRESS** - Critical incident stress is the stress reaction a person or group has to a critical incident. Critical incident stress is characterized by a wide range of cognitive, physical, emotional, and behavioral signs and symptoms. Most people recover from critical incident stress within a few weeks.

**CRISIS** – Crisis is an acute response to an event wherein:
• psychological homeostasis (balance) has been disrupted;
• one's usual coping mechanisms have failed; and
• there are signs and/or symptoms of distress, dysfunction, or impairment (Caplan, 1961, 1964).

**COGNITIVE IMPAIRMENT IN CRISIS** – It has been commonly observed that individuals in crisis routinely exhibit an acute cognitive dysfunction. This phenomenon has been referred to by terms such as cognitive distortion, cortical inhibition syndrome, and even the " dumbing down" effect. This may serve as an explanation for many of the "irrational," or "illogical" things people do in a crisis. A common cognitive error that is made by primary victims is a failure to understand the consequences of their actions while in a crisis state. Thus, people in crisis may be seen to act quite impulsively and often self-defeatingly. Similarly, those interventionists who commonly work with secondary victims, i.e., rescue workers, police and fire personnel, emergency medical personnel, and disaster workers, may prosper from the recognition that these professionals are often likely to make a second cognitive error of faulty self-attribution, i.e., they are likely to blame themselves for adverse outcome when no such causal attribution is appropriate.

**TRAUMA** – Trauma is an event outside the usual realm of human experience that would be markedly distressing to anyone who experienced it. In the most recent version of the Diagnostic and Statistical Manual of Mental

Disorders (DSM-IV; APA, 1994), a trauma is defined exclusively in terms of the exposure to human suffering, i.e., personal or vicarious exposure to severe injury, illness, or death. A trauma, therefore, may be seen as a more narrow form of critical incident.

**TRAUMATIC STRESS** - Traumatic stress is the stress response produced when a person is exposed to a disturbing traumatic event. "Traumatic stress" may be thought of as a subset of critical incident stress (Mitchell, Bray, 1990; Everly, 1989); the traumatic stress reaction may be immediate or delayed.

**POSTTRAUMATIC STRESS DISORDER (PTSD)** - PTSD is a formally recognized psychiatric disorder which may result from an exposure to a "traumatic event" (APA, 1980, 1987, 1994). Posttraumatic stress disorder is identified by three characteristic clusters of symptoms which follow a psychological trauma:
  • Intrusive recollections of the trauma
  • Physiological arousal,
  • Numbing / withdrawal / avoidance
The traumatic event is one that is closely associated with threatened or actual physical injury or death and produces intense fear, horror or helplessness (APA, 1994).

**CRISIS INTERVENTION** – Crisis intervention is the urgent and acute psychological support sometimes thought of as "emotional first-aid." The hallmarks of crisis intervention have historically been **immediacy** (early intervention), **proximity** (intervention is often done within close physical proximity to the critical incident), **expectancy** (both person in distress and interventionist have the expectation that the intervention will be acute and directed toward the goal of symptom stabilization and reduction, not cure), **simplicity** (relatively concrete, uncomplicated intervention strategies that avoid complex psychotherapy-oriented tactics), and **brevity** (the total duration of the intervention is short, typically consisting of one to three contacts). The goals of crisis intervention are:

• Acute stabilization of symptoms and signs of distress and dysfunction (to keep things from getting worse);

• Facilitation of symptom reduction (intervention aimed at the reduction of acute distress and dysfunction);

• Facilitation of a restoration of acute, adaptive independent functioning (successful reduction of impairment);

• Facilitation of an access to a higher or more continuous level of care, if needed (Caplan, 1961, 1964; Everly & Mitchell, 1999).

**CRITICAL INCIDENT STRESS MANAGEMENT (CISM)** is a comprehensive, integrated, multi-component crisis intervention system (Everly & Mitchell, 1999; Flannery, 1998). It has been recommended by the Occupational Safety and Health Administration (OSHA) and utilized by organizations such as the U.S. Air Force, U.S. Coast Guard, Airline Pilots' Association, U.S. Navy, the Bureau of Alcohol, Tobacco and Firearms (ATF), the Federal Bureau of Investigation (FBI), the Australian Navy, the Australian Army, the Hospital Authority of Hong Kong, the Armed Forces of Singapore, and numerous law enforcement agencies, fire departments, school systems, employee assistance programs, and hospitals throughout North America, Scandinavia, Europe, Australia, and/or Asia (see Everly & Mitchell, 1999). Just as a good golfer would never play a round of golf with only one golf club, a good crisis interventionist would never attempt the complex task of intervention in a crisis or disaster with only one crisis intervention technology. As noted above, CISM is an integrated, multi-component crisis intervention system. Table 1.1 summarizes the core elements of the CISM approach to crisis intervention.

The core crisis intervention components of the CISM system are further described below:

• **Pre-incident preparation.** Pre-incident preparation may be thought of as a form of psychological "immunization." The goal is to strengthen potential vulnerabilities and enhance psychological resiliency in individuals who may be at risk for psychological crises and/or psychological traumatization. One important aspect of pre-incident preparation is the provision of information. Sir Francis Bacon once noted, "Information itself is power." Many crises and traumas result from a violation of expectancy. Thus setting realistic expectations serves to protect against violated assumptions. But pre-incident preparation also consists of behavioral response preparation and rehearsal. This includes familiarization with common stressors, stress management education, stress resistance training, and crisis mitigation training for line personnel as well as management.

• Disaster or large scale crisis intervention programs including **demobilizations, staff advisement, and crisis management briefings (CMB)**. The demobilization is an opportunity for temporary psychological "decompression" immediately after exposure to a critical incident. This technique was originally developed for use by emergency services personnel. Staff

**TABLE 1.1**

Critical Incident Stress Management (CISM): The Core Components
(Adapted from: Everly and Mitchell, 1999)

| INTERVENTION | TIMING | ACTIVATION | GOAL | FORMAT |
|---|---|---|---|---|
| 1. Pre-crisis preparation. | Pre-crisis phase. | Crisis anticipation. | Set expectations, Improve coping, Stress management. | Groups/ Orgs. |
| 2a Demobilizations & staff consultation (rescuers). | Shift disengage-ment. | Event driven. | To inform and consult, allow psychological decompression. Stress management. | Large groups/ Orgs. |
| 2b Crisis Management Briefing (CMB) (civilians, schools, business). | Anytime | | | |
| 3. Defusing. | Post-crisis (within 12 hours). | Usually symptom driven. | Symptom mitigation. Possible closure. Triage. | Small groups. |
| 4. Critical Incident Stress Debriefing (CISD) | Post-crisis (1 to 10 days; 3-4 weeks mass disasters) | Usually symptom driven; can be event driven. | Facilitate psychological closure. Sx mitigation. Triage. | Small groups. |
| 5. Individual crisis intervention (1:1). | Anytime, Anywhere. | Symptom sdriven | Symptom mitigation. Return to function, if possible. Referral, if needed. | Individuals. |
| 6. Pastoral Crisis Intervention. | Anytime, Anywhere. | Whenever needed. | Provide spiritual, faith-based support. | Individuals, Groups. |
| 7a Family CISM. | Anytime. | Either symptom driven or event driven. | Foster support & communications. Symptom mitigation. Closure, if possible. Referral, if needed. | Families/ Orgs. |
| 7b Organizational consultation. | | | | |
| 8. Follow-up/ Referral. | Anytime. | Usually symptom driven. | Assess mental status. Access higher level of care, if needed. | Individuals/ Family. |

[From : Everly, G. & Mitchell, J. (1999) Critical Incident Stress Management (CISM): A New Era and Standard of Care in Crisis Intervention. Ellicott City, MD: Chevron Publishing.]

advisement refers to the provision of psychological consultations to command staff (emergency services personnel, military, disaster response teams), as well as management personnel in business and industrial settings. The crisis management briefing (CMB) refers to a four-step crisis intervention for large groups of individuals (up to 300 at one time). The CMB is ideal for responding to terrorism, school crisis events, business and industrial crisis events, community violence, and mass disasters (see Everly, 2000a; Newman, 2000).

• **Defusing**. This is a 3-phase, 45 minute, structured small group discussion provided within hours of a crisis for purposes of assessment, triaging, and acute symptom mitigation. In some cases, the defusing may do much to foster psychological closure after a critical incident.

• **Critical Incident Stress Debriefing (CISD)** is a proper noun referring to a specific model of psychological debriefing. The CISD is a 7-phase, structured group discussion, usually provided 1 to 14 days post-crisis (although in mass disasters it may be used three weeks or more post-incident). This form of group crisis intervention was developed by Jeffrey T. Mitchell, Ph.D. The CISD is designed to achieve the goal of psychological closure subsequent to a critical incident or traumatic event, or similarly serve as a forum for psychological triaging so as to facilitate access to a higher level of psychological support. Psychological closure, operationally, is generally thought to mean a facilitation of psychological and behavioral rebuilding in the wake of a crisis or trauma. The CISD is designed to be used with small groups of 4 to 25 participants, although 8 to 10 seems ideal. It is facilitated by the members of the "CISD team," usually consisting of 2 to 4 specially trained crisis interventionists.

The CISD begins with a set of introductory remarks which set the tone for the debriefing, motivate the participants to accept and cooperate with the process and establish the working rules for the discussion. The second phase of the CISD is the fact phase in which the participants describe what happened during the incident. The third phase is the thought phase in which the participants are asked about their first or most prominent thoughts while they were going through the incident. The reaction phase is the fourth phase. Here the participants discuss the elements of the situation which were the worst for them. The signals or symptoms of distress which were encountered during or after the critical incident are described in the fifth phase of the CISD, which is called the symptom phase. During the sixth phase, the teaching phase, team leaders and peer debriefers spend a fair amount of time providing information and suggestions which can be used to reduce the impact of the stress. In the seventh and final phase, re-entry, participants' questions are answered and loose ends are tied up. The last phase of the debriefing is where the intervention team summarizes the group discussion, attempts to facilitate closure, and responds to any remaining concerns.

The CISD is commonly confused with other "psychological debriefing" techniques which remain without standardization and are ill-defined (Dyregrov, 1997, 1998, 1999; Everly and Mitchell, 1999). The CISD intervention remains the only consistently validated form of group psychological debriefing (Everly & Boyle, 1999; Everly & Piacentini, 1999; Watchorn, 2000; Deahl, et al., 2000).

Due to its structure, the CISD may take up to two to three hours to complete. The CISD will sometimes be used subsequent to the crisis management briefing and the defusing. The CISD is almost always followed by intervention on an individual basis with those individuals who require such. Referral for more formal mental health intervention may then follow if necessary.

Although the aforementioned points may seem rather straightforward, historically there has been some confusion as to the actual nature of CISD. So a brief historical review seems useful at this point. Originally, Mitchell (1983) used the term CISD to refer to an overarching approach to crisis intervention which contained four elements:

a) individual or group on-scene crisis intervention,

b) initial small group discussions referred to as "defusings,"

c) formal 6-phase small group discussions referred to as the "formal CISD," and

d) follow-up services.

As can be imagined, the author's use of the term CISD to denote a) the overarching crisis intervention approach, as well as b) the "formal" 6-phase group discussion process, led to significant confusion. Later the term CISD as the label for the overarching crisis intervention system was abandoned in favor of the term Critical Incident Stress Management (CISM; Everly & Mitchell, 1999). More recently, the term CISD was reserved for a 7-phase group crisis intervention designed to facilitate psychological closure (rebuilding) subsequent to a critical incident or traumatic event for primary, secondary, and even tertiary participants.

• **One-on-one crisis intervention/counseling** or psychological support throughout the full range of the crisis spectrum (this is the most frequently used of the CISM interventions) typically consists of 1 to 3 contacts with an individual who is in crisis. Each contact may last from 15 minutes to more than 2 hours depending upon the nature and severity of the crisis. Although flexible and efficient, this form of crisis intervention lacks the added advantage of group process. Because of its extreme time-limited nature, it is especially important with this intervention, as with all crisis interventions, to avoid using paradoxical interventions, interpretation of unconscious processes, or confrontational techniques (see Everly & Mitchell, 1999).

• **Pastoral crisis intervention** (Everly, 2000b, 2000c), more than ministerial or chaplaincy services, represents the integration of traditional crisis intervention with pastoral-based support services. In addition to traditional crisis intervention tools, pastoral crisis intervention may employ scriptural education, prayer (personal, conjoint, intercessory), rituals and sacraments, and the unique ethos of the pastoral crisis interventionist. A specialized form of crisis intervention, pastoral crisis intervention may not be suited for all persons or all circumstances. Nevertheless, it represents a valuable addition the comprehensive CISM matrix.

• **Family crisis intervention, as well as organizational consultation,** represents crisis intervention at the systems level. Both family and organizational crisis intervention, when done most effectively, will possess proactive (pre-crisis) and reactive elements.

• **Follow-up and referral mechanisms for assessment and treatment**, if necessary. No crisis intervention system is complete without the recognition that some critical incidents are so toxic by their very nature that they will require a more intense and formalized intervention, perhaps even psychotropic medications. Therefore, it is important to build into any crisis intervention system a mechanism for follow-up and guidelines for psychological triage (see Everly, 1999).

The CISM system (Everly & Mitchell, 1999; Flannery, 1998) appears to be the most widely used crisis intervention system in the world and has been validated through narrative reviews (Everly & Mitchell, 1999; Everly, Flannery, & Mitchell, 2000; Flannery & Everly, 2000), as well as statistical reviews (Flannery, Everly & Eyler, 2000; Everly, Flannery & Eyler, in press). It may be suggested that CISM is the emerging standard of care in the crisis intervention field due to its high frequency of utilization and the extent of its empirical validation.

In an age of professional scrutiny and accountability, practitioners must be prepared to utilize the arguable "standard of care" or to defend a lack of adherence to such putative standards. The crisis intervention practitioner is encouraged to practice as current and comprehensive an approach to intervention as is reasonable.

**DEBRIEFING –** A debriefing is the generic term for the CISD process developed by Dr. Jeffrey T. Mitchell (see CISD). It is also a general term to describe a variety of not clearly defined psychological interventions called "psychological debriefings" that are applied in the aftermath of crisis events. It is suggested that greater precision be utilized when using terms such as "debriefing". Failure to be more precise with the utilization of terms produces an atmosphere of confusion in the field of crisis intervention.

**SPECIALTY DEBRIEFINGS** -These debriefing services are provided to people outside an intervention team's normal area of responsibility. The emphasis in such a debriefing is on the educational aspects of the debriefing rather than on the self disclosure aspects of the debriefing. There is usually more emphasis on the role of the mental health professional and less on the

### TABLE 1.2
### GROUP CRISIS INTERVENTIONS

| NAME | TARGET | TIMING | ELEMENTS |
|---|---|---|---|
| Crisis Management Briefing (CMB) | Large groups of primary victims or non-operational personnel. | During and/or after the event. 45-75 minutes duration. | Assembly, Information, Reactions, Coping Resources. |
| Demobilization | Large groups of operational emergency services, rescue, and public safety personnel. | Immediately after shift disengagement. 10-20 minutes duration. | Introduction, Information, Physical nourishment. |
| Defusing | Small groups. (3-20 persons) | 6 to 12 hours post event. 20-45 minutes duration. | Introduction, Exploration, Information. |
| Critical Incident Stress Debriefing (CISD) | Small groups (3-20 persons) | Usually 1 to 10 days post event. 3 to 6 weeks post disaster. 1 to 3 hours duration. | Introduction, Fact, Thought, Reaction, Symptom, Teaching, Re-entry. |

role of the peer support personnel.

**PEER SUPPORT PERSONNEL -** Peer support personnel are the members of the crisis response team whose primary professional training is not in mental health or religious/ spiritual studies. They may be drawn from rescue personnel, fire fighters, law enforcement agents, nursing staff, communications personnel, ATF, corrections, FBI, Marshals' Service, educational staff personnel, or the military. During the last decade, many organizations such as Amtrak, auto manufactures, and most major airlines have trained peer support personnel. Many other businesses and industries are following the example set by other professions in organizing peer support teams. Providing peer support personnel from within the profession is extremely important for stress interventions with groups that are insular, highly cohesive, and/or perceive themselves as very unique compared to the general population. Most commercial organizations usually rely more heavily on the skills of professional mental health support personnel. Occasionally, these organizations will utilize Employee Assistance Programs (EAP) or their own medical staffs to assist with trauma interventions.

**MENTAL HEALTH SUPPORT PERSONNEL -** These support personnel fall under two categories - mental health professionals and clergy. They have special knowledge and skills and have received specialized training within their professional fields. Ordinarily, mental health professionals have academic training, diplomas, certifications, licenses or some other form of recognition of their training and skills. For the clergy, it is expected that they are ordained clergy or appointed chaplains with special documented training and experience. Most hold academic degrees from colleges, universities or seminaries.

Likewise, mental health professionals must have the appropriate education, training and experience in the clinical areas to provide critical incident stress interventions. Mental health professionals are the psychologists, social workers, psychiatrists, psychiatric nurses or certified mental health counselors. The typical mental health professional serving in a professional support position on a critical incident stress team would have at least a master's degree in mental health.

**COMBINED EMERGENCY SERVICES CRITICAL INCIDENT STRESS (CIS) TEAM -** This is a fundamental concept in formulating an emergency services critical incident stress team. It means that there is one CIS team serving the needs of multiple agencies such as law enforcement agencies, hospitals, fire departments, emergency medical service agencies, communication centers, disaster relief personnel, ski patrols, corrections agencies, wild land fire fighters, park service agencies and other first response organizations. Each of the agencies or organizations supply personnel to one combined emergency services CIS team which provides consistent training, supervision, case reviews, support services, in-service education and team- building programs for the team members. This combined team then supplies the appropriate personnel to assist any of the first response agencies which might need help after a traumatic event. If a law enforcement agency needs assistance, then law enforcement personnel are chosen from the team pool to assist that agency. Fire personnel are chosen to assist fire agencies, nurses are utilized when nurses have been affected by the trauma and likewise for any of the other organizations. The combined emergency service CIS team keeps the cost of training down because the various agencies share CISM training. It is also a more efficient method of utilizing the limited number of mental health professionals available to serve the various emergency service organizations. But, most importantly, a combined emergency services CIS team reduces the need to use an agency's own personnel to provide services to its own traumatized workers. This is especially important since it is believed that psychological support services provided by people who are too well-known to the recipients may be psychologically unsound both for the recipient and for the provider of the services. It should be noted here that a combined CIS team does not eliminate the need for an organization to maintain a psychologist, an employee assistance program, a chaplain or any other human services program. CIS teams are a supplement to ordinary human services and personnel support services, not a substitute for those programs.

**ON-SCENE SUPPORT SERVICES -** Whenever direct support services are provided at the scene of a traumatic incident while the event is still going on, the services are called "on-scene" support services. There are three basic supports which are provided at the scene: 1) brief crisis interventions with emergency personnel who are showing signs of distress, 2) advice and counsel to the commanders and 3) assistance to victims, survivors and family members who are directly involved with the incident. It is important to remember that group services are seldom provided at the scene. On-scene support services to emergency personnel are typically limited to one-to-one contacts.

**SPOUSE AND SIGNIFICANT OTHER SUPPORT SERVICES -** Support for the emergency services personnel, and perhaps other groups, is inadequate unless it also includes special support services for the spouses and significant others. Greater emphasis is being placed on the loved ones of the emergency worker. They also may be negatively impacted, albeit indirectly, by the same traumatic events which affect the emergency services personnel. Many CISM teams are adding significant others to the teams in order to better serve the loved ones of emergency personnel who have been distressed by the traumatic events. Many special programs already exist to assist the significant others of emergency personnel. There are educational programs, debriefings after traumatic events, small on-going support groups, grief seminars and family fairs.

**FOLLOW-UP SERVICES -** Every time an on-scene support service, a demobilization, a defusing or a debriefing is provided, it is necessary to follow these actions with one or more types of follow-up services. In fact, any intervention, from an individual consult to a formal debriefing, should receive some type of follow up. Follow-up services include telephone calls, station or workplace visits, chaplain contacts, "ride alongs," small group meetings, contacts with commanders or managers, peer visits, one-on-one services, family contacts, etc.

# CATALYTIC SEQUENCES

The final section within this chapter addresses what may be the most advanced issue in the CISM model of crisis intervention: catalytic sequences. The term catalytic sequences refers to the manner in which the multiple CISM components will be paired or sequenced in order to achieve the most powerful effect. The term itself is borrowed from the work of Theodore Millon (Millon, Grossman, Meagher, Millon, & Everly, 1999). Millon discusses the importance of combining in potentiating and catalyzing sequences various and diverse psychotherapeutic interventions. In the context of this text, we are not referring to psychotherapy, but rather are addressing the manner in which the various and diverse CISM components may be best combined and sequenced. While there is no concrete approach to catalytic CISM sequences, there are some principles to keep in mind. For example,

1) CMB and demobilizations always precede the CISD.

2) Defusings precede the CISD.

3) The CISD is never used as a standalone intervention.

4) Individual one-on-one contacts are always considered following the CMB, demobilization, defusing, and CISD, as well as other interventions, if necessary.

5) On-scene support services will always require some form of follow-up intervention.

One approach to formulating the most effective catalytic CISM sequence is to use the concepts of TARGET, TYPE, and TIMING. Target refers to the groups that will be targeted for CISM intervention. Type refers to the specific CISM interventions that will be directed toward the target groups. Timing refers to the actual time and sequence in which the CISM interventions will be employed. The single best discussion of these concepts to date may be found in Everly and Mitchell (1999).

One further concept to be considered when using the TARGET, TYPE, and TIMING concepts described above is the concept of CONTEXT. The environment and circumstances of the critical incident should be considered as the target groups are identified and the choices of intervention and their specific application times are arranged. CONTEXT covers such issues as whether or not a suspect has been arrested after a police officer has been shot or the level of support or resistance from supervisors or the administration for the implementation of support services. When planning for crisis intervention services, it is important to determine if any danger still exists for those who are involved. The intervention teams should make sure that the incident is complete and that the groups that are designated for assistance are homogenous and that they have experienced roughly the same level of exposure to the traumatic event. Clearly, the circumstances that surround and are enmeshed with the event will have a substantial influence on when and how interventions can be made.

## SUMMARY

In this chapter, we have attempted to review the key terms and concepts that are important in achieving an understanding of the CISM model of crisis intervention. Representing a new standard of care in emergency mental health, the CISM approach is a comprehensive, integrated, multi-component approach to crisis intervention. Skill in CISM is based not only upon an understanding of how to implement the numerous and diverse CISM interventions, it is based upon an understanding of how to best combine and sequence the CISM interventions.

# Chapter 2

# THE NATURE OF HUMAN STRESS

Before we delve directly into the "how to" of Critical Incident Stress Management (CISM) interventions, it seems a worthwhile exercise to review the nature of stress and psychological trauma. Although it may seem obvious, let us emphasize that if there were no such thing as pathogenic stress nor psychological trauma, there would simply be no need for Critical Incident Stress Management services, including the specific group crisis intervention procedure known as Critical Incident Stress Debriefing (CISD). Thus the overall CISM field and the CISD process were actually created in response to the fact that excessive stress and psychological trauma are just as potentially disabling as is physical traumatization. Let's look at the basics.

## DEFINING STRESS

In 1676, Hooks's Law described a phenomenon in physical science where the presence of a "load" or physical "stress" was capable of causing a physical "strain" upon a given material. In 1926 an Austrian endocrinologist, Hans Selye, identified what he believed was a consistent pattern of mind-body reactions which he called the "nonspecific response of the body to any demand" (Selye, 1974, p. 14). Selye later referred to this pattern as "the rate of wear and tear on the body" (Selye, 1976). Early in his career, Selye was invited to discuss these concepts at the College de France. In search of a term that best summarized the aforementioned concepts, Selye went to the physical sciences and borrowed the term "stress." Thus, from the Selyean tradition, the term "stress" is used to denote the nonspecific response of the body to any demand placed upon it. Having created a new term for the body's response to a demand, it was then necessary to create a new term to describe the demand, or stimulus, itself. Thus, the term "stressor" was created. This relationship is depicted in Figure 2.1.

A major point of confusion is unveiled when authors refer to "mental

**FIGURE 2.1**

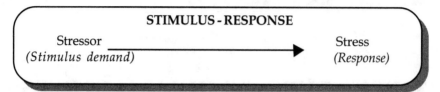

**STIMULUS - RESPONSE**

Stressor                                   Stress
*(Stimulus demand)*                        *(Response)*

stress" versus "physical stress." In such references, it is usually clear that the authors have departed from the Selyean notion of the nature of stress as a reaction or response to stressors that may be mental stressors or physical stressors. Despite the substantial historical precedents, there remains less than total agreement on the precise nature of stress.

Rather than discuss the myriad of alternative definitions, we shall define "stress" as it will be used in this book. In line with Selye's definition, stress is a mind-body response which mediates between stressor stimuli (a set of conditions or psychosocial events) and stress-related target organ diseases (see Everly and Sobelman, 1987; Everly, 1989). Figure 2.2 depicts this relationship.

As Figure 2.2 indicates, the stress response itself serves as a linking

**FIGURE 2.2**

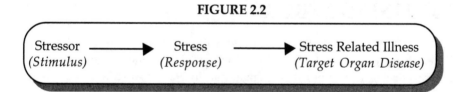

Stressor         →       Stress         →    Stress Related Illness
*(Stimulus)*             *(Response)*         *(Target Organ Disease)*

mechanism (mechanism of mediation) which explains how stressor stimuli can "cause" or be highly related to stress-related physical disease and dysfunction (target organ effects).

It is important to keep in mind that not all stress is undesirable. This notion is depicted in Figure 2.3

By looking closely at Figure 2.3, we can see that performance actually increases with an increase in stress arousal. This is the motivation underlying coaches' "pep talks" to athletes, or why some people try to "psyche" themselves up before some event which requires increased performance. Point (a) represents the point on the stress arousal axis that leads to maximal performance (a1). Yet look closely at Figure 2.3 and see what happens as stress arousal continues to increase from left to right on the horizontal axis. You can see that performance drops to point (b1) as stress increases to point (b). Selye (1974) refers to positive, motivating stress arousal as "eustress;" stress which leads to dysfunction (e.g., getting "psyched out") or disease, Selye terms "distress." So we see that stress is not always bad. In fact, Selye has argued that the absence of all stress is death.

In the 1940s, 1950s and early 1960s, stress-related diseases were termed "psychosomatic." These diseases were characterized by observable organic tissue pathology which was caused by excessive stress. In 1968, the American Psychiatric Association published the second edition of its Diagnostic and Statistical Manual of Mental Disorders (DSM-II). In this handbook of official psychiatric terms and diagnoses, stress-related diseases were referred to as "psychophysiological diseases." At the same time, neurotic disorders, which impaired sensory or motor functions but involved no actual organic tissue damage, were termed "conversion disorders" or "hysterical disorders." Psychosomatic disorders are often confused with conversion reactions. It is important to note that stress-related psychosomatic disorders are "real." They involve actual tissue damage and can even be life threatening in some cases. Conversion reactions are psychological dysfunctions and are not life threatening.

In 1980, the American Psychiatric Association revised its diagnostic

**FIGURE 2.3**

17

**FIGURE 2.4**

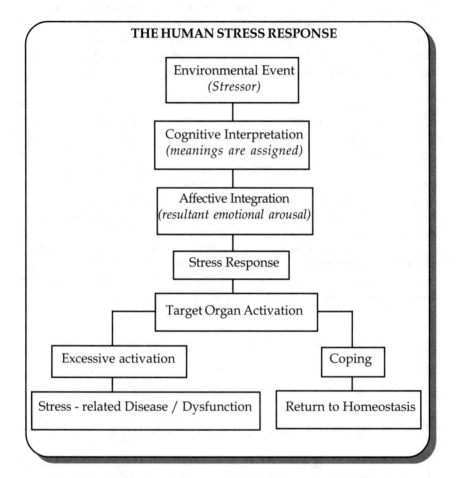

THE HUMAN STRESS RESPONSE

Environmental Event
*(Stressor)*

Cognitive Interpretation
*(meanings are assigned)*

Affective Integration
*(resultant emotional arousal)*

Stress Response

Target Organ Activation

Excessive activation

Coping

Stress - related Disease / Dysfunction

Return to Homeostasis

manual and created a third edition, the DSM-III. In this handbook of diagnostic nomenclature, stress-related diseases were no longer called psychophysiological, but now came under the diagnostic heading of "psychological factors affecting physical disease." This change greatly expanded the recognition of stress-related diseases. Neurotic-like conversion disorders were changed to a broader heading entitled "somatoform disorders." This taxonomy was retained in the DSM - IV (APA, 1994).

In the preceding section, we discussed basic terms and concepts relevant to the understanding of the human stress response. It is now time to put the "puzzle" together, that is, to explain why psychosocial events in one's environment can extract a "physical" toll from one's mind and body. It has long been known that the stress response is best viewed in the context of a multi-dimensional systems model. Figure 2.4 presents a detailed systems-based model of the human stress response.

The systems model of stress presented in Figure 2.4 is an integration of the work of Lazarus and Folkman (1984), Selye (1956), Everly (1989) and Smith and Everly (1992). Let's look at its components.

## STRESSORS

Stressors fall into two categories: 1) biogenic stressors and 2) psychosocial stressors (Everly, 1989). Biogenic stressors are stimulants which cause stress by virtue of the biochemical actions they exert on the human body. Preference, or even "addiction", to these substances fails to mitigate their ability to cause stress. Examples of biogenic stressors are:

- Caffeine

- Amphetamines

- Nicotine

- Phenylpropanolamine

- Theophylline

Caffeine is found in coffee, tea, many soft drinks and some medications. A 5-ounce cup of brewed coffee contains about 150 milligrams (mg) of caffeine. Tea (camellia theca) brewed for 5 minutes contains roughly 50-60 mg. A caffeinated 12-ounce soft drink contains 30-65 mg. A one-ounce chocolate bar has a caffeine content of approximately 40 mg. In addition, the following common medications contain caffeine: Anacin (32 mg), Cafergot (100 mg), Fiorinal (40 mg), No-Doz (100 mg), Prolamine (140 mg), Excedrin Extra (65 mg) and Midol (32 mg).[1]

(1) *Caffeine content is expressed per standard dosage and, without guarantee, is belived to be correct at the time of publication. Further questions should be directed to a qualified physician.*

The important point to remember is that, preference notwithstanding, biogenic stressors cause stress arousal. It is believed that dosages of 200-300 mg over several hours (3 - 6 hrs.) can be excessive for certain individuals, and can contribute to anxiety and stress-related symptoms (Greden, 1974; Girdano, Everly and Dusek, 1993). Common symptoms of excessive biogenic stressor consumption are sleep disturbances, irritability, jumpiness, nervousness, anxiety and excessive tension.

The second major category of stressors is referred to as "psychosocial" stressors. These stressors, unlike the biogenic variety, do not directly cause stress. Rather, they "set the stage" for stress responses to be initiated through intrapersonal mechanisms. That is, psychosocial stressors appear to be like beauty; they lie in the eye of the beholder. Simply put, although many psychosocial events can be potentially stressful, only those that are interpreted or appraised as being challenging, threatening or otherwise aversive will ultimately become psychosocial stressors. This brings us to the second stage of the model, *cognitive interpretation.*

## COGNITIVE INTERPRETATION

The 5th Century Greco-Roman philosopher Epictetus reportedly said, "Men are disturbed not by things, but the views which they take of them." Hans Selye, echoed the same sentiment when he said, "It is not what happens to you that matters, but how you take it." Finally, neurophysiologist Magda Arnold has noted, "the sheer experience of things around us cannot lead to action unless they are appraised for their effect upon us" (Arnold, 1984, p. 125). Simply stated, psychosocial events occur around us every waking moment. These events will not lead to excessive stress unless one or more of them are appraised or interpreted as being: 1) meaningful and 2) potentially challenging, threatening or otherwise aversive. The propensity to appraise / interpret events is a function of learning history and personality. Recent research by Smith and Everly (1992) has noted that interpretational mechanisms play what may be the primary role in occupational stress and illness among accountants.

# EMOTIONAL INTEGRATION

Magda Arnold (1970) noted that our emotions are caused by the appraisal of the psychosocial events that we encounter in the world around us. Further, Rosenman (1984) states that emotions are caused by the interpretation of events rather than the events themselves. The belief that emotions are caused by cognitive interpretations is referred to as the principle of "cognitive primacy." Not all authorities are in total agreement that emotions are always caused by cognitions. Nevertheless, there is agreement among authorities performing research in human stress that emotions and stress arousal function in such a manner so as to make cognitive primacy a functional and pragmatic reality if not a phenomenological one (Everly, 1989).

To summarize so far, the world is replete with sources of stress. Most of these potential sources of stress will only become stressors because we choose to, or have learned to, interpret them as challenging, threatening or aversive. Based upon such an interpretation, the mechanisms of human emotion are activated. To this point, however, the "stress response" is not physiologically manifest. On the basis of emotional arousal, the brain employs a "transducer" in order to convert psychological appraisals into somatic realities that affect our physical health. This "transducer" is called the "limbic-hypothalamic" complex. The more stress one experiences, the more likely this limbic circuitry may become neurologically "hypersensitive" (i.e., more easily activated with minimal stimulation over time).

# THE STRESS RESPONSE

An understanding of just what the stress response really represents may be derived from the study of neuroanatomy and neuroendocrinology. Let us briefly summarize the core features of the stress response.

The stress response itself consists of three major pathways, or axes: 1) the neural axis, 2) the neuroendocrine axis and 3) the endocrine axis (Everly, 1989). These mechanisms are always activated for they represent necessary aspects of normal human physiological functioning. They become of interest in the study of stress and disease when they become overstimulated and sustain their activation at excessively high levels.

The neural stress axis consists of the nerves of the sympathetic nervous system, the parasympathetic nervous system (collectively called the autonomic nervous system) and the neuromuscular nervous system (the nerves to the skeletal muscles).

The neuroendocrine stress axis consists of the sympathetic neural chain and its innervation of the adrenal medulae. Stimulation of this axis results in the release of the hormones epinephrine (adrenaline) and norepinephrine (noradrenalin) from the two adrenal medullae. This axis is responsible for the so-called "fight or flight" response studied by Walter Cannon in the early 1930s.

**FIGURE 2.5**

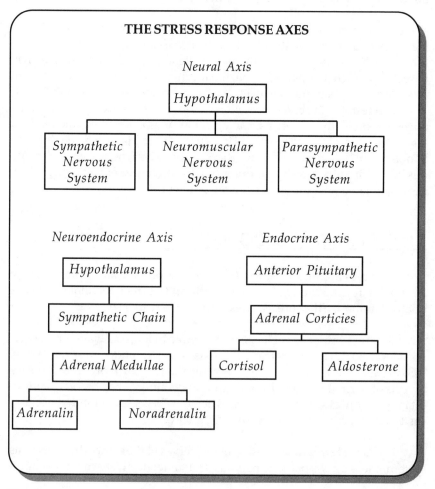

THE STRESS RESPONSE AXES

Neural Axis

Hypothalamus

Sympathetic Nervous System

Neuromuscular Nervous System

Parasympathetic Nervous System

Neuroendocrine Axis

Hypothalamus

Sympathetic Chain

Adrenal Medullae

Adrenalin

Noradrenalin

Endocrine Axis

Anterior Pituitary

Adrenal Corticies

Cortisol

Aldosterone

Finally, the endocrine axis consists of the anterior pituitary gland and its effector mechanisms such as the adrenal cortices which release hormones such as cortisol and aldosterone. Similarly, estrogen, progesterone and testosterone can all be altered during stress. Figure 2.5 shows these three stress response axes.

# TARGET ORGAN AROUSAL AND SYMPTOMS

"Target organs" refers to the bodily organs within any given person which may become the somatic "targets" of the stress response. Given the three stress responses axes just described, the potential range of target organs that could be affected by excessive stress is indeed wide. Table 2.1 summarizes some of the more common target organ signs and symptoms of excessive stress.

**TABLE 2.1**

| COMMON SIGNS AND SYMPTOMS OF EXCESSIVE STRESS | |
|---|---|
| **COGNITIVE** | **PHYSICAL** |
| Confusion in thinking<br>Difficulty making decisions<br>Lowered concentration<br>Memory dysfunction<br>Lowering of higher<br>  cognitive functions | Excessive sweating<br>Dizzy spells<br>Increased heart rate<br>Elevated blood pressure<br>Rapid breathing |
| **EMOTIONAL** | **BEHAVIORAL** |
| Emotional shock<br>Anger<br>Grief<br>Depression<br>Feeling overwhelmed | Changes in ordinary<br>  behavior patterns<br>Changes in eating<br>Decreased personal hygiene<br>Withdrawal from others<br>Prolonged silences |

# THEORIES OF STRESS-RELATED DISEASE

Figure 2.4, presented earlier, denotes that when coping strategies are successful, pathogenic stress arousal is reduced. However, if the coping strategies are unsuccessful, target organ activation will continue at excessive levels and target organ disease / dysfunction becomes a matter of time. That is, the target organs simply break down under the prolonged "wear and tear."

There exist several theories concerning just how and why stress leads to specific diseases or disorders. Let's briefly review them.

## Life Change Theory

The life change theory argues that "change" causes adaptation. The physiology of adaptation is stress. Too many changes or too extensive a change causes the body to become overwhelmed. The result is a stress-related disease. This major theory was first constructed considering major life changes, for example, moving, divorce, graduation (Holmes and Rahe, 1967), but has been modified to include the effects of minor "hassles" as well (Lazarus and Folkman, 1984). The life events theory fails to enumerate exactly how change leads to disease other than by stating that excessive stress causes the target organ to become exhausted.

## Weak Organ Theory

The weak organ theory states that all of us are either born with or, soon thereafter, develop a "weak" or highly vulnerable target organ. When we become aroused, it is this organ system that bears most of the strain. The more distressed the person becomes, the greater the strain on the weak organ, until it breaks down into a disease state. The key to pathogenesis is simply organ overload due to repeated activation.

## Homeostatic Failure Theory

The homeostatic failure theory was proposed by psychophysiologists in the 1960s and 1970s. It simply states that when aroused during stress, not all organs become equally aroused. Some organs will become more highly aroused and it will take longer to return to their baseline level of functioning. These organs ultimately become diseased from excessive stress (Sternbach,

1966). The key to pathogenesis is organ overload due to a failure to return to baseline levels of arousal quickly.

## Disorders Of Arousal Theory

One of the most recent theories to explain stress-related diseases is the "Disorders of Arousal" theory. Formulated by Everly and Benson (1989), this theory argues that if an individual is placed under a condition of excessive stress (excessively chronic or excessively high in magnitude), the stress arousal centers in the brain become hypersensitive. This hypersensitivity then leads to a condition where the stress response is too easily activated. This theory argues that all stress-related diseases are caused by excessively intense or excessively chronic arousal occurring within the brain and its effector systems. The target organs then undergo undue strain, that is, "wear and tear," and ultimately break down or become dysfunctional as a result.

## Hypokinetic Disease Theory

Postulated by cardiologists Kraus and Raab (1961), it states that stress is a normal preparatory mechanism that prepares one for physical exertion. It further notes that it is the failure to physically express the stress response that makes it pathogenic, not its mere presence. Thus, conceptually, stress that does not lead to physical activity is more likely to become pathogenic with time.

## <u>COPING WITH STRESS: STRESS MANAGEMENT</u>

While it is not the purpose of this text to provide an in-depth discussion of stress management techniques (see Mitchell and Bray, 1990; Girdano, Everly and Dusek, 1993), we will briefly highlight some key points.

A review of the myriad of coping strategies designed to manage stress while promoting health reveal four basic strategies:

1.   Avoiding Stressors

2.   Cognitive Reinterpretation

3. Reducing Arousal

4. Ventilating the Stress Response

# Avoiding Stressors

The most powerful means of coping with excessive stress is the avoidance of the source of stress or at least the reduction of exposure to such stressors. Techniques such as problem solving and time management are useful interventions. Something as simple as avoiding or reducing stimulant consumption can be a very powerful means of reducing excessive stress. It is important to keep in mind that the higher the stimulant intake, for example, methylated xanthines, the less stable the nerve cells of the limbic system and sympathetic nervous system (Everly, 1989). Furthermore, the less stable those nerves become, the higher the risk for excessive or traumatic stress sequelae in emergency personnel or anyone else.

# Cognitive Reinterpretation / Reframing

While there can be little doubt that removing a stressor is the most powerful means of coping, many stressors simply don't lend themselves to such an intervention. It has been said that "Stressors, like beauty, reside in the eye of the beholder." Similarly, "There are no things good nor bad, but thinking makes them so, Horatio," said Shakespeare's Hamlet. Cognitive therapies for depression, stress, and anxiety disorders have proven to be powerful and perhaps the most flexible means of coping with stress (Beck and Emery, 1985; Ellis, 1973). Cognitive-based coping strategies would entail the realization that by changing one's appraisal or interpretation of any given stressful or traumatic event, the negative impact of that event upon psychological well-being can be dramatically mitigated. Cognitive coping techniques might include finding a "silver lining" in a stressor, reinterpreting a "failure" into a "success," using the stressor to "learn a valuable lesson," viewing oneself as "lucky" that the stressor wasn't worse or perhaps seeing stress as a growth experience that "builds character."

# Reducing Arousal

The essence of stress is arousal, that is, "wear and tear" (Selye, 1974). The natural antithesis of stress, therefore, is what Herbert Benson has called the "relaxation response" (Benson, 1975). Research has demonstrated the health-promoting effects of reducing stress arousal via the relaxation response (Benson, 1983; Benson, Alexander, Feldman, 1975; Everly and Benson, 1989; Everly, 1989). The relaxation response may be defined as a state of lowered metabolic functioning. It can be engendered through a myriad of techniques such as meditation, biofeedback, deep breathing, hypnosis and neuromuscular relaxation techniques (see Everly, 1989, for a review and step-by-step guidelines).

## Ventilating the Stress Response

The ventilation or expression of the stress response is another effective means of coping (Roemer and Borkovec, 1994). Two primary techniques come to mind in this category: catharsis and exercise. Kahn (1966) discovered that expressing emotions served to lower psychophysiologic indices of stress. Similarly, in valuable reviews, Pennebaker (1985, 1990) has shown that verbally expressing emotions helps resolve traumas and reduce stress. With regard to exercise, it has long been known to have health-promoting and stress-reducing effects when applied in a safe and reasonable manner (de Vries, 1981; Weller and Everly, 1985; Sinyor, et al., 1983). In fact, in their "hypokinetic disease" theory, Kraus and Raab (1961) argue that it is the failure to physically express the stress response that makes it pathogenic!

## Maladaptive Coping

Upon occasion individuals will suffer excessive stress and be compelled to use self-defeating, health-eroding coping tactics rather than those described above. Such maladaptive coping tactics include alcohol and drug "self-medication," anger, violence and social withdrawal. The long-term effect of maladaptive coping will be the creation of problems above and beyond just stress alone.

## SUMMARY

The purpose of this chapter has been to provide a detailed analysis of the human stress response. Let us highlight some of the main points.

1. "Stress" describes the nonspecific responses of the body to any demand placed on it, that is, the "wear and tear" on an indi-

vidual. It acts as a link between given stressors and target organ symptoms.

2. Not all stress is bad. In fact, to a point, increased stress arousal motivates increased performance. However, as stress continues to increase beyond tolerable limits, dysfunctional consequences appear.

3. Stressors represent environmental events which either cause or set the stage for the stress response. Stressors can be categorized as either biogenic or psychosocial. Biogenic stressors are stimulants which cause stress via the biochemical actions they exert on the human body, for example: caffeine, nicotine, amphetamines and so forth. Psychosocial stressors are environmental events that set the stage for initiation of the stress response. It is one's appraisal or interpretation of these events as meaningful and potentially challenging, threatening or otherwise aversive which creates the stress response.

4. The cognitive-affective domain is crucial to most stress reactions. That is, one's interpretation of events as stressful causes emotional upheaval which results in a physiological stress response.

5. The physical stress response results from over-stimulation (cognitive-affective) of three major axes: 1) the neural axis, 2) the neuroendocrine axis and 3) the endocrine axis. Sustained activation of these axes eventually results in target organ symptoms of ill-health.

6. Coping may serve to mitigate the impact of the stress response on target organs. Coping represents environmental, behavioral or psychological efforts to deal with excessive stress and its correlates.

7. Excessive stress arousal coupled with unsuccessful coping strategies will inevitably result in target organ disease and / or dysfunction. Target organ systems that may eventually be affected by excessive stress include the neurological system, the cardiovascular system, the gastrointestinal system, the neuromuscular system, the immune system, the respiratory system and other body systems.

# Chapter 3

# PSYCHOTRAUMATOLOGY

## INTRODUCTION

Posttraumatic stress reactions may consist of a wide variety of clinical presentations.  Such presentations may include brief psychotic reactions, dissociative disorders, adjustment disorders, an acute stress disorder (APA, 1994) and perhaps even borderline personality disorder (Herman and van der Kolk, 1987).  Certainly the most widely known is Posttraumatic Stress Disorder (PTSD) (APA, 1994).

Contrary to "historic" opinion, PTSD may be engendered by events other than combat.  For example, PTSD may be engendered by:

- A serious accident
- The destruction of one's home or community
- Disasters
- Terrorism
- Natural catastrophes
- Rape
- Criminal victimization
- The threat of harm to oneself or others
- Experiencing / witnessing the actual physical harm to oneself or others (APA, 1987; WHO, 1992; APA, 1994).

Contrary to "popular" opinion, PTSD is shockingly prevalent.  For example:

- Nearly one-half of all patients admitted to urban trauma centers are likely to suffer from PTSD in addition to their physical trauma, while another 31% of these patients may suffer from a milder variant of posttraumatic stress reaction (Norman and Getek, 1988).

- The lifetime prevalence of PTSD is estimated to be 23.6% for those exposed to noncombat traumatic event (Breslau, et al., 1991).
- It has been estimated that there is an 80% prevalence of PTSD symptoms (any duration) among individuals who are victims of rape, physical injury, and threat of life combined (Kilpatrick, et al., 1989).
- It has been estimated that 16% of urban firefighters may be at risk of developing PTSD sometime during their career (Corneil, 1992).
- Finally, it is generally agreed that PTSD is grossly underestimated due to significant rates of under-reporting (Brett and Ostroff, 1985).

With regard to emergency services and disaster response personnel, the epidemiology of PTSD is further obscured by virtue of the fact that there exists an inherent resistance to acknowledge the presence of any psychological discord. Such an acknowledgment, it is feared, may result in alienation by peers, the destruction of the personal illusion of invulnerability, and the raising of concerns over some unique weakness or vulnerability being heretofore undiagnosed.

# PSYCHOTRAUMATOLOGY DEFINED

The term "psychotraumatology" was coined to define the study of psychological trauma. More specifically, psychotraumatology refers to the study of the processes and factors which:

1. Lie antecedent to psychological trauma

2. Exist concomitant with psychological trauma

3. Develop subsequent to psychological trauma
*(Everly and Lating, 1995; Everly, 1993a).*

This term was chosen in contrast to the term "traumatology" (Donovan, 1991) due to the fact that traumatology is already generally accepted to denote the study of "wounds" and thus is already inextricably bound to the practice of physical medicine (see Schnitt, 1993).

It is hoped that usage of the term psychotraumatology to define the endeavors enumerated above will reduce semantic confusion and will further assist in the development of the field (Everly and Lating, 1995).

As noted in the previous section, the most common and widely known variant of posttraumatic stress is PTSD. As such, it plays an important role in the field of psychotraumatology.

# PTSD - BACKGROUND

Posttraumatic Stress Disorder (PTSD) is the most widely used of the official diagnostic terms employed to denote the psychological sequelae that exist in response to a traumatic event. Nevertheless, the phenomenon was acknowledged to be in existence far before the advent of official diagnostic taxonomies.

Well-documented posttraumatic stress syndromes date back as far as 1666 as a result of the Great Fire of London (Trimble, 1981). But historical records reflective of posttraumatic stress are most commonly found in the archives of war. Army surgeons used terms such as "shell shock," "soldier's heart" and "posttraumatic neurosis" to describe combat related posttraumatic stress. Medical records dating back to the Civil War document the existence of combat-related posttraumatic stress. World War I, World War II and the Korean War all added their contributions to the history of posttraumatic stress. Yet it was the Vietnam conflict that ultimately forced modern psychiatry to officially recognize posttraumatic stress as a formal psychiatric disorder. This disorder was named Posttraumatic Stress Disorder (APA, 1980, 1987, 1994).

As noted earlier in this chapter, PTSD is now universally recognized as a potential response to any form of traumatic event, not just combat. Let's review its nature.

# PTSD (309.81) DIAGNOSTIC CRITERIA

PTSD was first officially recognized in the psychiatric taxonomy of the American Psychiatric Association's *Diagnostic and Statistical Manual of Mental Disorders* (DSM) in the year 1980 (APA, 1980). PTSD has been retained in the subsequent editions of the DSM, specifically DSM-III-R (APA, 1987) and DSM - IV (APA, 1994). Let's examine the four specific diagnostic criteria: the traumatic event, re-experiencing the event, avoidance and numbing reactions and symptoms of increased arousal.

## Traumatic Event

The sine qua non of the PTSD diagnosis is the existence of a traumatic stressor. Exactly what constitutes a traumatic event may be open to some debate; however, according to the DSM-III-R (APA, 1987, p.250), a traumatic event may be defined as "an event outside the range of usual human experience and that would be markedly distressing to almost everyone."

The DSM-IV (APA, 1994) denotes a traumatic event as "... directly experiencing or witnessing actual or threatened death or serious injury or experiencing a threat to one's own physical integrity or the physical integrity of someone else." In addition, the DSM-IV mandates that the individual's response must be characterized by fear, helplessness or horror. Thus, the DSM-IV has somewhat restricted the definition of a traumatic event and personalized it more so than the DSM-III-R. DSM-IV has also chosen to underscore the critical role that perception or interpretation actually plays in the determination of a traumatic event. A weakness inherent in the DSM-IV is the failure to recognize environmental/ ecological disasters or catastrophes that don't actually represent a direct threat to human life.

What may be a more realistic definition of a traumatic event comes from the World Health Organization in its International Classification of Disease taxonomy, 10th edition (WHO, 1992). A traumatic event is defined therein as "exceptionally threatening or catastrophic." The ICD-10 goes on to note that predisposing factors may serve to lower the threshold for PTSD but are neither necessary nor sufficient etiologically. Finally, the ICD-10 notes that PTSD may be so chronic as to transition into an enduring personality change as a direct result of the traumatic stressor, a "trauma personality" of sorts.

Table 3.1 enumerates some of the major factors which predict psychological trauma.

## Re-experiencing the Event

The key element of this cluster of symptoms is that the individual experiences intrusive recollective ideation pertaining to the traumatic event. The re-experiencing may take the form of "recurrent and intrusive distressing recollections of the event," "recurrent and distressing dreams of the event, " "a sense of reliving the experience," "intense psychological distress at exposure to ... cues that symbolize or resemble ... the event" or "physiological reactivity on exposure to ... cues ... of the traumatic event" (APA, 1994, p. 428).

**TABLE 3.1**

## MAJOR FACTORS PREDICTING PSYCHOLOGICAL TRAUMA

- Actual severe physical injury, disfigurement, dismemberment or disability
- Fear of severe physical injury, disfigurement, dismemberment or disability
- Fear of losing one's life
- Torture
- Fear of torture
- Sexual assault
- Fear of sexual assault
- Watching someone else die, experience extreme pain or physical inury
- A belief of failed resonsibility that results in harm to others
- The belief of unjustified survival or escape / avoidance from harm
- The belief of betrayal
- Death or injury to children
- The violation or contradiction of a "core belief" or "critical expectation" (e.g., God, friendship, loyalty, fairness, justice, fidelity or competence)
- Shame associated with factors other than those listed above
- Guilt associated with factors other than those listed above
- War
- Environmental or ecological catastrophe

*Note: fatigue, dehydration, extreme heat, extreme cold or certain chemical substances may be presumed to augment the risk of subsequent psychological traumatization from the aforementioned factors*

## Avoidance and Numbing Reactions

The key element of this cluster of symptoms is that the individual persistently avoids things that are associated with the traumatic event. Numbing of general responsiveness may also be noted.

## Symptoms of Increased Arousal

The key element of this symptom cluster is the presence of symptoms of increased arousal, or stress, that were not present prior to the traumatic event. Such symptoms might include sleep disturbances, irritability, anger, rage, hypervigilance or exaggerated startle response.

## ACUTE STRESS DISORDER (308.3) DIAGNOSTIC CRITERIA

It should be noted that the diagnosis of PTSD cannot be made until the symptoms have persisted for more than one month. The diagnosis of acute stress disorder (308.3) fills the temporal gap from stressor through the subsequent four weeks (APA, 1994). Acute Stress Disorder first appeared in the American taxonomy in the DSM-IV (APA, 1994).

The essential feature of the diagnosis is the development of the characteristic stress, dissociative, recollective ideational and numbing / withdrawal symptom complex as seen in PTSD, but this disorder may be diagnosed as soon as the symptoms have persisted for at least two days. The duration of the symptoms can, obviously, persist for only one month as this is when the PTSD diagnosis becomes relevant.

## AN INTEGRATED THEORY OF POSTTRAUMATIC STRESS

In an effort to add greater overall phenomenological significance to the aforementioned diagnostic criteria of PTSD, as well as to attempt to provide greater clinical insight into the disorder, Everly (1993a and 1993b) has constructed a model which integrates the various constituents of the disorder itself. This model is presented in Figure 3.1.

Figure 3.1 demonstrates how the various components of posttraumatic stress may relate to one another (adapted from Everly, 1993a, 1993b).

Let us briefly examine this interpretation of posttraumatic stress.

As noted earlier, the sine qua non of PTSD is the traumatic event itself, that is, some aversive event outside the usual realm of human experience which overwhelms the victim's coping and ego defense mechanisms. As emphasized by Pierre Janet in the late 1800s, to some degree the psychic toxicity of the traumatic event is either augmented or mitigated by the psychological appraisal, or interpretation, of the traumatic event itself by the victim. This is a critical aspect of the model for clinicians to note for it is the

**FIGURE 3.1**

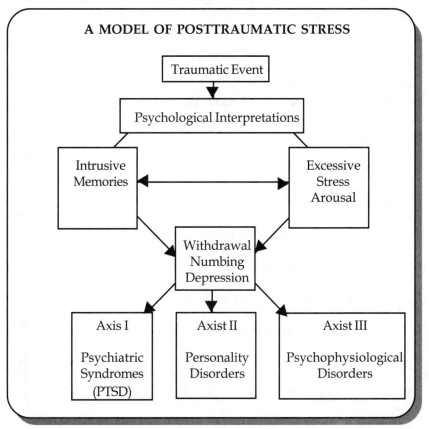

alteration of this element that is so important in the recovery process (Everly, 1994).

Phenomenologically, close examination of the model in Figure 3.1 reveals the intrusive memories of the trauma (which may occur hourly, daily, etc.) combined with excessively chronic and intense levels of arousal (Everly, 1990) constitute the key elements of PTSD. The third major symptom cluster is seen as secondary and reactive to the intrusive memories and arousal. That is, the withdrawal symptoms are seen as resulting from and therefore contingent upon the severity of the interaction between the intrusive recollections and arousal.

Finally, the model (Figure 3.1) extends the symptoms beyond that of mere PTSD and sees other disorders as being potentially trauma related. PTSD, some panic attacks, amnestic syndromes and some substance abuse seem likely candidates for trauma reactive syndromes. Likewise, borderline and "multiple" personality disorders may be manifestations of traumatic stress. Trauma may also be capable of creating almost any psychophysi-

**TABLE 3.2**

## EARLY INDICATIONS OF POSSIBLE PTSD

- Flashbacks

- Traumatic dreams

- Memory disturbances

- Self medication (e.g., alcohol abuse)

- Anger, irritability, hostility which is difficult to control

- Persistent depression, withdrawal

- A "dazed" or "numb" appearance

- Panic attacks

- Phobia formation

ologic reaction or disorder.

Early diagnosis and treatment of PTSD is a desirable goal since the proper treatment depends heavily on a precise diagnosis of the condition. Table 3.2 provides a list of useful diagnostic signs and symptoms of PTSD. These are considered "early warning" signals of the potential for PTSD.

As pointed out in the preceding paragraphs, PTSD is not the only psychiatric manifestation of posttraumatic stress. There will be many victims who will suffer the ill effects of posttraumatic stress yet will not meet all of the diagnostic criteria for PTSD. Table 3.3 lists a variety of potential posttraumatic stress syndromes.

**TABLE 3.3**

**POTENTIAL POSTTRAUMATIC STRESS SYNDROMES**

- Acute stress disorder

- Posttraumatic Stress Disorder

- Complex partial seizures

- Adjustment disorder

- Depression

- Self medicating or substance abuse

- Personality disorders (borderline, antisocial, multiple personality, schizotypal)

- Panic syndromes

- Irratic work-related behavior

- Memory dysfunction without traumatic amnesia

- Amnestic syndromes regarding traumatization

- Virtually any psychophysiologic medical disorder

Finally, a wide variety of stress-related (psychophysiologic) physical illnesses, for example, acute hypertension, inflammation of the gastrointestinal system, tension headaches, migraine headaches and so forth, may arise as a result of psychological traumatization. Thus, coordination between medical therapeutics and psychotherapeutics is important.

## TWO FACTOR THEORY OF POSTTRAUMATIC STRESS

While it is clearly important to recognize and understand the signs and symptoms of PTSD diagnostically, these signs and symptoms represent only the "skeleton" of the disorder. In order to be better able to prevent and treat this disorder, we must learn to understand it on a far deeper level. We must search for its foundation or core if we are to best target our interventions.

In a phenomenological analysis of PTSD, Everly (1993a, 1993b) has postulated that this disorder actually consists of a two-factor disposition: 1) neurological hypersensitivity and 2) psychological hypersensitivity.

## Factor One: Neurologic Hypersensitivity

Traumatic stress appears to represent a cascade of neural and endocrine events that are capable of altering normal neurologic processing. For example, the physiology of traumatic stress not only results in higher than normal levels of available neurotransmitters, but it may also bias, or predispose, otherwise normal neurons toward a condition of phasic hyperactivity or tonic hyperactivity. This condition has been referred to as neurologic hypersensitivity.

The neurological hypersensitivity just described as being inherent in PTSD is believed to consist of a lowered depolarization threshold within the nerve cells of the amygdala and hippocampal regions (Everly, 1989; Everly and Benson, 1989). There appear to be several mechanisms which potentially underlie the neurologic hypersensitivity in PTSD.

- A functionally excessive amount of excitatory neurotransmitters available at the synaptic cleft

- A functional paucity of the inhibitory neurotransmitter gamma-aminobutyric acid (GABA)

- Micromorphological changes to the neurons themselves that serve to dysfunctionally facilitate neural excitation, for example, an increase in dendritic spine and a decrease in alpha-2 inhibitory receptors (see Everly, 1993a and 1993b for reviews of primary research)

Post (1992) has even postulated that the biochemistry of extreme stress may be able to alter genetic transcription factors creating a condition of genetically based neurologic hypersensitivity that may endure indefinitely. Finally, Everly and Horton (1989) found evidence of an immediate to short-term memory consolidation dysfunction in PTSD patients. This dysfunction was in no way content-specific to any particular event, task or theme. It may be that the biochemistry of extreme stress can not only create a status of neurologic hypersensitivity, but it may also be capable of destroying brain cells via some excitotoxic mechanism (Sapolsky, Krey, McEwen, 1984; Olney, 1978; McGeer and McGeer, 1988).

Resolution of the neurologic hypersensitivity depends upon lowering the levels of arousal experienced by the individual. Medications and the "relaxation response" have proven useful in this regard.

# Factor Two: Psychological Hypersensitivity

The psychological hypersensitivity inherent in PTSD appears to arise from the fact that some aspect of the victim's worldview, that is, "Weltanschauung," has been contradicted. Thus the trauma represents a piece of the puzzle of life that simply refuses to be normally integrated into the overall picture. It was Abraham Maslow (1970) who told us that other than the need for physical survival, the need for "safety" was the most powerful human need of all. In order to make a complex and otherwise indefinable world "safer," humans tend to construct overarching schematic worldviews (ideologies, "Weltanschauung") which help explain the human experience. When something terribly aversive happens that doesn't fit into the scheme, (e.g., a trauma) the effect is posttraumatic stress. The world is no longer safe and will not be safe until some understanding and predictability can be brought to the world again (Everly, 1993a, 1993b, 1994).

Resolution of the psychological hypersensitivity appears contingent upon following one of three possible therapeutic tacks:

1. Integrating the trauma into the existing worldview

2. Creating an "exception to the rule" parallel worldview

3. Abolishing the old worldview and creating a new worldview (Everly, 1994).

PTSD and related posttraumatic stress syndromes have the potential to literally consume an individual's life. The reiterative nature of the disorder is nothing less than a potentially never-ending effort to make sense out of the world in the face of traumatic evidence that one's worldview is inadequate and therefore no longer protective. Horowitz (1976) refers to the reiterative quality of posttraumatic stress as the "completion tendency." It seems reasonable that any therapeutic formulation should be directed toward both "factors" in the posttraumatic phenomenon.

# A PROGRAM FOR PSYCHOLOGICAL TRAUMA IMMUNIZATION

In the years since the "official" recognition of PTSD and related posttrauma syndromes, we have made tremendous advances in our ability to understand and treat these problems. No longer does PTSD mean an end to a career. Now, the overwhelming majority of individuals who develop PTSD can return to their chosen line of work, often very rapidly. Many individuals never have to leave active duty even temporarily. The key to effective treatment is early aggressive treatment by a knowledgeable psychotraumatologist, (i.e., a mental health professional) who has received specialized training in psychological trauma and who specializes in its treatment.

Having said those words about treatment, however, there exists a compelling logic to aggressively pursue the prevention of PTSD and related syndromes. Peer counseling, crisis intervention, defusings and Critical Incident Stress Debriefings (CISD) are designed to prevent or mitigate PTSD and other stress-related syndromes. These techniques can now be structured into a form of "psychological trauma immunization program." Listed below is one approach to such a program.

# Orientations

Prior to becoming "operational," all recruits, trainees, volunteers and other personnel should receive an orientation, or indoctrination, to the psychological demands or aspects of their "career." Any orientation should include videos, sound tracks and photographs that orient the trainee to the "sights and sounds" of the endeavor they are about to pursue. A basic orientation to stress, anxiety, stress-related physical illness, signs and symptoms of excessive stress and psychological trauma should be mandatory. A brief review of PTSD should be included. Trainees should also receive basic training in personal stress management techniques as reviewed in chapter 2. In fact, any of the adaptive, health-promoting stress management techniques briefly enumerated in chapter 2 can be of great value in diminishing the risk of excessive stress before, during and after highly stressful incidents and even disasters.

All responders should be briefed in the staging area before deployment at a disaster scene. They need to be oriented to the nature of the specific disaster facing them. Videos and photographs may be very helpful during the incident orientation. They should also be reminded of signs and symptoms of excessive stress and trauma. This tactic may obviously be impossible if there is no opportunity to prepare prior to tactical engagement. This system is recommended, however, in large-scale disasters.

## On-scene Crisis Intervention

All emergency service workers should be encouraged to use stress management techniques as reviewed in chapter 2 as on-going means of coping with the stress of high-demand shifts, prolonged incidents, or major disaster situations. Every effort should be made to ensure that disaster workers are properly fed, sheltered, rested and rotated from difficult tasks to less difficult tasks. They should be regularly monitored for both the physiological and psychological effects of traumatic stress. When necessary, on-scene support personnel should be available to provide quick one-on-one consultations to reduce the harmful effects of stress (Mitchell and Bray, 1990). On-scene support personnel may consist of mental health professionals, peer support personnel or teams of both. Refer to chapter 6 on acute crisis intervention for a detailed discussion.

# Aftercare

Defusings and CISD are useful following the critical incident or disaster. We believe that early cathartic intervention may impact some level of understanding or at least provide some normalization and may assist in reestablishing the viability of one's worldview following a trauma. CISD and defusings are designed to do just that. Early intervention tends to reduce subsequent arousal and the tendency to "concretize" the trauma, as will be discussed later in this book. In addition, basic stress management techniques can be effectively applied as emergency service personnel recover from a stressful shift or decompress from a disaster scene. Again the fundamentals of personal stress management will prove of great value.

These same techniques can be applied in the context of family support for all family members. Formal family support services can be very valuable. Both formal and informal family support groups may be considered. Some form of formal or informal follow-ups are recommended for personnel if such a need is assessed. Referral to professional mental health services always remains an option. Table 3.4 provides a summary of a standard program that could be used for "psychological trauma immunization."

## SUMMARY

In this chapter, we have discussed the most severe variation of human stress, that is, posttraumatic stress. The term psychotraumatology was introduced and defined as the study of psychological factors antecedent to, concomitant with or subsequent to trauma. The chapter focused upon the official variations of posttraumatic stress, that is, Posttraumatic Stress Disorder (PTSD) and acute stress disorder from the perspectives of the DSM-IV and the ICD-10. Recent advances in the nature, prevention and treatment of PTSD were briefly discussed in this chapter. These advances have the potential, we believe, to reduce the long-term adversity that this disorder may cause within the emergency service and disaster response professions.

It seems appropriate at this juncture to reiterate the point made early in chapter 2. CISM exists because of a generally perceived need. That need is recognized as the fact that emergency service personnel, as well as many others, are at risk for the development of disorders of excessive stress, especially PTSD. As Leonardo da Vinci said "First study the science, then practice the art." In the final analysis, effective prevention and intervention programs are based upon an analysis of understanding of the problem being faced. Although admittedly not comprehensive, chapters 2 and 3 were designed to provide an initial lesson in "the science" of stress and trauma so as to allow a more potent "practice" of "the art" of CISM. These chapters should be seen as introductions, or overviews, rather than definitive reviews. Thus, more exploration of "the science" may be desirable before engaging in CISM interventions.

TABLE 3.4

## BASIC OUTLINE FOR PSYCHOLOGICAL TRAUMA IMMUNIZATION

1. Pre-service orientation
   a. Prior to active duty
   b. Career in-service education
   c. Briefing prior to deployment at a specific incident

2. On-scene support
   a. Mental health support
   b. Peer support
   c. Rest, food, altering assignments and limiting exposure
   d. Brief support for individuals who are obviously distressed
   e. Advice to supervisors when necessary
   f. Limited support to actual victims, family members and bystanders as required

3. After-care
   a. Defusings
   b. CISD
   c. Family interventions
   d. Follow-up
   e. Referral options
   f. Post-incident education

# Chapter 4

## HISTORY AND BACKGROUND OF CRITICAL INCIDENT STRESS MANAGEMENT SERVICES

### INTRODUCTION

Few of life's most important pursuits are fully meaningful without an understanding of the historical roots which made them possible. There is great value in the theories and experiences of people who worked in both the distant and immediate past. Much can be learned from a review of the mistakes and successes of the past. In fact, the lessons from the past are vital in ensuring competency in present day services in the relatively new field of Critical Incident Stress Management (CISM). Learning from the past can guide CISM teams in taking the right steps to help stressed emergency personnel. In addition, following the course of action of past experts can save us time and ensure superior services by eliminating unnecessary guesswork. A thorough theoretical and historical foundation can serve as protection against serious mistakes in the provision of CISM services, especially the complex group intervention process known as CISD.

The following chapter will review the basic historical and theoretical foundations of CISM as well as the special group intervention - Critical Incident Stress Debriefing (CISD).

### MAJOR INFLUENCES IN CRITICAL INCIDENT STRESS MANAGEMENT

Without "critical incidents," (those significant turning point events, traumas and disasters which have occurred throughout history), the field of Critical Incident Stress Management and its well-known component, "Critical Incident Stress Debriefing," would never have been developed. Human beings tend to be reactive to situations and not necessarily proactive in their approach to managing human problems. History is filled with instances of catastrophic events which have changed peoples' thinking and behaviors. When people suffered great disruption and pain in their lives, they frequently attempted to change the way they did things. Tragedies have frequently been the source of new ideas, discoveries and technologies. The current knowledge base in the fields of traumatic stress, critical incident stress management and CISD had its origins in the conflicts and turmoil of the past.

Four major influences which set the foundation for Critical Incident Stress Management can be identified. They are:

- Warfare

- Disasters

- Law enforcement psychology

- Emergency medical, fire and hospital services

Each of these fields of human experience, over the course of thousands of years, gradually built a base on which the current concepts of traumatic stress, as well as the present day support services, could stand. From our past we draw understanding, a drive to make things better and a hope for a healthier future.

## THE INFLUENCE OF WARFARE

Stress has been part of the human experience since the very beginning of time. No one would survive without it. At best, it is a creative, driving force which can drive people to survive, to find great happiness and to achieve incredible accomplishments. At worst, it is a destructive force which can deprive people of joy, health, sanity, relationships and even life itself (Selye, 1980).

Among the many stressors which affect the human race, few can be imagined that are as destructive and psychologically debilitating as warfare. Few who have experienced its terror would disagree with General William T. Sherman's famous quote during the American Civil War - "All war is hell" (Holmes, 1985). War is a dramatic concentration of the most extremely powerful, destructive stressors known to humanity. With few exceptions, virtually every generation has experienced the trauma of war. The victims of war are practically uncountable. War psychologically scars almost all who participate in it and even most who observe it from afar. The stress of war has the power to change individuals and entire communities forever.

Combat stress has been observed and recorded in military forces since about 603 B.C. Most armies are familiar with its harmful effects. During the American Civil War, for example, literally thousands of soldiers suffered from combat stress and many were seriously incapacitated by its effects. In the Napoleonic wars, Lieutenant-General Sir Thomas Picton once wrote to complain about his own combat stress to Lord Wellington, who commanded the British forces at Waterloo. He stated the following:

> "My lord, I must give up. I am grown so nervous that when there is any service to be done it works upon my mind so that it is impossible for me to sleep at nights. I cannot possibly stand it, and I shall be forced to retire."
>
> (Holmes, 1985)

Unfortunately, little was understood about traumatic stress and almost nothing was known about its treatment. In fact, in all wars prior to World War I, stress reactions were left untreated. Instead of treatment, many soldiers were ridiculed, imprisoned or even killed by their fellow warriors who believed that they were insane, lacking in moral fiber, cowards or traitors (Holmes, 1985; Nakanomiya, 1975).

Warfare changed dramatically between the time of the American Civil War and World War I. Both the technology and tactics of waging war had changed. As a result, a widespread, insidious enemy became more apparent in twentieth century warfare. For the first time in history, huge numbers of psychiatric casualties were encountered during battles. The Civil War experience of psychiatric casualties was between 2.34 and 3.3 per 1,000 troops. In World War I, the incidence of psychiatric casualties rose to 4.0 per 1,000 troops. Some combat units with sustained combat experience encountered even higher levels of psychiatric casualties (Holmes, 1985).

A successful army had to be maintained at relatively full strength to accomplish its mission. It was important to restore wounded and "shell shocked" soldiers to front line duties as soon as possible. In World War I, new techniques were being tested to ensure a greater return of experienced soldiers to the front. This included better medical services as well as psychiatric interventions. "Shell shocked" (stressed) soldiers were being treated in field hospitals near the front lines instead of in remote hospitals far from the front. About 65 percent of those who received immediate treatment for stress were able to return to combat. Approximately 40 percent of soldiers were able to return to combat if treatment for stress was delayed and given only when the soldiers reached a rear hospital (Holmes, 1985; Brown and Williams, 1918; Salmon, 1919).

Most of the support services in the First World War were individual, one-on-one psychiatric-based interventions. Little thought and no action was given to group interventions. There was no formal program of peer support. The same situation prevailed into the early to middle stages of World War II. Nearly 10 percent of all battle casualties in the Second World War were psychiatric in nature. Some units, such as the US 2nd Armored Division, experienced 44 days of sustained combat operations in Italy in 1944 and sustained psychiatric casualty rates as high as 54 percent (Holmes, 1985; Appel, Beebe and Hilger, 1946).

By mid 1944, around the time of the D-Day invasion by the allies, the military had learned that the application of certain basic psychiatric intervention principles had an enormous impact on reducing the rate of combat stress casualties. Combat stress casualties dropped from a rate of 20 percent at the beginning of the invasion of Europe in June and July, 1944, to 8 percent in April and May of 1945 (Holmes, 1985; Appel, et al., 1946). Those principles still are applied in current military stress relief operations and are essential in today's "on-scene" support services and in certain aspects of defusings, demobilizations and debriefings with emergency personnel. The principles are:

- *Simplicity*
- *Innovation*
- *Brevity*
- *Pragmatism*
- *Immediacy*
- *Proximity*
- *Expectancy*

In crisis intervention, which CISM happens to be, the *simple interventions* appear to be most successful. *Innovation* is vital in the field of crisis intervention. Not every circumstance is going to be outlined in a book. Whenever CISM services are provided, they must be *brief*. There is no time for long , involved interventions when people are in pain. *Pragmatism* is also essential. Any intervention which is too theoretical will be impossible to apply and is doomed to failure. *Immediacy* means, of course, that support services for the distressed should be applied as quickly as possible after the traumatic event. *Proximity* means that the intervention should take place as close to the scene as is safe and controlled. Removal to rear areas should only happen when the circumstances warrant it or when an individual's distress is so severe that effective intervention near the field of operations is not possible. *Expectancy* is defined as the expectations which are set up in the affected person's mind by the suggestions of the helper. When a person believes that they will recover and that they will be able to resume their normal duties and their usual life's activities when the stress reaction lessens, they are more likely to work toward those goals (Appel, et al., 1946; Noy, 1991).

The most rudimentary of debriefings were performed on the beaches of Normandy during the D-Day operations on June 6, 1944. These services were not named "debriefings" nor were they very structured. In fact, the neuropsychiatrist who provided "psychiatric first aid" on Utah beach, Dr. Glenn Srodes of Pittsburgh, Pennsylvania, mostly sat with groups of soldiers and let them talk about the traumatic experiences they had during the invasion. He found that those who were afforded this opportunity to ventilate were more alert and ready for battle the next day. The word quickly spread to other psychiatric aid stations during the remaining one and a half years of the war and other psychiatrists tried these loose knit debriefings. Both those receiving the services and those supplying it felt that these unstructured sessions were quite helpful (staff, Pittsburgh Post Gazette, 1984). Units not receiving such help had many more combat stress casualties. The greater the delay of intervention, the less likely it was that soldiers would return to military duties (Appel, 1966).

Until the late 1980s, little changed in the interventions applied by psychiatrists assigned to combat units. Psychological interventions, despite the apparent successes of small group processes which were utilized at the end of World War II and during the Korean conflict, remained essentially a one-on-one process. For example, in the late 1970s and early 1980s, the US Navy developed the "SPRINT" program. The initials stood for "Special Psychiatric Rapid Intervention Team." Several teams were established at naval hospitals and responded to special requests when traumatic events occurred which had a negative effect on naval personnel. The teams were led by psychiatrists and used psychiatric care workers to assist the psychiatrists. They were helpful, but they maintained a strong emphasis on one-on-one contact and on the psychiatric nature of the intervention. It should be noted that during the last decade the teams have changed their name to *Special Personnel Rapid Intervention Teams* and have trained in the CISM program and the CISD model, which they now use to alleviate traumatic stress in groups of naval personnel. Both individual and group Critical Incident Stress Management interventions were utilized after the October, 2000 terrorist attack on the USS Cole in Yemen (Kennedy and Hartiens, 2000).

Although some sporadic group interventions were used with US combat forces in Vietnam, group interventions were not formalized until after the Vietnam war. Even then, they were formalized in the nonmilitary arena (Mitchell, 1983). The Israeli army, on the other hand, did employ a more structured form of group interventions with its troops. In addition, the use of peers to support other soldiers was initiated during the war in Lebanon in 1982. Of the 600 soldiers who were evacuated from the front with psychiatric distress problems, only 60 required further treatment and none required long-term care. Overall, the use of support services for combat troops reduced the incidence of psychiatric disturbance in Israeli combat forces by 60 percent (Holmes, 1985; Breznitz, 1980; Solomon, 1986).

The Israeli military is also credited with the first serious research projects on the effects of psychological first aid and the use of group support interventions on combat personnel. Their well-managed studies and clearly documented results have laid a solid foundation on which to build the Critical Incident Stress Management movement and the group CISD process which is such a major aspect of CISM (Pugliese, 1988).

## DISASTERS' INFLUENCE ON CISM

Disasters have been occurring throughout recorded history. Their highly negative, psychological impact on their victims had been assumed for centuries although no formal studies of disasters took place until the twentieth century. As was the case in warfare, before the twentieth century psychological casualties were essentially left untreated. Little was known about the psychological impact of disasters on individuals or the community. Psychiatry was still a relatively new science and had not yet developed any effective means to intervene in a disaster (Raphael, 1986).

A catastrophic occurrence in 1943 set the stage for the development of practically all of the crisis intervention theory and practice which has evolved since that time. The Coconut Grove night club fire in Boston, Massachusetts, killed more than 400 people. It led effectively to the improvement of the fire protection codes in the United States and in many other countries throughout the world. The disaster also left major scars on the psyche of the American population as well as the survivors and the bereaved. Mental health professionals scrambled to make sense out of chaos and disorder. The work of Dr. Gerald Caplan and, especially, Dr. Eric Lindemann with the survivors and the bereaved became a keystone to present day crisis intervention principles. This work continues to serve as a core theoretical and practice component of Critical Incident Stress Management and Critical Incident Stress Debriefing (Caplan, 1964; Lindemann, 1944).

The emphasis of the crisis intervention work of Caplan, Lindemann and other theoreticians and practitioners was on the actual victims of disastrous events. Disaster literature and research reports are, in fact, filled with information on the plight of the victims (Cohen and Ahearn, 1980; Gist and Lubin, 1989). Little thought was given to the stress encountered by police officers, ambulance personnel, fire fighters, nurses, dispatchers, physicians and disaster workers. There was an assumption that training alone was sufficient to overcome the stress of the disaster. For example, in 1954, a document, *Psychological First Aid in Community Disaster*, which was prepared by the American Psychiatric Association's Committee on Civil Defense, warned that disasters could have some negative psychological effects upon disaster workers themselves. The same warning was presented in the 1964 revised edition of that document. In the next paragraph, however, the text quickly dismissed or attempted to downplay this possibility by stating, "The training you receive as a disaster worker will in itself protect you somewhat in time of stress." (American Psychiatric Association, 1964).

An extensive review of disaster literature between 1900 and 1975 reveals extremely little information on the effects of disasters on the workers. Beginning in 1975, a few hints about the potential negative impacts of disaster work on emergency personnel appear in the literature (Kliman, 1975). Dr. Beverly Raphael of Sydney, Australia, was another rare exception to the significant lack of attention paid to the stress on emergency personnel. She applied loose knit stress debriefing techniques in the late 1970s (Raphael, 1986).

Two very tragic and highly publicized disasters brought into focus the reality of the negative psychological effects of disasters on both the victims and the emergency personnel. The first event was the crash of a Pacific Southwest Airlines plane into a residential neighborhood in San Diego in 1978.

The second event was another plane crash, American Airlines Flight 191, which crashed near Chicago in 1979. These two events accelerated the trend to recognize and attempt to intervene against the stress encountered by emergency personnel. In both events, field personnel as well as hospital staff experienced significant stress reactions for as long as a year after the events (Graham, 1981a, 1981b; Mitchell, 1982; Duffy, 1979; Freeman, 1979).

It was yet another air crash disaster which motivated the finalization of the development of the CISD process. On January 13, 1982, Air Florida Flight 90 failed to achieve altitude after lifting off from National Airport in Washington, DC. The aircraft slammed into the 14th Street Bridge over the Potomac River and 76 people lost their lives. No immediate support was provided to the emergency personnel. Within three weeks, significant stress symptoms began to appear and personnel were asking for some help. A decision was made to provide a CISD. The debriefing process was still considered an experimental intervention. It had been applied on much less intense events for about eight years prior to the Air Florida incident (Mitchell, 1976, 1981). The Washington air crash was the first application of a formal CISD on a large scale incident. Emergency personnel in attendance included fire fighters, police officers, paramedics and disaster managers. The feedback from the personnel was quite positive. They reported that the debriefing process was very helpful to them (Mitchell, 1982).

The CISD has been utilized on numerous disasters since the Air Florida crash. Some of the more notable disasters in which debriefings were provided include:

Barneveld, Wisconsin - Tornado, 1984
Mexico City - Earthquake, 1985
Cerritos, California - Air disaster, 1986
El Salvador - Earthquake, 1986
Palm Bay, Florida - Mass shooting, 1987
Bridgeport, Connecticut - Building collapse, 1987
San Francisco, California - Earthquake, 1989
New York - Fire bombing, 1990
Charleston, South Carolina - Hurricane Hugo, 1990
Persian Gulf - Desert Storm, 1991
Los Angeles, California - Civil riots, 1992
Miami, Florida - Hurricane Andrew, 1992
Hawaii - Hurricane Iniki, 1992
Kuwait - Combat, 1992
Yugoslavia - Civil war, 1993

Rwanda - Mass murder, 1994
Japan - Earthquake, 1995
Oklahoma City, Oklahoma - Terrorist bombing, 1995
Long Island, New York- TWA aircrash, 1996
Kentucky - Severe statewide flooding, 1997
Germany - High-speed train crash, 1998
Honduras - Hurricane, 1999
Fiji - Civil uprising, 2000
Yemen - Terrorist bombing of USS Cole, 2000
Austria - Ski resort tunnel fire, 2000
El Salvador - Earthquake, 2001

# LAW ENFORCEMENT AND CISM

Although structured police services have been in operation in Europe for almost 2,000 years and in the United States for about 350 years, behavioral science applications to policing did not take place until the beginning of the twentieth century. The very first behavioral applications to police work came in the form of psychological evaluations of police recruits (Reese, 1987). This application was important because it laid the foundation for understanding the personality of emergency personnel, specifically the police officer.

It did not take long to recognize that police work was extremely stressful. In the mid 1930s, for example, the mayor of New York City, Fiorello H. La Guardia, ordered a study of police officer suicides. The suicide rate in police officers was found to be considerably higher than the rate of suicides in the average population (Heinman, 1975). Unfortunately, recognizing a stress problem is insufficient in and of itself to solve the problem. The absence of an easily applied intervention program to assist stressed law enforcement personnel only seemed to enhance the further neglect of the problem. In 1976 two police stress researchers stated, "There are few experts in the job stress field and even fewer in the area of stress in policing ...." (Kroes and Hurrell, 1976, p. iii). The majority of the research in the field of police stress was performed during the last two decades. The development of police stress intervention strategies came about only during the last few years (Reese, 1987).

Helping strategies for police officers, including counseling services, spouse support programs, marriage and family counseling, stress inoculation training and other police stress education projects, were pioneered in the late 1960s. Dr. Martin Reiser was the first full-time law enforcement psychologist. He was hired in 1968 by the Los Angeles, California, police department. San Jose, California, soon hired Dr. Michael Roberts as their police psychologist. Other cities such as New York followed the lead of Los Angeles and San Jose. By the early 1980s the number of active police psychologists in the United States had climbed into the hundreds. In 1980, the FBI added a psychological services program to provide counseling to its employees (Reese, 1987).

The first "police stress" programs, which were developed in the mid-1970s, were offshoots of the earlier alcohol counseling programs of the 1950s and 1960s. Police stress programs, in fact, were modeled on the Alcohol Anonymous programs. They were often peer support type programs and can be credited with establishing the use of peers in support services for emergency personnel.

A form of debriefing was offered to police officers who had worked at the 1979 crash of American Airlines Flight 191 outside of Chicago. The process was described as helpful by the police officers who attended. Unfortunately, the literature available did not describe the process in sufficient detail (Wagner, 1979, a-b). It was not until 1983 that the debriefing process in use today was described in sufficient detail to serve as a model for the development of debriefing teams (Mitchell, 1983, 1991).

Today police departments are using the CISM program and the CISD process more frequently. Many police officers are joining the more than 700 CISM teams throughout the United States and in other nations. In addition, the work of many police psychologists and the leadership of the FBI's behavioral sciences services unit has contributed to a wider acceptance of numerous support functions such as pre-incident stress education, family and marriage counseling, post-shooting trauma teams and individual counseling (Reese, 1991).

# HOSPITAL, EMERGENCY MEDICAL, AND FIRE INFLUENCES

The last major influence on the development of the comprehensive CISM program with its many services, including the CISD group crisis intervention process, was, in fact, not a single group but a combined set of influences.

Stress management work in hospitals, emergency medical services programs and fire departments set the final segment of the CISM foundation. All of the influences were interdependent upon one another. In fact, the final stages of development of the process could never have been accomplished without the history established by the military, law enforcement and disaster fields.

The Shock Trauma Center in Baltimore was the first major medical trauma facility known to provide support services to its trauma staff. Marge Epperson-Sebour, a social worker in the family services section, was concerned with the turn-over of experienced staff nurses. She developed a series of educational stress management and crisis intervention programs in the mid-1970s. There was a remarkable decrease in the turn-over rate among the trauma nurses and other staff (Epperson, 1977; Epperson-Sebour, 1985). Some of the theory and applications developed at the Maryland Shock Trauma Center became a core for the eventual development of the CISM field and the CISD process in use today.

Nancy Graham's articles on stress and burnout in the emergency medical services field were some of the very first to describe the stress problems being encountered by emergency medical technicians and paramedics (Graham, 1981a,b). But the United States was not the only place where there was interest in the field of stress effects on emergency workers. Dr. Tony Taylor of New Zealand was interested in the effects of body-handling on disaster workers after an air crash in Antarctica (Taylor and Frazer, 1982). Dr. Robyn Robinson in Melbourne, Australia, and Dr. Beverly Raphael in Sydney, Australia, were working with fire, emergency medical and hospital staffs to reduce the negative impact of stress on staff members (Robinson, 1986). Dr. Robinson was responsible for the development of a sophisticated peer counseling and debriefing unit which serves Melbourne's fire and emergency medical services. Dr. Atle Dyregrov, a Norwegian psychologist who specialized in pediatric traumatic stress, also was very interested in workplace trauma among hospital workers, military police, fire fighters and industrial employees (Dyregrov and Thyhodt, 1988). He has published extensively in European psychological journals and is credited with the spread of CISM services throughout Europe.

The first article which specifically addressed the details of the Critical Incident Stress Debriefing process was written by Dr. Jeffrey T. Mitchell and published by the *Journal of Emergency Medical Services* in January, 1983. It was this article which described the debriefing process and stimulated the development of CISD teams throughout the world (Mitchell, 1983, 1988).

Although the 1983 article is the most frequently cited CISD article, it is not the most up-to-date as these concepts were updated in 1984 and again in 1988. The CISD model has remained essentially intact since it was first described in 1983, but a few changes have been made. What has occurred is the natural refinement process of the concepts and procedures which would occur in any new stress intervention process. Originally, the CISD had only six phases. Articles written shortly after the 1983 article show seven phases. A "Thought" phase, which was assumed under the "Fact" phase in the original article, was added as a transition between the "Fact" and "Reaction" phases. The "Reaction" phase was originally named the "Feeling" phase. The name was changed from "Feeling" to "Reaction" for several reasons. First, the word "feeling" was found to be somewhat uncomfortable for emergency operations personnel who resisted any efforts to discuss feelings. Secondly, it was recognized that people have many ways to react to a traumatic situation. Feelings are only one of those ways. The differences between the original CISD process and the one in use today are outlined in Table 4.1 for the convenience of the reader.

**TABLE 4.1**

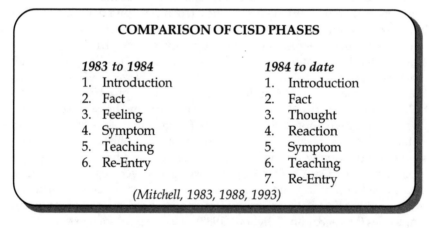

### COMPARISON OF CISD PHASES

| *1983 to 1984* | *1984 to date* |
|---|---|
| 1. Introduction | 1. Introduction |
| 2. Fact | 2. Fact |
| 3. Feeling | 3. Thought |
| 4. Symptom | 4. Reaction |
| 5. Teaching | 5. Symptom |
| 6. Re-Entry | 6. Teaching |
| | 7. Re-Entry |

*(Mitchell, 1983, 1988, 1993)*

It should be noted that the 1983 article by Mitchell did not suggest the use of only one intervention technique as has been mistakenly reported in the literature. It instead suggested a comprehensive, systematic and multi-tactic approach to managing stress within an organization. The 1983 article, which is the first stepping stone in the development of the CISM program, urged emergency services organizations to have a complete program that would include pre-incident education, defusing, family support, on-scene support services and follow-up services and referral mechanisms. In fact, it suggested all of the core elements of today's CISM program.

Several other developments are important to note before concluding this chapter. The descriptions of the various types of debriefings have changed during the last decade as debriefers have learned more about the CISD process. Today there is a greater emphasis on the role of peer support personnel. This does not diminish the importance of the mental health professional. The importance of that role remains consistent. But there is an expanded and enhanced role for the peer support personnel. The on-scene support functions are no longer considered a type of debriefing. Instead, they are one-on-one services provided primarily by well-trained peer support personnel and only rarely, under the most extreme circumstances, by mental health professionals. They are always individual interventions and never a group process.

The name "initial defusing" has been dropped and only the name "defusing" remains. Additionally, the services of the defusing are more often provided by peers. Debriefings, defusings or any group process for that matter, are never provided at the scene. They are reserved for when the incident is complete and personnel are no longer at the scene. New adaptations of large group interventions, such as Demobilizations, and more recently, Crisis Management Briefings, have been developed and described in the literature. Significant changes and improvements to the follow-up services have been made and they will be described in a later chapter in this book.

Finally, CISM and its group process, CISD, are no longer seen as being reserved for emergency service workers. CISM services are now seen as viable interventions for the prevention of traumatic stress among all high-risk professions as well as businesses, industries, school systems and communities (Everly and Mitchell, 1992).

## SUMMARY

This chapter has described the major influences which have enhanced the development of the CISM field and its specific group intervention, CISD. The contributions of several notable researchers, mental health professionals and emergency personnel to the field have been briefly described. Those whose works were mentioned are indeed luminaries in the field.

There were, of course, many others who contributed to the development of the CISM field and CISD model. It would be impossible to list every contributor because of the limitations of space and time. But it should be recognized that no single person can be credited with the development of a major movement in the field of CISM. Many dedicated experts contributed a piece to its history. Many more continue to make contributions of their talents and energies as they provide CISM services to their communities. Those who benefit from the CISM program owe their gratitude to the many who suffered stress in their lives and especially to the stress management pioneers in the military, disaster, law enforcement, hospital, fire service and emergency medical services fields.

# Chapter 5

# CISM: MECHANISMS OF ACTION AND EFFECTIVENESS

In previous chapters the CISD and post-trauma defusings, as well as other CISM services, were operationally defined. As noted, the CISM "field" has proliferated. The CISM program and the group interventions of CISD and defusing have become widely adopted (more than 500 teams world-wide) and have been generally accepted based upon what may be considered by some a rigorous, grueling, and adversarial mechanism of appraisal (i.e., over a decade of empirical field testing performed by and upon a population which was professionally, and perhaps at times personally, inclined to disprove any need whatsoever for CISM or CISD). Despite this gauntlet of administrative, professional and personal resistance, the use of CISM has grown dramatically to the point that psychological debriefing has emerged as a virtual field, or subspecialty, of its own. Upon what factors can this success be based? Let us first look at the mechanisms at work in the defusing and debriefing processes. Then we will turn to a discussion of the rationale for the establishment of any form of CISM program.

## POSSIBLE MECHANISMS OF ACTION

Let us consider mechanisms which may underlie the effectiveness of defusings and debriefings. Consider the following aspects as they are represented within CISD and related processes:

1. EARLY INTERVENTION .... CISD is most typically utilized as an early intervention strategy, oft-times employed within hours of the actual traumatic stressor. Friedman, Framer and Shearer (1988) found that early detection of and early intervention with PTSD or posttraumatic stress syndromes led to lower costs and more favorable prognoses associated with victims of trauma. Two hundred clinical PTSD cases receiving treatment in the Los Angeles area were divided into two groups: 100 individu-

als who were diagnosed and treated within 6 months of the trauma were compared to 100 individuals who were diagnosed and treated from 6 to 36 months after the trauma. The average costs attributed to the "early" (within 6 months) cases were $8,300, while the costs attributable to the "late" cases were $46,000. The "early" cases averaged 12 weeks of recovery prior to return to work, the "late" cases required 46 weeks to recover. Finally, 13% of the "early" cases entered litigation while 94% of the "late" cases pursued legal action. Indeed, it is almost universally recognized that prevention and early intervention are preferable to having to pursue traditional treatment strategies (Yandrick, 1990; Duffy, 1979; Kentsmith, 1980; Butcher, 1980).

The concept of the "trauma membrane" may help explain why early intervention in the trauma process appears important. Lindy's notion of the "trauma membrane" (Lindy, Grace and Green, 1981) argues that after a traumatic event, victims begin to be insulated from individuals and processes that are external to the immediate trauma sequelae. This insulation process is thought to be analogous to the formation of a protective, insular membrane serving as a protective barrier. While this barrier attempts to protect from further intrusion, it may also inadvertently isolate victims from healing interventions as well. Thus, it becomes of paramount importance to intervene early while the trauma membrane is still permeable. Early intervention, then, allows for help prior to "concretization" of traumatic memories and perhaps prior to the formation of a potential host of maladaptive coping mechanisms (e.g., substance abuse, social alienation, acting out, etc.). Post (1992) argues that early intervention may prevent a neurologically based lowered threshold for excitation from developing within the central nervous system subsequent to intense stress. Thus, early intervention may prevent the development of a cellular "memory" of the trauma from forming in excitatory neural tissues.

2. OPPORTUNITY FOR CATHARSIS .... According to Heider (1974), there are few conditions that cannot benefit from catharsis. Catharsis refers to the ventilation of emotions. CISD provides a safe, supportive, structured environment wherein individuals can ventilate emotions. Kahn (1966) showed that expressing emotions lowers levels of arousal. In a review of studies specifically investigating the relationship between the disclosure of traumatic events and stress arousal, Pennebaker and Susman (1988) concluded that disclosure of traumatic events leads to reduced stress arousal and improved immune functioning. Most importantly, however, Roemer and Borkovec (1994) found that suppressing emotions was related to increased anxiety and depression over time, almost a sensitiza-

tion effect, while expression of emotions was related to the habituation of anxiety over time. The importance of expressing one's emotions is not a very new concept. Shakespeare's MacBeth said, "Give sorrow words: the grief that does not speak whispers the o'er-fraught heart and bids it break." Getting emotions out in the open improves psychological and physical well being (Pennebaker, 1990). Emotional catharsis or ventilation is a critical feature of the healing process (Meichenbaum, 1994; Pennebaker, 1999).

3. OPPORTUNITY TO VERBALIZE TRAUMA .... CISM interventions, including CISD, not only give individuals the opportunity to release emotions, but the opportunity to verbally reconstruct and express specific traumas, fears and regrets. Van der Hart, Brown and van der Kolk (1989) recount the views of master traumatologist Pierre Janet who noted at the turn of the twentieth century that the successful treatment of posttraumatic reactions was largely based upon the patient's ability to not just express feelings (catharsis) but was based upon the patients ability to reconstruct and integrate the trauma using the verbally expressive medium. The work of Pennebaker (Pennebaker, 1985; Pennebaker and Beall, 1986) appears to confirm the critical role that verbal reconstruction and expression of the traumatic event play in the successful resolution of post-trauma syndromes for many individuals (Pennebaker, 1999).

Bruno Bettleheim who studied holocaust survivors and other traumatized individuals stated, "What cannot be talked about can also not be put to rest; and if it is not, the wounds continue to fester from generation to generation." (Bettleheim, 1984, p.166). When people cannot put their traumatic experiences into words, they tend to dream about those experiences more often and they tend to obsessively think about those experiences for longer periods of time in an unresolved manner which creates more distress for them (Silver, et al., 1983; Harvey, et al., 1991). In a review of the literature on the benefits of verbalizing traumatic experiences Meichenbaum (1994) describes an unpublished work of Pennebaker and Francis in which they conclude that, either verbally or in writing, the expression in language of one's traumatic experiences will:

• Organize a person's thoughts and feelings about the event

• Facilitate the labeling of feelings

• Lower preoccupation with event related thoughts and feelings

- Enhance insight and reframing and allow acceptance

- Allow for an exploration of the meaning of the event

- Encourage new perspectives and problem solving activities

The collective value of catharsis and the verbalizing of the trauma appear to reside in their ability to: a) reduce stress, b) reduce strain on the homeostatic mechanisms of the body, c) reduce tendencies to ruminate / obsess and d) increase the likelihood of "making sense" out of the trauma (reintegration of the individual's "Weltanshuuang" or "Worldview").

4. BEHAVIORAL STRUCTURE .... CISD provides a finite behavioral structure, that is, a group debriefing represents a process with a finite beginning and a finite end, superimposed upon a traumatic event representing chaos, suffering, and a myriad of unanswered questions. CISD is the antithesis of the traumatic milieu. Borkovec, and others, (1983) found that providing a structured environment within which to "worry" actually reduced the tendency for worry to contaminate or interfere with other activities on a daily basis.

5. PSYCHOLOGICAL STRUCTURE .... CISD and defusings follow a well-conceived structured psychological progression. The process is initiated engaging the cognitive domain (Introduction and Fact Phases in the CISD). This structure is ideal for those persons already engaged in that domain using cognitive analysis or even denial mechanisms. It aligns with their psychological posture rather than contradicting or opposing it, thereby avoiding the risk of initiating group conflict. Consistent with a crisis intervention model, this structure is similarly useful for those engaged in the affective domain for it gently superimposes a cognitive structure so as to set some boundaries with the "promise" of the opportunity for further affective expression later in the process. It, thus, represents an exercise in self-control and self-efficacy as well. As the process moves through the Thought Phase, the cognitive domain is left and the affective domain may be entered. Affective ventilation may be achieved in the Reaction Phase. Being careful not to leave any "emotional loose ends," the process then passes through the Symptom Phase, moving from the affective domain back to the cognitive. Lastly, the cognitive domain dominates the Teaching and Re-Entry Phases. This overall structure allows the affective domain to be experienced in the most useful manner possible, given an acute, crisis intervention (not therapeutic) format. The cognitively based phases serve as entrance and exit portals to and from the affective domain, while also

**TABLE 5.1**

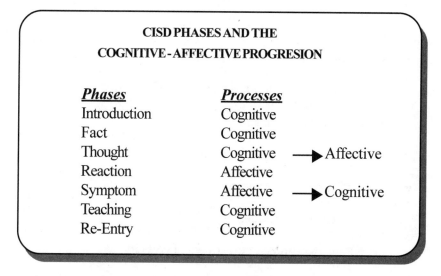

**CISD PHASES AND THE**
**COGNITIVE - AFFECTIVE PROGRESION**

| *Phases* | *Processes* | |
|----------|-------------|---|
| Introduction | Cognitive | |
| Fact | Cognitive | |
| Thought | Cognitive ⟶ Affective | |
| Reaction | Affective | |
| Symptom | Affective ⟶ Cognitive | |
| Teaching | Cognitive | |
| Re-Entry | Cognitive | |

providing a useful cognitive structure and information in their own right. See Table 5.1 for a summary of this process.

6. GROUP SUPPORT .... CISD, in the classic application, employs a group model. The value of using a group format to address distressing issues is well-documented. Yalom (1970) notes that the group process provides numerous healing factors intrinsic to the group format itself. Among them are the exchange of useful constructive information, catharsis, the dissolution of the myth of a unique vulnerability or weakness among individuals, the modeling of constructive coping behavior, the opportunity to derive a sense of group caring and support, the opportunity to help oneself by helping others and, perhaps most importantly with regard to trauma, the generation of feelings of hope. As Jones (1985) commented on the value of using group discussion formats following trauma, "There is real value, especially for young men, in understanding that others feel the same strong emotions under such circumstances, that each is not alone in the strength of his shock, grief, and anger" (Jones, 1985, p.307).

Numerous clinicians and researchers in the fields of crisis intervention, post-trauma treatment and group work suggest that the resolution of traumatic experiences is facilitated when people discuss those experiences in the presence of others who have lived through the same or similar situations (Yalom, 1970; Smith, 1985; Scurfield, 1985; Roth and

Newman, 1993; Courchaine and Dowd, 1994). Some of the benefits of group process are:

- Exchange of useful constructive information

- Reduction of the sense of isolation

- Provision of mutual comfort and support

- Reduction of stigmatization

- Identification of common issue and goals

- Opening up of communication

- Safe exploration of hidden issues

- Encouragement and empowerment of participants

- Restoration of individual and unit pride

- Diminishing of guilt and shame

- Generation of feelings of hope

- Generation of optimism

- Enhancement of group cohesiveness

- Encouragement of mutual help

- Normalization of the experience

- Opening up paths of potential change (Meichenbaum, 1994)

7. PEER SUPPORT .... Although mental health professionals oversee the CISD process, peers actively participate. Carkhuff and Truax (1965) long ago demonstrated the value of lay support models. Indeed, peer support interventions offer unique advantages over traditional mental health services especially when the peer-group views itself as being highly unique, selective or otherwise "different" compared to the general population. Peers can most effectively eradicate the myth of unique vulnerability or

weakness and can also most effectively offer advice on effective coping / stress management techniques. In the final analysis, peers have a unique credibility (the Aristotelian concept of "ethos") that no mental health professional could possess (unless he/she is also an operations person).

Peer counselors have been used in various settings including disaster situations (Orner, 1994). Peers who have been well-trained in the following peer counselor skills can be very effective in assisting people in their own professions through the turmoil produced in the aftermath of a traumatic event. The peer skills are:

- Attending

- Communicating

- Empathizing

- Summarizing

- Questioning

- Being genuine

- Being assertive

- Confrontation

- Problem solving (Tindall and Gray, 1985)

8. STRESS EDUCATION .... The stress education information provided in debriefings is not a lecture, but an interactive learning experience which helps people to leave the debriefing and cope better with more knowledge about the natural consequences of traumatic stress. Education in a debriefing is used to debunk myths; to provide information about possible stress triggers to be avoided and the symptoms which might arise and linger; to provide specific information on managing flashbacks, memory problems and relapse prevention. Stress education in debriefings instills hope, engenders meaning, and helps people to cognitively reframe their experiences (Meichenbaum, 1994). Often the education segment of a debriefing and many therapy programs is used to "normalize" an experience (Lipton, 1994). Providing an education segment in a debriefing provides people with a guide or a "road map" which helps them to recover from the traumatic experience (Ochberg, 1991; Herman, 1992).

9. ALLOWS FOR FOLLOW-UP .... The CISD process represents an entry portal where potential victims can engage in group discussion, information exchange and support. It also represents a mechanism wherein individuals who do indeed require formal psychological care can be identified and helped so as to maximize the likelihood of rapid and total recovery. (A point completely neglected in outcome research).

10. ACTION ORIENTED .... The CISD process and other CISM tactics follow a key principle of crisis intervention. It is a process of direct intervention during a period of extreme stress. The CISD process does not allow people to remain in a state of confusion and disequilibrium. Instead the team providing the CISD organizes the group, stabilizes the situation, mobilizes resources, actively normalizes the experience and encourages those affected by the trauma to take responsibility for their own recovery. When action is taking place, participants in a debriefing feel that their concerns are being taken seriously and that the leaders of the group are in control and knowledgeable about trauma support.

# A RATIONALE TO CONSIDER

Having examined how CISD and other group interventions may work, the question becomes, "Why establish such programs?" According to the National Council on Compensation Insurance, excessive stress accounts for about 14% of all "occupational disease" workers' compensation claims (McCarthy, 1988). The Council notes that medical and other benefit payments average $15,000 for stress-related claims. This amount is twice the average amount paid per claim for workers with physical injuries.

Although even more difficult to document, the total financial costs of excessive stress to business and industry, beyond just workers' compensation claims, appear quite formidable. Estimates place the overall cost of stress on the economy as high as $150 billion per year (Miller, et al., 1988).

In an epidemiological investigation conducted by Helzer, and others, (1987), it was discovered that PTSD occurred in the general population of the United States at a prevalence of about 1%. This prevalence is comparable to that of schizophrenia. In a population of young urban adults the prevalence was found to be over 9%, lifetime (Breslau, et al., 1991). The statistical risk of PTSD can be very misleading, however.

For those in high risk professions, any single traumatic incident could engender symptoms of posttraumatic stress or fully developed PTSD. Consider, then, the following:

1. Work-related stress claims represent the fastest growing and most costly, per incident, type of workers' compensation claim affecting American commerce (McCarthy, 1988).

2. PTSD is a severe and incapacitating form of stress-related disorder, capable of ending its victim's functional life in a matter of moments while changing, forever, the life of the victim's family, (Everly and Lating, 1995).

3. The risk of becoming a victim of PTSD is primarily a function of being in a high-risk, potentially traumatizing situation / experience, thus individuals in "high-risk" occupations (such as emergency services professions) are at a higher than normal risk for PTSD.

4. The career prevalence of PTSD in a major urban fire department was estimated at over 16% (Corneil, 1993); and it may be that the risk of developing PTSD over the span of a career in any of the emergency service professions is in the 15% to 20% range.

In a study of the London Ambulance Service in the United Kingdom, 40 randomly selected ambulance personnel were tested to determine if they were stressed by the types of calls they handled. Sixty percent (60%) could be classified as having stress responses and 17% of the personnel were in the severe category of symptoms on the General Health Questionnaire and on the Impact of Events Scale (Thompson and Suzuki, 1991).

In another study of 1,420 personnel of the London Ambulance Service, which happens to be the largest ambulance service in the world, it was found that 15% of front line staff crossed the threshold for the diagnosis of posttraumatic stress disorder and had as many as 16 symptoms of the disorder at significant levels. For example, in addition to the key PTSD symptoms of intrusion, avoidance and arousal, 46% of the group felt angry; 43% had lost hope in the future; 25% felt "coldness" toward the patients; 33% were having sleep disturbance; 29% were restless and "jumpy" (Ravenscroft, 1994).

Similar results were found among ambulance personnel on another continent. The Victoria Ambulance service in Australia performed an extensive study of 1380 ambulance officers and 1223 of their significant others. Dr. Robyn Robinson (1994, p. 3) stated,

"A disturbing finding is that sixty-five percent of Officers report that they currently experience trauma reactions as a result of prior ambulance jobs [calls]. Seventeen percent report pervasive, strong response. Though this study does not define staff with Posttraumatic Stress Disorder, the findings suggest that a high incidence exists."

1. The suicide rates in some law enforcement agencies may be three times the national average and have been associated with the stress of being exposed to, and dealing with, other people's traumas (see for example, Newsweek, Sept. 26, 1994).

2. It is generally accepted that the psychological states of first responders greatly affect the overall outcome of any given emergency situation to which these personnel are asked to respond, including the health of the primary victims themselves.

3. These points and more argue compellingly for intervention efforts to be directed toward the prevention of posttraumatic stress syndromes (Duffy, 1979; Kentsmith, 1980; Butcher, 1980).

4. CISD and traumatic stress defusings have over a 17 year history of application in high risk occupational venues across the globe making them the most widely used formalized intervention for the prevention of traumatic stress in the world.

## EFFECTIVENESS OF CISD: EARLY RESEARCH

Since the first edition of this book was published in 1993, new data on the effects of CISD have become available and other studies are currently underway. Each piece of this body of research is welcomed because it sheds further light on the evolving field of Critical Incident Stress Management and the use of debriefing services. Research will help to determine what is working and why, and it will help us to make plans, modifications, more effective protocols and procedures and set a direction for additional research in the future. The following paragraphs will shed some light on the latest research which has been accomplished to date.

While true experimental designs are difficult to achieve in field research, Rogers (1992) has conducted a quasi-experimental analysis of the effects of CISD on emergency personnel. Data suggest that there may be a powerful symptom mitigation effect achieved from the use of CISD. This effect may not be evident, however, until several weeks after the CISD. According to Rogers' data, the immediate 36 - hour post - CISD effect appears minimal. This study, obviously, needs to be replicated and expanded. The use of comparable control groups needs to be pursued as does the general quest for valid and reliable outcome data subsequent to defusings and CISD interventions.

Tables 5.2 and 5.3 compare the severity of two air disasters. Table 5.3 contrasts the effects of those disasters, given very different post-disaster interventions. The Cerritos disaster was the beneficiary of CISD and related interventions. The results seem striking in this naturalistically derived empirical comparison.

Dr. Atle Dyregrov, a key European researcher in the field of traumatic stress, suggests that the early use of Critical Incident Stress Debriefing is helpful for disaster victims (Dyregrov, 1989). His suggestions for the use of group debriefings are supported by other researchers (Turner, Thompson and Rosser, 1993). The CISD process was utilized after a ferry, bearing British school children, sank in the Mediterranean Sea (Johnston, 1983). In the United States it has been suggested that debriefings would be useful in a variety of workplace traumas (Williams, 1993). Critical Incident Stress Debriefings are recommended for police officers (Blau, 1994) and for nurses (Burns and Harm, 1993). CISDs have been utilized extensively in the military (Miller, 1994). Numerous clinicians and researchers have employed various forms of debriefings in their work with traumatized individuals and groups (Wilson and Raphael, 1993; Mitchell and Dyregrov, 1993; Meichenbaum, 1994).

Other studies also suggest rather positive benefits from debriefings. Robyn Robinson's study of ambulance personnel indicates that 45% state that one or several major critical incidents were the cause of significant stress reactions for them. Of the 823 ambulance officers surveyed, 64% were aware of the debriefing services which were offered to them by the Victoria Ambulance Crisis Counselling Unit. Of these, 71% felt that debriefing services were very important, 26% felt that debriefing services were quite important and only 3% felt debriefings were not important (Robinson, 1994).

When the debriefings themselves were evaluated, 37% of ambulance personnel in the study found them very helpful. Another 45% found the

**TABLE 5.2**

## COMPARISON OF SAN DIEGO AND CERRITOS
## AIR DISASTERS

|  | San Diego | Cerritos |
|---|---|---|
| Total killed | 125 | 82 |
| Plane survivors | 0 | 0 |
| Homes destroyed | 16 | 16 |
| Civilians killed on the ground | 15 | 15 |
| Emergency personnel engaged | 300 | 300 |
| Body parts recovered | >10,000 | >10,000 |

*(compiled by J. T. Mitchell, Ph.D. from NIMH, 1979; 1983; Duffy, 1979; Freeman, 1979; Honig, 1987)*

**TABLE 5.3**

## SAN DIEGO AND CERRITOS AIR DISASTERS' IMPACT
## ON EMERGENCY WORKERS WITH AND WITHOUT
## CISD INTERVENTION

|  | San Diego | Cerritos |
|---|---|---|
| Intervention | Sporadic 1 on 1 Crisis Intervention | 12 CISD Demobilizations Hotline Follow-up |
| Loss of Ranking Police | 5 in one year | Total of 1 in one year |
| Loss of Fire Personnel | 7 in one year | |
| Loss of Paramedics | 17 in one year | |
| Increase in mental health utilization | 31% in one year | 1% in one year |

*(compiled by J. T. Mitchell, Ph.D. from NIMH, 1979; 1983; Duffy, 1979; Freeman, 1979; Honig, 1987)*

debriefings moderately helpful and 18 % found them not helpful.

Since the CISD process is believed to lower stress symptoms (Rogers, 1992), specific questions were asked about symptom reduction in Robinson's study. Twenty-one (21%) of the personnel who went through a debriefing said that they had considerable lowering of symptoms. Another 51% said their symptoms lowered a little, and 28% said the debriefing had no effect on their symptom levels.

When asked how long the benefits of CISD lasted, 48% believed the benefits of CISD were long lasting. Another 10% said the benefits of CISD lasted a few weeks; yet another 14% said the benefits lasted up to a few days and 28% said they did not perceive any benefits of the CISD (Robinson, 1994).

The effectiveness of CISDs was evaluated in a study of 288 emergency, welfare and hospital workers who were involved in 31 "Mitchell Model" debriefings held between 1987 and 1989 in Melbourne, Australia. The incidents which were debriefed included a line of duty death, five multi-casualty (with multiple fatalities) incidents, child fatalities, injury of a colleague, a patient suicide and other traumatic situations. All respondents in the study agreed that the critical incidents had moderate to considerable impact upon them.

Two weeks after each of the debriefings, questionnaires were distributed to all of the CISD participants. The two week time frame is important to note because a number of other studies have allowed much greater times to elapse and those delays may distort the results.

The majority of the participants in the Melbourne study indicated that the CISDs were considerably helpful to themselves and they perceived that the process was considerably helpful to others in the group. In fact, "96% of emergency service personnel and 77% of the welfare / hospital staff who experienced stress symptoms after the incident stated that they had experienced a reduction of stress symptoms which they attributed, at least in part, to the debriefing." (Robinson and Mitchell, 1993, p. 376).

The most prominent reasons presented by the participants for why the debriefings were helpful were:

- Talking with people involved in the event about the incident helped to deal with it better

- Talking about the incident (which they stated they would not have done without the debriefings)

- The debriefings helped personnel to gain better understanding of themselves

Although the questionnaire contained questions which invited criticisms of the CISD process, the only substantial criticisms offered by the participants revolved around procedural issues such as the lack of comfort of the chairs, the debriefing was held too long after the event and everyone involved in the event should have been present in the debriefing. Others

**TABLE 5.4**

**NURSING STUDY ON CISD**

| *CISD Helpful* | *% indicating* |
|---|---|
| 1. Talking about the incident helped | 86.6% |
| 2. Realizing that I wasn't alone in my responses to the incident | 85.1% |
| 3. Hearing others talk about the incident | 83.0% |
| 4. Being part of a group that had also experienced the incident | 73.2% |
| 5. Hearing how others were handling the stress | 58.2% |
| 6. My stress responses decreased in intensity | 46.9% |
| 7. Learning about stress from the leaders | 22.2% |

| *CISD Not helpful* | *% indicating* |
|---|---|
| 1. The leaders had no relevant experience | 26.9% |
| 2. There were people present in the group with whom I was uncomfortable | 23.1% |
| 3. Too long after the event | 19.2% |
| 4. I was not comfortable discussing the event in a group | 9.6% |
| 5. I resented the time the debriefing took from my personal life | 9.6% |
| 6. Too soon after the event | 3.8% |

*(Burns and Harm, 1993)*

cited the fact that the process was a new one and they did not know enough about it in advance. They suggested that if they had known more about CISD they might have gotten more out of the sessions. No one reported experiencing harm from the debriefings (Robinson and Mitchell, 1993).

Overall, CISDs were found to be generally positive for the participants in the Melbourne study. "The positive impact and the value of debriefing on personnel was marked. Most personnel who reported symptoms of stress following a critical incident also stated that these had been reduced as a consequence of attending the debriefing. Further, the greater the impact of an event on staff, the greater was the rated value of the debriefing." (Robinson and Mitchell, 1993, p. 380).

In another researcher's study, similar reasons were given for the effectiveness of the debriefings. Of 219 nurses who received CISDs 193 reported the process was helpful to them. Twenty-six (26) reported that the process was not helpful. The nurses stated reasons why the debriefings were helpful or not helpful. (Burns and Harm, 1993) See Table 5.4 for these reasons.

It is important to pay attention to the reasons given for the ineffectiveness of debriefings. Not following the basic CISD principles outlined in this book and in numerous articles can set the stage for a "failed" debriefing or at least one that is uncomfortable for the debriefing team. Such a violation of core CISD principles is described in a paper on the Lockerbie air disaster. One "debriefer" wrote:

> "We also rapidly learned a cardinal rule in debriefing - that it is not advisable to begin with inquiring about the emotional reactions of 'exposure hardened' individuals. It was more effective (and easier) to collect together the overall experience of the group before exploring individual reactions. The correction of individual misinterpretations and misconceptions using this technique was very impressive." (Meichenbaum, 1994, p. 521).

Debriefing processes have been used on children with positive results. For example, one and one half years after the Armenian earthquake, children were given debriefing sessions and individual and group follow-up sessions. The debriefing significantly reduced the severity of posttraumatic stress reactions in the children. Control groups did not fare as well (Pynoos, et al., 1994).

As can be seen by the numerous articles cited in the preceding paragraphs, CISD and its associated interventions have entered the realm of research and an expanded literature base. Shalev (1994, p. 209) notes that the works of Raphael and Mitchell are the "most widely cited" in the debriefing field. Meichenbaum (1994) echoes Shalev's comment and provides a description and critique of the "Mitchell Model" of CISD.

# EFFECTIVENESS OF CISD: RECENT RESEARCH

As might be expected, there is not total agreement on the effectiveness of group crisis intervention, especially "debriefing." Initial concern over the effectiveness of psychological debriefings arose in the relevant literature with the publication of two Australian studies. McFarlane (1988) reported on the longitudinal course of posttraumatic morbidity in the wake of bush fires. One aspect of the study found that acute posttraumatic stress was predicted by avoidance of thinking about problems, property loss, and not attending undefined forms of psychological debriefings. However, chronic variations of posttraumatic stress disorder were best predicted by premorbid, non-event related factors, such as a family history of psychiatric disorders, concurrent avoidance and neuroticism, and a tendency not to confront conflicts. The delayed onset posttraumatic stress group not only had higher premorbid neuroticism scores, and greater property loss, but also attended the undefined debriefings. While these factors, when submitted to discriminant function analysis, only resulted in the correct identification of 53% of the delayed onset group, this study is often reported as evidence for lack of effectiveness of debriefings.

The second of the early negative outcome studies was that of Kenardy, et al., (1996). Kenardy's investigation purported to assess the effectiveness of stress debriefings for 62 "debriefed helpers" compared to 133 who were apparently not debriefed subsequent to an earthquake in New Castle, Australia. This study is often cited as evidence for the ineffectiveness of debriefings, yet the authors state, "we were not able to influence the availability or nature of the debriefing…" (p. 39). They continue, "It was assumed that all subjects in this study who reported having been debriefed did in fact receive posttrauma debriefing. However, there was no standardization of debriefing services…"(p.47). These rather remarkable epistemological revelations by the authors have failed to deter critics of the "debriefing" process, whatever the term may mean.

Unfortunately, those who cite these investigations as "evidence" of the lack of effectiveness of "psychological debriefings" appear to have neglected the immutable empirical reality that failure to insure the standardization and reliability of the independent variable (debriefing) renders the results of the investigations unintelligible, ungeneralizable, and certainly not supportive of the null hypothesis, as some would contend.

Perhaps the greatest contention regarding the utilization of debriefings has arisen from reviews constructed by Wessely, Rose, & Bisson (1998), sometimes referred to as the Cochrane Report, and by Rose & Bisson (1998). These reviews are held out to be methodologically robust because they employ only investigations using randomization, however, these reviews suffer from the inconsistent use of the term "debriefing," as evidenced in constituent studies below:

Bisson, Jenkins, Alexander, & Bannister (1997) randomly assigned 110 patients with severe burns to either a "debriefing" group or a control group. The clinical standard group debriefing was abandoned for an individual adaptation. Despite the lack of equivalent groups (more severe burns in the debriefed group), despite a plausible alternative explanation for poorer psychological outcome (greater financial problems for the debriefed group), despite the inappropriate use of the debriefing with medical patients who were either in pain or on analgesic medications, and despite the failure to follow standard clinical protocols for group debriefings, these authors contend that the results cast serious doubt upon the utility of debriefings.

Hobbs, Mayou, Harrison, & Warlock (1996) performed a randomized trial of debriefings for 106 (54 debriefed; 52 control) motor vehicle accident victims. Despite, non-equivalent groups (the debriefing group was more severe at pretest), despite the failure to use the clinical standard group -based intervention, these data have been used to argue that debriefing may be injurious. Yet closer scrutiny reveals that while the debriefed group evidenced statistically higher trauma scores at posttest, the difference was not clinically meaningful. In a four-year longitudinal follow-up investigation, Mayou, Ehlers, and Hobbs (2000) found the intervention group (individualized debriefings) remained symptomatic. It seems a non-sequitur to conclude that psychological debriefing is ineffective and to further conclude that it is inappropriate for trauma patients when the debriefing process was individualized, as opposed to the group format, and when the debriefing was taken out of its prescribed multicomponent context.

Lee, Slade, & Lygo (1996) assessed the effectiveness of individual debriefing on women following miscarriages. No significant changes were attributed to debriefings. In a more recent variation, Small, et al. (2000) used "debriefing" subsequent to operative childbirth (Caesarean, forceps, or vacuum delivery). Once again individual debriefing was employed, as opposed to group debriefing. The debriefing took place prior to hospital discharge, while the psychological assessment took place at six months post childbirth. Unfortunately, the debriefing process, as operationalized in this study, was not specifically described, other than being at variance with the prescribed group-based intervention. Nevertheless, the reported results indicated that 94% of the women in the debriefing group found the debriefing either "helpful" or "very helpful" (n = 437/463). As would be predicted, the intervention was found to be ineffective as a treatment for the symptoms of depression.

In support of debriefings, but specifically the CISD model of group psychological crisis intervention, we find several investigations: Nurmi (1999) with rescue personnel in the wake of the sinking of the Estonia; Wee, et al., (1999) with emergency medical technicians subsequent to the Los Angeles riots; Bohl (1991) with police; Bohl (1995) with fire personnel; Chemtob, et al. (1997) with healthcare providers subsequent to Hurricane Iniki; and Jenkins (1996) with emergency medical personnel in the wake of a mass shooting. All of these investigations offer varying degrees of evidence for the effectiveness of the CISD intervention. Each of these studies, however, may be criticized for their lack of randomized subject assignment. However, five of the seven aforementioned studies possessed a static control condition, while one possessed a time-lagged control. These research designs are known to be vulnerable to selection, mortality, and maturation as threats to internal validity and the selection-intervention interaction threat to external validity (Campbell & Stanley, 1963). In order to partially compensate for the vulnerabilities and derive greater insight from their collective findings, Everly and his colleagues subsequently meta-analyzed the six of the aforementioned studies possessing control conditions. The results of the meta-analyses found cumulative evidence suggesting that the CISD is, indeed, clinically effective across applications (Everly & Boyle, 1999; Everly & Piacentini, 1999). These meta-analytic investigations revealed statistical sufficiency criteria far in excess of that required to demonstrate reliability of the clinical effect. One observation that may be noted concerning the CISD studies cited, as well as the meta-analyses, is that in some instances the CISD intervention was followed by other interventions. While confounding a strict components' analysis, such follow-up interventions are actually part of the prescribed CISD protocol. More specifically, follow-up intervention is always indicated subsequent to the actual CISD group discussion. Further, failure to follow-up with CISD participants is a violation of the CISD protocol.

Most recently, Watchorn (2000) has shown that group debriefings serve to prevent the development of PTSD. More specifically, the author concludes that peritraumatic dissociation predicts long-term impairment, but for those who dissociated, subsequent debriefings were associated with less long-term impairment. Similarly, Deahl, et al. (2000), in the only randomized investigation of the CISD model of debriefing, found CISD effective in reducing alcoholism and symptoms of anxiety, depression and PTSD. This investigation was conducted with 106 British soldiers involved in a United Nations' peacekeeping mission. Soldiers were randomly assigned to a debriefing condition or a no debriefing condition. In addition, all soldiers received an Operational Stress Training Package. At the six month follow-up, the debriefed group evidenced a lower prevalence of alcohol abuse and lower scores on psychometrically assessed anxiety, depression, PTSD symptoms. Thus current evidence is supportive of the CISD model of debriefing as a means of mitigating adverse psychological responses to critical incidents and even more severe traumatic events. But, again, it should be kept in mind that debriefings were not designed to be a standalone intervention. Rather, as noted earlier, the British Psychological Society (1990) and Mitchell & Everly (1997; Everly & Mitchell, 1999) argue that crisis intervention should be multifaceted. Crisis intervention should be a multicomponent endeavor, a fact that is often forgotten in actual practice.

# EFFECTIVENESS OF CISM

The effectiveness of integrated multicomponent CISM programs has now been suggested through thoughtful qualitative analyses (Everly, Flannery & Mitchell, 2000; Everly & Mitchell, 1999; Miller, 1999; Dyregrov, 1997, 1998 1999), as well as through empirical investigations, and even meta-analyses (Flannery, 1998; Flannery, Penk, & Corrigan, 1999; Flannery, et al., 1995; Flannery, et al., 1998; Flannery, et al., 2000; Mitchell, Schiller, Everly, & Eyler, 1999; Everly, Flannery, & Eyler, in press; Flannery, Everly, & Eyler, 2000; Western Management Consultants, 1996).

In 1985, the Commonwealth Banking Corporation in Australia experienced 30 holdups affecting 107 employees. No debriefing or traumatic events response team was in existence in that year. The bank totalled 281 lost staff work days directly related to the holdup and another 668 sick days within six months of the holdups. The average cost of compensation to employees was $18,488 (Aus.). A critical incident stress team called the "Post Hold-Up Support Program" was established in late 1986 and early 1987. In 1987-88, after the team had been established, there were a total of 36 holdups which also affected 107 staff members.

With trauma support by the Post Hold-Up Support Team there was a lowering of lost days and a lessening of workers compensation payments. Only 112 sick days directly related to the holdups were utilized by affected staff members. This was a 60 percent reduction over the 1985 statistics. Or'.y 265 other sick days were used within six months of the holdups. This figure also represents a 60% reduction over the 1985 figures. Even more dramatically, the compensation payouts decreased substantially. The average after the support team was put in service was $6,326 (Aus.). This is a 66% decrease in workers compensation payouts. See Table 5.5 for a summary of these statistics (Leeman - Conley, 1990).

Flannery's Assaulted Staff Action Program (ASAP) is a more recent CISM crisis intervention approach (Flannery, 1998, 1999a, 1999b, 1999c) used in

**TABLE 5.5**

## COMMONWEALTH BANK OF AUSTRALIA
## WORKERS COMPENSATION COMPARISONS

|  | 1985 | 1987-88 | Change |
|---|---|---|---|
| • hold-ups | 30 | 36 | + 20% |
| • staff affected | 107 | 107 | 0% |
| • support services | none | support team |  |
| • sick days directly related to hold-up | 281 | 112 | - 60% |
| • other sick days not directly related | 668 | 265 | -60% |
| • compensation payments | $18,488 | $6,326 | - 66% |

*(Leeman-Conley, 1990).*

hospitals, clinics, and schools. Research has consistently shown the ASAP program to be an effective crisis intervention. A recent meta-analysis of five ASAP studies found the meta-analytic coefficient to be highly significant and indicative of a powerful clinical effect (Flannery, Everly, & Eyler, 2000). The latest and largest of the meta-analytic studies conducted on CISM coalesced eight investigations. Results of the combinatorial analysis of a wide variety of subjects across diverse settings revealed evidence of a clinically significant effect with a failsafe number far exceeding the sufficiency criterion (Everly, Flannery, & Eyler, in press). As would be predicted, Richards (1999) has demonstrated the relative superiority of the multicomponent CISM compared to the singular CISD, consistent with expectations and prescription.

Critics of CISM point out that the investigations supporting such forms of crisis intervention are of a quasi-experimental nature. Clearly, randomized research designs which can assess the effectiveness of crisis intervention are certainly welcomed, if they can be instituted without sacrificing internal content validity. It was noted earlier that CISM has been submitted to meta-analytic scrutiny and initially found to be effective on the basis of empirical investigations (Everly, Flannery, & Eyler, in press; Flannery, Everly & Eyler, 2000). Although the component investigations were quasi-experimental they are not without epistemological value for several reasons. First, the use of such designs, even single case designs can be useful in contributing meaningful data to the conduct of inquiry (Herson & Barlow, 1976; Blampied, 2000). Second, faithful adherence to the standardized protocols (specifically CISD or CISM) serves as the foundation of internal validity and serves to enhance specified external validity. Third, the use of meta-analysis serves to diminish the likelihood of systematic error across the participant investigations and compensate for specific threats to internal validity. Fourth, the use of meta-analysis with diverse recipient groups also serves to enhance the external validity of the meta-analytic findings supporting the effectiveness of CISD and CISM. Fifth, the use of combinatorial meta-analytic strategies increases to power of the findings by increasing the sample population thus increasing the credibility of the subsequent findings (Seligman, (1995). Nevertheless, randomized designs are certainly welcomed in the future.

To summarize so far, we see that the semantics surrounding crisis intervention has clouded the conclusions we may reach concerning the clinical utility of such interventions. Fortunately, we can trace the semantic evolution and extract useful conclusions, nevertheless:

1. The earliest of research investigations into debriefing seemed to focus upon the CISD model using self-report survey designs. Their contribution was to begin to systematize anecdotal evidence in support of the CISD model of debriefing.

2. The second generation of "debriefing" studies (McFarlane, 1988; Kenardy, et al., 1996) could not define the term debriefing, nor could they describe what actually happened, if anything, during the debriefing. Their contribution to our understanding of debriefing is to underscore the need to verify the nature and existence of the intervention.

3. The third generation of "debriefing" studies was conducted with medical patients using an individualized intervention format (Bisson, et al., 1997; Hobbs, et al., 1996; Mayou, Ehlers, & Hobbs, 2000; Lee, Slade, & Lygo, 1996; Small, et al., 2000). Their contribution to our understanding of debriefing is that a) crisis intervention is clearly not a substitute for psychotherapy, but may be very helpful nevertheless (Small, et al., 2000), b) crisis intervention is probably not suitable for patients in acute medical distress in that it is not a substitute for analgesia, physical rehabilitation, psychological rehabilitation, reconstructive surgery, or financial counseling. These studies have also clearly shown that it is premature to reach any adverse conclusions with regard to debriefings (Bisson, McFarlane, & Rose, 2000).

4. The fourth generation of debriefing studies once again employed the CISD model of group-format debriefing using improved research designs compared to the first generation. These studies Nurmi (1999), Bohl (1991, 1995), Chemtob et al. (1997), Wee, et al. (1999), Jenkins (1996), Everly & Piacentini (1999) in a meta-analytic investigation, Deahl, et al. (2000) in a randomized design, and Watchorn (2000) clearly support the assertion that the CISD model of "debriefing" can be an effective clinical tool for reducing psychological distress, reducing alcohol use, and in preventing PTSD. Their contribution to our understanding of "debriefing" is demonstrating the value of a standardized, theoretically based, empirically developed protocol for small group crisis intervention.

5. Finally, the use of the term "debriefing" to refer to multicomponent crisis intervention programs is clearly a misnomer. The term Critical Incident Stress Management (CISM), as defined earlier, is the term indicative of a comprehensive, multifaceted approach to crisis intervention (Everly & Mitchell, 1999; Flannery, 1998). Studies such as the randomized trial conducted by Bordow & Porritt (1979) and the pretest post-test open outcome inpatient investigation conducted by Busuttil, et al (1995) provided early

support for the necessity of a multifaceted, CISM-like approach. Later studies by Flannery (Flannery, Everly, & Eyler, 2000), Everly (Everly, Flannery, & Eyler, in press), and Richards (1999) have shown repeatedly that the CISM approach to crisis intervention is a clinically effective intervention. The contribution of these studies to our current understanding of the larger field of crisis intervention is the notion that crisis intervention should not consist of a single intervention, but rather, should be an integrated multifaceted intervention (British Psychological Society, 1990; Mitchell & Everly, 1997; Turnbull, Busuttil & Pittman, 1997; Richards, 1999; Bordow & Porritt, 1979). As Bisson, McFarlane, & Rose (2000) have stated, one-shot debriefing as a standalone crisis intervention cannot be recommended at this time, but there is evidence that debriefing, as part of a multifaceted crisis intervention, is well received by most people.

# CISM RESEARCH: A SUMMARY OF KEY POINTS

1. Swanson and Carbon (1989) writing for the American Psychiatric Association Task Force Report on Treatment of Psychiatric Disorders (American Psychiatric Association, 1989) state, "Crisis intervention is a proven approach to helping in the pain of an emotional crisis" (p.2520). Based upon evidence dating back to the 1960s, crisis intervention (rapid and acute psychological intervention following critical incidents and traumatic events) has demonstrated itself to be an effective means of reducing psychological morbidity (see American Psychiatric Association Task Force Report, 1989; Everly & Mitchell, 1999). Parad & Parad (1968) reviewed 1656 social work cases and found crisis-oriented intervention to be effective in reducing florid psychiatric complaints and in improving patients' ability to cope with stress. Langsley, Machotka, & Flomenhaft (1971) followed 300 psychiatric patients randomly assigned to inpatient treatment or family crisis intervention groups. The crisis intervention group was found to be superior in reducing the need for subsequent hospital admissions at 6 and 18 month intervals. A similar finding was recorded by Decker & Stubblebine (1972) using a single group 2.5 year longitudinal design. Finally, it was Bordow & Porritt (1979) who initially demonstrated, through randomized experimental design, that multicomponent crisis intervention was superior to single crisis tactics. While there is a compelling logic to support the notion of early psychological intervention subsequent to a critical incident, while there is evidence to support the utilization of CISD and CISM, continued empirical validation and clinical re-

finement are worthy pursuits for the future.

2. A review of current literature reveals a rather spirited discussion on the value of crisis interventions, especially "debriefing" (see Raphael & Wilson, 2000; Everly & Mitchell, 2000). Dyregrov (1998) has stated, "In my opinion the debate on debriefing is not only a scientific but also a political debate. It entails power and positions in the therapeutic world. As a technique…[debriefings] represented a threat to the psychiatric elite." Certainly, at the very least, the debriefing "controversy" is grounded in semantics.

3. Although not always obvious, at the heart of these discussions resides considerable confusion surrounding the use of the various key terms and concepts. More specifically, there exists considerable confusion regarding the use of the terms: "debriefing," Critical Incident Stress Debriefing (CISD), crisis intervention, and Critical Incident Stress Management (CISM). The confusion stems largely from the liberal interpretation and inconsistent use of these terms (Bisson, McFarlane & Rose, 2000; Everly & Mitchell, 2000).

4. Contrary to the most current and common usage, some authors use the term "debriefing" to refer to virtually any form of acute crisis intervention, whether standardized or non-standardized in implementation, and whether implemented on an individual basis or in a group format. Unfortunately, the lack of a standardized terminology makes it difficult to make meaningful empirical comparisons. Rational discourse is necessarily predicated upon the consistent use of terms!

5. However, the preponderance of papers written on these respective topics agree on the following:

   a) "Crisis intervention" refers to acute, psychological first-aid, the goals of which are to assist in the reduction of acute distress and dysfunction following a trauma or critical incident; and/or, psychological triaging, i.e., the identification of those who appear to need a more advanced level of psychological care (e.g., counseling or psychotherapy) and the facilitation of access to that care; regarding psychotherapy it should be noted that although there exist numerous models of "brief" psychotherapy, it is largely contraindicated in acute crisis situations (Debenhan, Sargent, Hill, & Slater,1941), and the use of such brief psychotherapy models, by definition exclude the valuable resource of trained and experienced "peer" interventionists.

b) Critical Incident Stress Debriefing (CISD) refers to a seven stage group discussion usually instituted 1 to 10 days after a critical incident (3 to 4 weeks after a mass disaster). The process is only performed in small groups typically consisting of 3 to 20 persons. The CISD is the oldest, most widely used and research validated standardized model of group crisis intervention. CISD is NOT psychotherapy. CISD was NOT designed to be a substitute for psychotherapy. CISD was NOT designed to be a substitute for traditional EAP services. CISD was NOT designed to be a substitute for psychological or physical rehabilitation. CISD is NOT an operational critique. Finally, CISD was NOT designed to be a stand-alone intervention. Rather, CISD was designed to mitigate acute distress, serve as a forum for triaging, and to be but one component within a comprehensive crisis intervention program referred to as Critical Incident Stress Management (CISM; Everly & Mitchell, 1999).

c) Consistent with Millon's integrative synergistic approach to psychological intervention, Critical Incident Stress Management (CISM) refers to a comprehensive, integrated multi-component approach to crisis intervention, wherein CISD is but one component. See Table 1.1 – CISM: The Core Components for a listing of the core elements of CISM. The CISM approach, contrary to other models of crisis intervention, encourages a "best practices" approach to crisis intervention wherein the most appropriate interventions are matched to the needs of the situation. Similarly, when dealing with "high-risk" occupations such as law enforcement, fire suppression, emergency medical services, nursing and other healthcare professions, airline pilots, the military, and other similar professions, the use of mental health professionals in combination with specially trained "peer support" personnel is encouraged.

6. There now seems to be a general agreement amongst the most prolific of contributors to this field that: a) there has, indeed, been an inconsistent utilization of the key tactics relevant to the field of crisis intervention; b) most of the randomized outcome investigations assessing the effectiveness of "debriefing" have suffered from a bias toward an inconsistent application of individual debriefing as a standalone process and, c) these randomized studies, which show largely no positive outcome or negative outcome, have incorrectly attempted to assess effectiveness on target populations that appear to be inappropriate for the assessment of crisis intervention outcome (Bisson, McFarlane, &Rose, 2000; Everly & Mitchell, 1999, 2001).

7. Research (Two meta-analyses and seven primary empirical studies including: 1 randomized design, 5 two-group static control designs, 1 time-lagged design) has shown the CISD model of psychological debriefing to be effective in reducing symptoms of acute distress after a critical incident or trauma. Meta-analytic assessment revealed CISD to possess a meaningful positive clinical effect (Everly & Boyle, 1999; Everly & Piacentini, 1999).

8. Research (Two meta-analyses and eight primary empirical studies) has shown the CISM multicomponent approach to crisis intervention to be consistently effective in reducing symptoms of distress and dysfunction. Meta-analytic assessment revealed these studies to possess a significant clinical effect (Flannery, Everly & Eyler, 2000; Everly, Flannery, & Eyler, in press).

9. Using an assessment of empirical sufficiency, it was discovered that both CISD research and, more importantly CISM research, have amassed a sufficiently large and diverse constituency of supportive investigations that proves their clinical effectiveness far beyond reasonable doubt, as verified by empirical sufficiency and power analyses (Everly & Boyle, 1999; Everly, Flannery, & Eyler, in press; Flannery, Everly, & Eyler, 2000; Everly, Flannery, Eyler & Mitchell, in press).

10. In sum, when implemented as prescribed, CISM appears to be an effective crisis intervention, capable of reducing signs and symptoms of distress associated with an acute psychological crisis. However, when implemented without proper training and experience, when implemented as a standalone intervention, when implemented as a substitute for psychotherapy, when implemented with patients in acute medical crises, and when implemented without concern for standardization and quality assurance, crisis interventions, even CISM, are likely to be ineffectual, and perhaps harmful. All of the aforementioned points argue cogently that proper training is required in order to realize the clinical effectiveness of crisis intervention, especially the CISM comprehensive approach to crisis intervention (Dyregrov, 1997, 1998).

## CISD CAUTIONS

No one psychological support process, no matter how well-designed and practiced, can be equally effective for all people under all circumstances. Where some gain maximal benefit others may feel little or no effect. The success or failure of the Critical Incident Stress Debriefing process depends on several interlocking factors which include, but are not limited to the following:

1.  **Using the CISD for its intended purpose** (*mitigation* of the impact of a traumatic event, *prevention* of posttraumatic stress reactions and *acceleration* of recovery processes in non-psychiatric populations who have experienced significant psychological trauma)- It should be noted that the CISD process was *not* developed as a treatment for Posttraumatic Stress Disorder (PTSD) or any other mental disorder. Its main usefulness has been and continues to be as a tool which may prevent or mitigate various forms of traumatic stress including PTSD. One recent review of the broad utilization of CISDs in disaster work cautioned, "We recognize that CISD procedures may help some disaster victims. We are concerned, however, that an unreasonable expectation of CISD usefulness may be developing among field practitioners." (Hiley-Young and Gerrity, 1994, p. 17).

2.  **Timing-** Interventions which are too early or too late after a traumatic event may be ineffective (Burns and Harm, 1993).

3.  **Readiness of the group members for help-** All the help in the world will be useless if those who need it are not ready to accept it (Mitchell, 1994).

4.  **Level of involvement in the traumatic incident-** It appears that the more intimately involved in an incident a person is, the more likelihood there is that debriefings alone will not be sufficient to overcome the negative impact of the trauma. For instance, a fire fighter or police officer who helps others who are victims of a natural disaster may feel that the debriefings were especially helpful after the event if his home and family were not personally affected. If an emergency services person, on the other hand, not only had to help others after a natural disaster, but also suffered the loss of his or her home or injury or death to a family member, the debriefing is not likely to be very helpful by itself (Raphael and Wilson, 1993; Hiley-Young and Gerrity, 1994).

5.  **Level of concurrent psychological distress in a person at the time of the critical incident-** Some people will need more assistance than just a debriefing because they had already been dealing with significant stressful situations before they encountered the current critical incident or because they have several current stressful circumstances which are occurring simultaneously (Raphael and Wilson, 1993).

6. **Level of psychiatric disturbance which might exist before a traumatic event occurs**- In some cases people may have a serious psychopathology. Then they encounter a significant stress. The end result is that they are unable to cope with the stress of a critical incident and decompensate further. Psychotherapy is clearly indicated in these circumstances and CISD is not likely to be effective by itself (Hiley-Young and Gerrity, 1994).

7. **Applications of the CISD by properly trained mental health professionals and peers**- Inadequately trained debriefers and those who apply the process inappropriately because of a lack of experience may cause the CISD process to fail (Mitchell and Everly, 1993).

8. **Adherence to basic CISD policies and procedures**- The CISD process has been well-documented and significant variations from the commonly accepted procedures may cause harm to the recipients or may cause the process to fail (Mitchell and Everly, 1993).

9. **Level of pre-incident education on traumatic stress and the CISD process**- Pre-incident education may be helpful in mitigating the impact of a traumatic event and may also make the participants in a debriefing more ready to accept and utilize the process effectively (Mitchell, 1994).

10. **Level of follow-up services provided**- It would be fool hardy for anyone to believe that support services of any kind can be provided without appropriate follow up services. It is very important to check repeatedly on the well-being of those who have been given support services. Some will not need further assistance. Others may need additional support or possibly a referral for professional counseling (Mitchell, 1992; Mitchell and Everly, 1993).

11. **Intensity of the critical incident**- Some events are so powerful that the CISD cannot eliminate all of the negative effects. Even months after a debriefing some symptoms of traumatic stress may linger and may need additional work to clear them up (Sloan, et al., 1994).

12. **Level of exposure over time to critical incidents**- Time may not heal as effectively as some might wish to believe. Recent studies of emergency personnel indicate that there may be a link between time in the service, the types and number of critical incidents which emergency personnel encounter and the persistent long range stress symptoms which can be found in emergency personnel (Moran and Britton, 1994).

13. Level of administrative support

14. Level of family and social support

15. The existence of a comprehensive critical incident stress management program which has many more components than just debriefing (Robinson and Mitchell, 1993).

# CAUTIONS IN CISD RESEARCH

If anyone plans to do research on CISD, or if they plan to read research projects developed by others, the following guidelines would be worth considering. The end product of the research would then be more useful to CISD providers everywhere.

1. Obtain appropriate training in the specific model of debriefing which is to be researched. This will ensure that the appropriate applications of the debriefing model are understood by those who will be researching it. Training in a specific process eliminates guess work and faulty assumptions. Reading about a model is insufficient since many gaps in learning may be caused by incomplete understanding of the process which comes from a review of only the writings in the field.

2. Define the model to be researched and describe it in detail. Many researchers today are claiming that they have studied debriefings, yet they cannot describe a specific debriefing process. They may refer to everything from a brief unstructured interview to a highly structured group process as a "debriefing." Their research would be more useful if they described what is meant by "debriefing." A lack of definition of the process causes significant confusion in those who study the research articles.

3. Clearly define the population to be researched. To state that one is studying "firefighters" gives a very different impression to the reader than to state that one is studying average citizens whose homes were threatened by a fire storm and thus fought the fire to save themselves and their property. Clearly the groups are different in training, experience and in their reactions.

4. Do not mix groups within a population which is being studied. A police

officer who provided perimeter control at a scene has a very different experience and a different viewpoint than a police officer who was on an assault team which was involved in a fire fight at the same incident. It is also not a good idea to lump average citizens or victims together with rescue personnel even though they experienced the same event. Their training, experience, personalities and reactions may be very different from each other.

5. Make sure that those who are providing the debriefings as part of the study are well-trained and experienced in the provision of the service. Also be aware that one person's style of providing a debriefing service may vary substantially from the style of another debriefer. Likewise, one team's skills may vary considerably from that of another. As much consistency as possible needs to be built into the design of a study. **In the final analysis what we measure in any outcome research is *not* so much any given model or behavioral protocol, but rather *is* the clinicians' ability to implement or operationalize a given model or protocol.**

6. Compare events that are as similar as possible. For example, comparing the effectiveness of the CISD process when used on a multiple vehicle accident with multiple fatalities and another multiple vehicle incident with only minor injuries is not a fair evaluation since the stress effects of the two events are very dissimilar.

7. Compare people who experienced roughly equal levels of exposure to the same event.

8. Do not discuss items in the research paper which were not actually studied. In other words good researchers avoid writing in such a manner as to imply certain findings which were not actually included in the research project. It would be inaccurate to state that only voluntary debriefings have a positive effect if the only thing the project was designed to study is whether or not debriefings should occur within 24 hours of an incident.

9. Avoid drawing conclusions which are well beyond the data. For example, if a study on the effectiveness of utilizing CISD for the treatment of schizophrenia were to conclude that the CISD process had no positive effect on the schizophrenia patients, it would be inappropriate to conclude that debriefings do not work on emergency personnel who are not schizophrenic.

10. Perform the research in close time proximity to the occurrence of the debriefings. Many researchers have waited several months to collect the

data. Long time lapses from the time of the intervention subject the study to many variables which can cloud the overall picture and distort the results.

11. Never allow ongoing research projects to interfere with the provision of support services to groups who might benefit from the processes after a traumatic event.

12. Take into consideration the previously published works which address the same issues.

There is clearly a great need to have research in the CISM field. But research projects should be carefully designed and managed. The minimal guidelines above should be helpful to potential researchers and readers as well.

## SUMMARY

In this chapter, we've tried to offer insight into the "whys" and "hows" undergirding the impetus to establish and maintain debriefing and defusing protocols.

As for mechanisms of action, the following concepts appear important:

- Early intervention

- Opportunity for catharsis

- Opportunity to verbally reconstruct the trauma

- Establishment of a behavioral structure within which to conduct the group process (a sort of behavioral "road map")

- Establishment of a structured psychological progression (a psychological "road map")

- Group support

- Peer support

- Opportunity for follow-up

In the final analysis, debriefings and defusings demonstrate that someone cares.

To paraphrase William James, the deepest craving of human nature is the desire to be appreciated! Upon such a foundation there may be no limit to what humanity can achieve for itself.

Finally, there now exists a corpus of research data that strongly suggests the clinical utility of not only CISD but CISM, the emerging standard of care.

# Chapter 6

## ON-SCENE SUPPORT SERVICES

### INTRODUCTION

Distress in people who function on the front lines is unpredictable. Most events have a routine about them and cause little noticeable stress. Every once in awhile, something happens or a circumstance exists which turns the routine into a significant stress for one or two people or perhaps for an entire group. When that happens it is a good idea to have trained CISM personnel on the scene to help manage the personnel experiencing stress reactions. This chapter will present some guidelines to assist organizations and CISM teams in responding to a call for on-scene support services.

### THE SCENE DEFINED

A "scene" is where the action takes place; where people work. For law enforcement personnel it is the patrol sector. For emergency medical services, a scene is the ambulance or the place where the accident or sick person is located. For a communications officer, it is the operations center. For a nurse, the scene is the emergency room or other in-hospital facilities.

Whenever a distressing situation occurs in any place where people work (the scene) and support services are initiated at or very near that location, those services are called "on-scene support services." Services provided under "on-scene" conditions are brief, practical crisis intervention functions to limit the level of distress encountered by the workers. The crisis intervention provided on scene is individual in nature. Only rarely are group services provided while on the scene of an event. It is hard to envision any group activity taking place on a scene other than a very brief informative meeting of working units.

# METHODS OF APPROACH

There are two main approaches to on-scene support services. The first approach is a haphazard method in which services are provided if a trained person just happens to be on the scene during the incident. If that person is not too busy with other duties, they may be able to direct a little attention toward distressed fellow workers. Obviously, the services provided with a haphazard approach are limited.

The second approach to on-scene support services is a planned and organized approach. With this method, trained CISM personnel are organized in advance of an incident. They may have regular duties, but be assigned to a specialty team which is released from normal duties to provide on-scene support services. Or they may volunteer to be on call a few days or nights per month. If needed, they can be called to the scene to provide support services. In some jurisdictions, members of CISM teams are automatically dispatched on certain events to standby in case they might be needed at the scene. There are clearly many advantages to an organized approach.


# GOALS OF ON-SCENE SUPPORT

The goals of on-scene support are identical to the goals for crisis intervention because these services are crisis intervention. The goals of on scene support services are:

- Stabilize the situation and protect the personnel from additional stress.

- Mitigate the impact of a traumatic event

- Mobilize a wide range of resources to assist the distressed person.

- Normalize the experience and reduce the feelings of uniqueness and abnormality.

- Restore to adaptive function as quickly as possible.

# USUAL EFFECTS OF ON-SCENE SUPPORT

The early intervention achieved by on-scene support services disrupts the person's movement toward "freezing up" or dysfunction. Early recognition of distress allows for a low-profile and inexpensive intervention which encourages a rapid return to normal functions. On-scene support services may lessen the impact of a traumatic event and block further deterioration of the individual, reducing the need for time off or prolonged physical and emotional distress. People who are given the brief breaks provided by on-scene support services feel cared for and respond quickly, moving away from being emotionally overwhelmed. They return to the normal cognitive defenses which help them to perform their jobs.

# TARGET GROUPS

There are only three groups who are targeted for field interventions by CISM members. They are:

- Individuals with obvious signs of distress

- Command and supervisory personnel who receive only advice and consultation

- Distressed primary victims, their families and witnesses or bystanders who are involved in the actual incident

Most on-scene support services are provided during prolonged field incidents or during incidents which have become large-scale. An incident of any magnitude, however, may involve distressing conditions which could cause an individual to become temporarily overwhelmed and in need of quick individual support from CISM team members.

# PROVIDERS

On-scene support services are provided by peer support personnel who have been trained in Critical Incident Stress Management processes and who have a good working knowledge of crisis intervention. Chaplains and clergy personnel who have been trained in crisis intervention and CISM are often called upon to assist people at the scenes of tragedies. Likewise, CISM trained mental health professionals are called upon when the situation is so huge or so overwhelming that the peer members of the CISM team are too busy to provide support services or are overwhelmed by the incident themselves. Well-intentioned but untrained people can inadvertently make a situation worse by choosing the wrong techniques in attempting to help others. Therefore, trained CISM team members provide the very best services.

## TIMING

There is only one word to describe the time frame of on-scene support services and that word is *immediate*. On-scene support services are provided immediately, while an incident is in progress. The services are provided in a location as close as possible to the actual situation. However, it must be a relatively secure area in which those involved will not be endangered. One key to successful intervention is that the support is very short in duration.

## CORE RULES

The intensity of field operations and the defense systems of people who work in such conditions do not allow for complex interventions at the scene. Everything the CISM team members do must be short and simple. There are three core rules to follow:

- Provide support services only to obviously distressed individuals. Those who are functioning well should be left to do their jobs without any interference. Do not interrupt those who are functioning well to check on their emotional status. Just let them work.

- Interventions should be very brief. Sometimes only a few seconds are necessary. A five minute intervention is considered reasonably long and fifteen minutes is extremely long. In fact, if a person at a scene does not show marked improvement by the end of fifteen minutes it is unlikely that the person will recover sufficiently to go back to work at that scene. Distress which does not dissipate after fifteen minutes away from the disturbing stimuli may indicate that the person should not be returned to the work site.

- Focus on immediate concerns. There is no need to explore old history. Support personnel should stick to "here and now" issues. The current issues are the only issues that the CISM team members might influence. Anything that is part of the person's past history is too set and complex to be resolved in the midst of a crisis reaction.

# GUIDELINES FOR EFFECTIVE ON-SCENE SUPPORT SERVICES

- Be safety conscious both for yourself and for the personnel working in the situation.

- Do not get physically involved in the situation if your assigned job is CISM support. You cannot do both jobs adequately at the same time.

- On-scene support service is a common sense approach. Think first before intervening. Anticipate the reaction the "help" you are contemplating is going to have on the person.

- If your only duties are CISM services, stay outside of the internal perimeter.

- Never criticize the performance of the personnel involved in the incident.

- Avoid drawing unnecessary attention to the distressed individual.

- Look for signs of obvious distress:

  * wandering about aimlessly

  * unjustified angry outbursts

  * overall loss of emotional control

* shock-like state

* crying

* "thousand mile" stare

* unusual behaviors

* inappropriate behaviors

* exaggerated behaviors

* isolation from the group

* others

- Advice-giving should be limited to only what the scene requires.

- Reinforce any activity which seems to help in the situation.

- Fulfill first request if possible.

- Avoid asking "feeling-loaded" questions. Ask about what happened and let the affected individual tell the story in his or her own words.

- Listen carefully. Use the best listening skills.

- Dispel feelings of uniqueness and abnormality.

- Let the individuals know that the reactions they are having are normal and temporary and that they can return to work as soon possible after the reactions subside.

- If the stress subsides, restore people to function as quickly as possible after a brief break.

- Sometimes an alternate duty station at the scene is required to reduce the possibility that the same duty will stir up the distress again.

- If necessary, encourage the distressed person to make contact later or to go to a defusing or a debriefing if one is to be provided.

# MENTAL HEALTH AND CLERGY AT SCENES

Occasionally, mental health and clergy personnel are requested to assist at the scene of a tragedy. There are several things they should keep in mind to ensure that their services are accepted and helpful.

First they should not go to a scene unless they are called upon to do so or perhaps if they are part of prearranged and normal response system. To show up at scenes without being called in or designated as part of a normal response team can generate anger and resentment in the personnel at the scene. Many fear that these "uninvited guests" at the scene will take some personnel out of action unnecessarily and cause embarrassment and interference with their jobs and possibly with their advancement in the system.

If their presence is requested at a scene, the clergy personnel and mental health professionals should report into the command center. They should never wander about the scene without checking in first. Additionally, they should keep a low profile, being discrete as they check out a person who shows obvious signs of distress. They should always avoid bringing any unnecessary attention to an individual. Neither should they wear clothing that attracts unusual attention from the personnel at the scene. Blending in at an emergency is very important. Keeping a low profile also entails avoiding the media unless they have been requested to render assistance to the organization by making a specified and approved statement to the media.

Again, they should approach only those demonstrating obvious signs of distress. Everyone else should be left to do their work. Mental health professionals and clergy should avoid getting physically involved in the work. It will distract them from their primary duties of rendering support. There have been several cases in which clergy or mental health professionals became involved in recovery of body parts at a disaster. It so seriously impacted them that they were unable to carry out their primary support duties at the scene. When they are not needed immediately, they should stay near the command post or some other designated area. They usually are assigned to the safety officer at the scene.

Staying out of the internal perimeter is very important because there are inherent dangers at scenes and one could get injured very easily. An injury would complicate an already complex situation and cause more work for the overburdened operations personnel.

Mental health professionals and clergy do their best work when they provide consultations to command staff and supervisors. They are, of course, helpful in their brief contacts with obviously distressed individuals. They are providing a support service, not psychotherapy or a religious service. Mental health and clergy are at their best at a scene when they are displaying good listening skills and care and concern. They should also be ready to point out appropriate resources which might be helpful after the incident concludes. These resources might include defusings, debriefings and other CISM services.

One requirement for participation at the scene of a major incident should be a special orientation program to the emergency services. Mental health professionals and clergy should go on ride-alongs and tour facilities and talk to operations personnel so that they can learn as much as possible about the personnel and the jobs they perform. The more a CISM trained mental health professional or clergy person knows about the services they are supporting the better able they will be to render the best possible services.

## FOLLOW-UP SERVICES

With on-scene support services there is a need to draw a careful balance between providing inadequate services and too much service. Too limited an approach to distressed personnel leaves them hurting and uncomfortable. To avoid under-serving people involved in a significant event, it is necessary to contact people when they are resting. The approach should be a friendly, casual, conversational one that occurs when operations personnel are on rest breaks. If they see that the members of the CISM team have interest in them and are friendly, they may initiate contact later on their own.

Constant checking and rechecking, on the other hand, will eventually annoy people and result in rejection of the help being offered. Likewise, following people around with a clipboard with a check list of signs and symptoms of distress will cause the operations personnel to go into a rage. This actually happened in a recent plane crash situation. People who were not trained in CISM procedures tried to be helpful by "assessing" the signs and symptoms of distress in the emergency personnel at the scene. The emergency personnel found the procedure to be intrusive and they freely vented their anger on those who were holding the checklists.

The key rule of thumb for on-scene support services is to do only that which is absolutely necessary and no more. The scene is simply not the place to try to fix everything. Many things must be left alone. Remember, the personnel at a major incident know their jobs, do them well and are generally quite healthy and normal in their reactions to a situation. There is virtually no need to "fix" them, especially at the scene of a major incident. Leave people alone to perform their jobs. If there is any need to provide brief support services, that will become clearly evident.

## SUMMARY

This chapter covered the topic of "on-scene" support services. It defined the processes and discussed the scope of the interventions. The targets, timing and providers (CISM trained peers, mental health professionals and clergy) of on-scene support services were addressed. The core rules of on-scene support services were also presented. Many cautions designed to make the process run smoothly and effectively were discussed. Specific instructions were provided for the peer support personnel and the mental health professionals and clergy members.

The overall objective of on-scene support services is to provide only as much support as is actually necessary and to ensure that help is provided by trained people who avoid the extremes of too little or too much.

# Chapter 7

# DEMOBILIZATION

## INTRODUCTION

In previous chapters, various CISM interventions designed for rapid stabilization and accelerated recovery from stress were briefly described. Defusings will be helpful when the CISM team is able to intervene in a traumatic situation within hours of the incident. They are aimed at small core groups which have been traumatized by their exposure to an incident. The Critical Incident Stress Debriefing (CISD) is most helpful several days after the incident when personnel have had the time to mentally process some of their experience in a traumatic event. A CISD may be provided after a defusing if the incident is very intense and the CISM team believes that the defusing was insufficient to satisfy the needs of the group. The size of the groups to be managed in either defusing or CISD interventions is generally small. Most defusings have six to eight people and debriefings generally have ten to thirty participants.

When an incident draws a great many emergency personnel who may need some immediate support after the incident, it will be very difficult to manage those people with a defusing. Defusings are designed for small groups and they take more time than is available in a disaster. The task of working through defusings with hundreds of emergency personnel would be a monumental one. The defusing team would be quickly drained and there would be a backup of people waiting.

Likewise, the CISD was not developed with immediate applications in mind. Most emergency personnel need about twenty four hours before they begin to react to the emotions associated with the incident. Again, hundreds of personnel in need of something more immediate could not be processed through debriefings.

This chapter contains information on a CISM technique which has immediate applicability for the large scale incident.

# DEMOBILIZATION DEFINED

The demobilization is a primary stress prevention and intervention technique which is applied immediately after the personnel are released from a large scale scene and before they return to normal duties. The demobilization consists of two main segments. The first is a 10 to 15 minute period in which personnel are given information which might be helpful to them in understanding and managing their stress reactions. Only 10 minutes of lecture are necessary for most emergency personnel. Non-emergency populations may need more time. The second segment of the demobilization is a 20 minute period of time to rest and eat before they return to the routines in their lives.

# USES

The demobilization has only two uses. It has been developed for use when emergency personnel have encountered either:

1. A disaster, or

2. A large scale traumatic event

Demobilizations have already been successfully applied to numerous major disasters in the United States. They may be difficult to organize, however, so CISM teams should be very familiar with the process before they attempt to provide demobilizations.

# CAUTION

Demobilizations are only applied once to personnel working in the first two or three shifts of work at a disaster. That is, demobilizations are provided after personnel have completed their first exposure to the disaster scene. Then they are not used again for the same personnel. The first two or three shifts in a disaster are made up of personnel who have not had previous exposure to the disaster. They are exposed to the disaster when it is most chaotic and shocking. That is when the demobilization is most useful. The information presented in the demobilization has the effect of lowering the anxiety and stress reactions that are prominent in the early exposures to the disaster. The demobilization is not helpful, however, after the first two or three shifts because the scene becomes more organized and the surprise elements of the disaster become less volatile.

Disaster operations that are prolonged beyond a few shifts begin to re-cycle disaster workers to the scene. To continue to use a group process such as demobilization may be dangerous or disruptive because the demobiliza-tion process raises the consciousness of stress reactions in the disaster work-ers and they must then work harder to suppress their emotions in order to do their jobs. Each additional group process makes the rescue workers more vulnerable to significant stress reactions. When a disaster is prolonged, group processes beyond the first few shifts should be avoided and only one-on-ones should be utilized with obviously distraught individuals.

If a severe trauma occurs to a small group during the disaster, a defusing might be applied for that small group of traumatized workers. Disaster workers should be allowed to complete their daily assignment with a mini-mum of support by CISM teams.

## AN INNOVATION

The Oklahoma City CISM team and the statewide Oklahoma CISM team were faced with a huge challenge after the terrorist bombing in 1995. Many thousands of workers were repeatedly exposed to the traumatic scenes of the bomb site. In addition, new personnel were being brought in from all over the United States to supplement or replace worn out workers. Demobiliza-tions were beyond their usefulness. Yet personnel needed something to support them that would not lower their guards and cause them to work harder to suppress their emotions in order to do their jobs. An innovative process was devised to manage the situation.

With the approval of command staff, the CISM team became part of the daily deployment program that was provided during this very complicated and prolonged incident. When a shift was coming off duty, CISM team members would meet with them and inform them that they were going to help with the deployment of the next group for work in the bomb site. The group coming off duty was asked if there was anything that they could tell the CISM team about work in the site that might be helpful to reduce the stress and strain that the in-going group would likely face. The personnel would then tell the CISM team members about the difficulties they encountered during their work shift. No efforts were made to get the workers to lower their guards and talk about their emotions.

When the short meeting with the off-duty shift was completed, the CISM team would then meet with the shift coming on duty. The CISM team would inform the new shift regarding the difficulties of work at the bomb site, shared by the previous shift. After the CISM team finished, the command staff would then brief the new shift on their assignments at the site.

This innovation was extremely useful in cutting down on the surprises faced by new groups of workers. With fewer surprises there is usually less anxiety and stress and groups can work more effectively. This model would be advisable in any prolonged operation in which people are continuously re-exposed to the traumatic scene. The Oklahoma CISM teams are to be congratulated for developing an innovative and effective CISM tool for use in prolonged and complicated events.

The sections below will be helpful to any CISM team which is trying to plan a demobilization program for a disaster or other large scale event.

## GOALS AND OBJECTIVES

The goals and objectives of a demobilization are the following:

- to provide a transition from large scale traumatic event back to the routine

- to reduce the intensity of immediate stress reactions

- to provide a preliminary assessment of group needs for additional support services

- to forewarn participants about potential reactions

- to provide information about the incident and the reactions of the personnel involved

- to provide practical information for stress management and the establishment of linkages for additional support

- to establish positive expectations about outcome

# PROVIDERS

The demobilization should be provided only by people trained in CISM. The actual demobilization is handled by a team of CISM personnel. It usually takes one or two demobilization center managers and six to eight team members who make the presentations at the demobilization center. Presenters are CISM trained mental health professionals, members of the clergy and peers, either from other jurisdictions or off duty and not directly affected by the disaster. Presenters should not be involved in the actual operations at the scene of the incident.

# DEMOBILIZATION REQUIREMENTS

The arrangement of the demobilization center can be a challenge to the CISM team members. Many elements must be brought together to ensure the success of the demobilization. This list should be helpful to the organizers on a CISM team. It can be used as a check sheet.

- Several pre-designated centers in a jurisdiction

- Two large rooms in each center

- Moveable furniture

- Adequate supplies of chairs and tables to handle the group

- Ample supplies of food, juices and so forth

- Resources from which to obtain food if it is not at the center chosen for the demobilization

- At least one demobilization manager

- Six to eight CISM team members to present the information

- A check-in desk

- Staff to keep the food stocked

- Parking to accommodate several emergency vehicles at a time

- Several people to control or deny access to the media and other interested parties

# **ORGANIZATION**

Having the right facilities, staff and materials is only a part of the establishment of a demobilization center. There are many other considerations which must be addressed or the demobilization will fail. Success in a demobilization can be achieved only when there has been considerable planning and practice before the large scale incident occurs. If a demobilization is arranged successfully during a disaster without a plan, the success is probably fortuitous and not apt to be repeated in the future. Demobilizations demand thought, organization, practice, and planning. Here are some of the most important considerations for the development of a demobilization pre-plan:

- Presentation of the idea to administration and command

- Authorization of the administration and command

- Cooperation of administration and command

- Instructions for use to administration and command

- Pre-designation of sites

- Pre-incident arrangements for food

- Preprinted handouts for the demobilization

- Additional training to CISM team members

- Written plan

- Agreements with all neighboring jurisdictions

- Development of brief (ten minute) stress presentation

- Practice sessions for the CISM team in classrooms

- Practice with emergency operations people at disaster drills

- Written authorizations from the pre-designated sites

- A list of emergency numbers for officials who control the sites

- Education sessions to the rank and file personnel so that they know what to expect

- Pre-incident briefings to the media so that they know that the demobilization is simply a method to rest crews and give them information before they are returned to their normal duties. Letting the media know this in advance will generally prevent the disruption of trying to explain demobilizations when a real event is actually occurring

## DIFFICULTIES

It should be clear from the preceding sections that the organization and management of a demobilization can be a difficult process. No CISM team should go into it blindly. A demobilization can be a marvelous success or an abysmal failure. Much will depend on the organization which took place before the disaster or other large scale incident occurred. Some of the difficulties which must be overcome by CISM teams who are trying to organize a demobilization are presented here as a forewarning to teams. These are the practical realities which will make a demobilization difficult. They are most common (and most destructive) when there has been no pre-planning for the demobilization. Good pre-planning could eliminate most of these problems:

- Supervisors or commanders unfamiliar with the process or the need for it.

- Poor communications at the scene from upper level to lower level supervisors.

- The overwhelming nature of the incident which makes the demobilization a very low priority in the minds of the leaders.

- Delayed notification of the team.

- Delayed opening of the demobilization center.

- Insufficient availability of CISM team members.

- Personnel kept at the incident too long, resulting in extreme exhaustion and resistance to the demobilization.

- Insufficient food and fluids.

- Considerable distance from the scene to the center.

- Premature notification of release from duty before completing the demobilization process.

- Difficulty in locating the demobilization center.

- No communication system between the demobilization center and the command post.

- CISM members trying to help too much or too often.

- CISM members attempting to provide debriefings or defusings when only the demobilization should be provided.

## OVERVIEW

The demobilization is more difficult to set up than it is to run. The simplest solution is to think TWO. There are two key segments to a demobilization and each takes place in a separate room. So there are two segments and two rooms. This may sound a little simplistic but it can help the pressured CISM team to pull the demobilization together when it is necessary. The diagram, Figure 7.1, will help to conceptualize the overall structure of the demobilization center.

In this diagram the presentation room is on the left and the food room is on the right. Personnel receive the ten minute presentation first and then

**FIGURE 7.1**

move to the food room where they have twenty minutes to one half hour of rest and food.

Once the demobilization center has been arranged, the supervisors are advised that, when they are ready, they can begin to move people to the center after they have completed their work. It is very important to note that a demobilization is a group process and it is never provided at the scene of an incident. The demobilization only occurs away from the scene. The only people sent to the demobilization center are those who have completed their work at the scene and are being released from the scene by their supervisors. They will NOT be returning to the scene to continue to work for at least eight hours. Once a supervisor makes the decision to send his or her personnel to the demobilization center, they no longer need those people and are releasing them from any further activity at the same scene for the remainder of the shift or until the next day. The personnel may work elsewhere but not at the disaster or large scale incident scene from which they have just been released. Returning people to the scene of a stressful incident immediately after they have undergone the demobilization process may make them more vulnerable to intense stress reactions at the scene. They should not have that problem if they work at different scenes. They usually see a different scene as not associated with the disaster and they can handle it without problems.

The next step in the demobilization process is the transport of the personnel from the scene to the demobilization center. This is usually accomplished by using the same piece of apparatus or unit that they used to get to the scene. The equipment from that unit will be collected and placed in its proper places on the unit before it is released from the scene. Equipment still in use may be left at the scene. If the unit is hopelessly caught at the scene and blocked by other emergency vehicles, arrangements may be made to move the personnel by means of utility vehicles. The drivers are ordered to take the unit and its personnel to the demobilization center (which should be close by, if properly pre- planned).

When the personnel arrive at the center, they are directed to the presentation room where they are assigned to a set of seats which are arranged in a circle. It is best to keep units together. People who work together on the same operations units sit with their own group. It is also important to keep law enforcement personnel with law enforcement personnel from their own units. Likewise, fire personnel stay with fire personnel and emergency medical services stay with their own. If the demobilization is being provided for disaster workers such as Red Cross personnel, they are handled as a "unit" in the demobilization. Avoid mixing up the groups. They need to be with their own people because they derive support from their fellow workers.

When the personnel from a particular unit are settled into the seats in their unit's assigned circle, one of the presenters from the CISM team will begin the demobilization. The remarks presented by the team member will be described in more detail in the section to follow, "The Process." The comments made by the presenter are the same for each group. Usually each presenter has the same outline from which to work. The presenter spends ten minutes (maximum time) providing information to the group. They are then asked if they have any questions of if they would like to say anything. It is very rare that they have either comments or questions. Once the questions have been handled and the statements accepted, the demobilization leader disengages from the group and sends them to the food room.

In the food room the personnel will have approximately twenty minutes to eat and rest and prepare to return to routine functions. At the end of their twenty minutes the personnel are given instructions about their functions or about their release to go home. Often, at the end of the rest phase, a supervisor will join the group and provide further information or instructions to the crew(s) who are preparing to leave the demobilization center.

More than one group is handled in a demobilization at one time. While the first group of emergency personnel is being given its ten minute presentation, a second, third or fourth group of emergency personnel might be released from the scene and arrive at the demobilization center. Each group is assigned to its own circle of chairs in the presentation room. A different CISM team member will approach one of the new groups and begin the same presentation which is already in progress for the first group which arrived earlier.

At the conclusion of the presentation the group which has just finished listening to its presentation will proceed to the food room. The groups which are in progress will continue until their presentations are completed. They, in turn, will depart the presentation room for the food room when their presentation session is complete. New groups just released from the scene will arrive and the cycle begins again and continues until all operations personnel who were working at the scene for the first or second shift have received their demobilization. Remember, personnel undergo demobilization only once, directly following their first exposure to the disaster. After that, the previously described innovation developed by the Oklahoma City CISM team or one-on-ones are the services provided for thew remainder of the operation.

## THE PROCESS

During the demobilization the following topics are usually covered in this predominantly didactic presentation:

- Introduction of the presenter

- Brief description of the demobilization

- A statement that the presentation portion of the demobilization will only take ten minutes and that the information is important and it may prevent painful stress reactions or help the personnel to cope with those reactions faster and better

- A statement that some may already have stress symptoms, some may develop them later and that some may escape them altogether

- Assurance that stress symptoms are normal under the circumstances

- A warning that stress symptoms could become more severe or disruptive to the personnel if they are ignored

- Descriptions of common cognitive, physical, emotional and behavioral signs and symptoms of stress

- Specific advice on eating, resting, avoiding alcohol and drugs, conversing with loved ones, coping with the media and other helpful hints to recover from stress

- An announcement of the debriefings to follow in a week or so after the demobilization

- A brief statement to encourage the participants to ask questions or make any comments they might wish

- A summary and distribution of handouts

Unlike the defusing or the debriefing, participants in a demobilization rarely ever speak unless they really want to. The demobilization process is a *passive process*. Only the CISM team member presenter is active. The participants simply listen and take in the information that is provided to them. The CISM presenter does NOT try to question the participants to get them to speak. The main objective of the demobilization is to give information. If participants wish to discuss their experiences they are invited to do so either at the end of the demobilization or privately afterwards. Just before ending the demobilization, the CISM team member making the presentation usually says, "Does anyone have any questions or comments before we wrap this presentation up?"

## MILITARY ADAPTATIONS

In enormous operations, such as a military operation, where thousands of personnel are involved, the demobilization changes its structure to conform to the special needs of the group. With thousands of people to serve, it would be impossible to provide formal debriefings for all of the personnel. The aim would be to debrief only those groups which saw the most action and provide an adaptation of the demobilization process to all of the others.

In emergency service operations, there are usually groups of six to eight demobilized as a unit immediately after their work at the scene is complete. In military operations there may be one hundred or more in a unit being demobilized at the same time. The demobilization may be given several days to several weeks later, when the personnel are returning home from the operation. The delay is necessary because their operations were prolonged over several days or weeks and a demobilization given earlier would have interfered with their ability to perform their duties.

Under the circumstances described in this section, the demobilization begins to look more like a lecture in a large classroom rather than a small group of people gathered in a circle. It is important to make sure that each person in a unit demobilization was involved in the same event or performed the same type of service or was part of a team dealing with a specific objective or task. The ten minute information-giving session may need to be expanded to twenty to forty-five minutes because the demobilization may be the only type of group support service which will be offered to the many thousands involved in the incident. More information is provided and a larger handout packet is developed and distributed for this special type of operation. In the handouts, a great deal more emphasis is placed on providing information regarding many other resources which may be available to the service personnel. It is particularly important that they know what types of services are available on their own bases or at other bases near their own.

## CONTRAINDICATIONS

The demobilization was designed to provide a minimal amount of stress control information to large numbers of people in a very short period of time. The events for which a demobilization has been designed are large scale events such as disasters, major wildland fires, and large search operations. The technique is inappropriate for a small event involving few emergency service personnel and adequate time to provide other types of services such as defusings or debriefings. Those other interventions would then be preferable.

It was mentioned earlier that a demobilization is easy to perform as far as the actual delivery of the service is concerned. It does not take much energy for trained CISM team members to give a ten minute talk on critical incident stress management and then tell people to go and eat and rest in the next room. What is very difficult to manage is the logistics behind this type of support service. If food is unavailable for the hundreds of personnel in the operation, about one half of the demobilization service has just been disrupted. If operations people have not been educated about the demobilization process they will resist it. If the CISM team has not arranged in advance for the demobilization service with the various emergency organizations involved in operation , it may become an impossibility to carry out in the chaotic atmosphere of a disaster. If the supervisors have not learned about the process in advance and agreed to it, the demobilization is doomed from the very start. Instead of cooperation, the demobilization team will encounter resentment and resistance.

Pushing the concept of a demobilization without the necessary support, cooperation and logistics from the organizations involved can be a self-destructive endeavor for the CISM team. There is a fall-back position for the CISM team when it becomes obvious that the demobilization, although a generally good idea, is not going to work in this particular disaster. The team must quickly modify its approach and provide defusings for selected groups that were exposed to the worst parts of the incident. A defusing is a direct substitute for the demobilization. Either one or the other is provided, not both. They may also provide on-scene support services on a one-on-one basis to individuals involved in the incident who are showing obvious signs of distress. Station visits, post-incident educational sessions and a schedule of CISD's can help to compensate for the lack of a demobilization. Those services are not the ideal but they can be helpful if the demobilization is not possible.

Multiple demobilizations of the same personnel during the disaster should be avoided since they may stir up more symptoms than they resolve. A demobilization one time is helpful, more often and it is perceived to be intrusive and annoying.

The demobilization process is simply one step in a whole series of steps to render support to emergency personnel after a large scale event or a disaster. It should never be looked at as a one-time process which will help everyone. The demobilization is quite limited. It is only a tool with which a CISM team can address the needs of many hundreds of personnel after a chaotic situation. It may not be the best intervention overall, but it is the best under very strenuous circumstances.

## FOLLOW-UP SERVICES

The demobilization is *always* followed up with a CISD several days or weeks after the end of the disaster work. The large scale event is generally so distressing to emergency personnel that debriefings will be required anyway. Numerous debriefings may need to be set up in the weeks following the incident. It is best to start with the groups which were most seriously affected by an incident such as the first arrivals or those who had to deal with the dead or dying. Once debriefings have been provided to those groups, the CISM team organizes CISDs for groups less seriously affected, until there are no other groups which need support.

Individual sessions with single emergency service personnel are always indicated when the personnel are requesting them. In a disaster, it is not uncommon to find that about ten percent of the personnel seek out individual support through the CISM team or in private therapy. Sometimes, the first contact with CISM team members in the demobilization session helps with subsequent contacts and facilitates contact with other CISM services or referrals, should those be necessary.

## SUMMARY

This chapter describes a process which has been developed to provide support services to many hundreds of personnel who may be involved in a disaster or other large scale incident. The advantages and disadvantages of the process were described. It was noted that the demobilization process is easy to apply but very difficult to manage because of the needs for logistical support and the pre-incident agreements which are necessary.

The chapter entitled, "Mass Disaster CISM Interventions and Community Response Teams" will provide considerable additional information on disasters and the functions of CISM and Community Response Teams with non-emergency service populations. It is also recommended that the reader become familiar with the chapter on Crisis Management Briefing.

# Chapter 8

# CRISIS MANAGEMENT BRIEFING (CMB)

Community violence, acts of terrorism, and mass disasters all share a common element: they all affect large groups of individuals. As such, they threaten to quickly overwhelm the mental health resources of any given community or organization. Traditional crisis intervention methods have been labor-intensive, often consisting of one-on-one interventions. The advent of group crisis intervention technologies have served to not only enhance the effectiveness of crisis intervention, but to enhance its efficiency as well. The most popular group crisis intervention technology in the world is the Critical Incident Stress Debriefing (CISD), as noted previously. However, the CISD is a **small** group (20 individuals or less at a time) crisis intervention. Although effective, the CISD is not suited for large numbers of primary and vicarious victims. As a result, a **large** group crisis intervention had to be developed. The Crisis Management Briefing (CMB) is a large group (up to 300 people at a time) crisis intervention. It is designed to last 45 to 75 minutes. The CMB may be thought of as a form of "town meeting" for the expressed purpose of crisis intervention.

Initially referred to as a group informational briefing (Everly & Mitchell, 1999), the process was refined and later referred to as the CMB (Everly, 2000). It appears to be ideally suited for business and industrial applications, schools (Newman, 2000), large scale community critical incidents, and even military applications. The CMB was first formally used in response to a natural disaster which occurred in a rural township in the early 1990s. The next noteworthy application of the CMB was in response to the TWA 800 air disaster. Since that time, the CMB has been reportedly employed in numerous school crises and incidences of community and workplace violence. The United States military has even explored the use of the CMB for large combat groups.

# FOUR PHASES OF THE CMB

The CMB consists of four phases:

**PHASE ONE – ASSEMBLY.** In this initial phase of the CMB, crisis interventionists identify the target group(s) for the intervention. The logistics of determining how and when to bring these individuals together is addressed. In a school setting for example, each grade may be brought together, one grade at a time, in the school auditorium for the purpose of conducting the CMB. In the case of a high school, four sequential CMBs would be conducted. In the case of business and industrial applications, employees may be brought together in a large meeting room, either all at one time, or in large sequential groups. In the military, combat groups may be aggregated. When working with naval groups on shipboard, the closed circuit TV system may be useful, or the overhead message system may be employed. In large community incidents, the community may be divided into voting districts, or school districts with the primary voting venue or high school utilized as the location for assembly, respectively. Also useful in community incidents will be houses of worship which will be of value to those inclined to seek faith-based support in times of community distress.

The CMB may be all that is needed to reach large groups of individuals who are only peripherally involved in a critical incident. For example, if an employee of a business that has offices throughout the nation is violently murdered at work in Washington, D.C., not only will the locally based employees be in need of intervention, but the employees in other offices will also be in need of intervention because they may share the potential risk.

The CMB may be used while a protracted critical event is unfolding, or it may be used immediately after the event has resolved. Thus, the CMB may be repeated as many times as needed.

**PHASE TWO – INFORMATION.** In this phase, level of anxiety is reduced and rumors are controlled by a direct presentation concerning what is known and what is not known about the critical incident. Care is taken not to breach boundaries of confidentiality or to disseminate information which might negatively impact emergency operations. Usually, the person responsible for conducting this phase is one with technical credibility in the eyes of the target group. A physician may address the "facts" of a medical emergency. A high-ranking law enforcement official may address the facts of a criminal action. A representative of management may provide information in business and industrial settings.

**PHASE THREE - REACTIONS.** In this phase, the discussion turns to common psychological and behavioral reactions engendered by similar critical incidents. Major psychological themes are anticipated and discussed. An effort is made to normalize and demedicalize reactions as much as possible. Once again, the person responsible for conducting this phase of the CMB should possess content credibility, e.g., a psychologist or psychiatrist.

**PHASE FOUR – COPING STRATEGIES AND RESOURCES.** This final phase of the CMB consists of providing the group with specific personal and community resources that may assist in the restoration and recovery process. Stress management techniques are often discussed. Final questions are answered. Each person leaves the CMB with a hand-out listing common reactions, common coping techniques, and community resources that may be used to facilitate the recovery process.

The CMB can also be used to triage individuals for more intense and appropriate intervention, such as CISD, individual crisis intervention, etc. Thus in some critical incidents, victims may attend three or four serial crisis interventions. For example, victims may first receive the CMB, later those who require further attention may receive the CISD, and a smaller number yet may receive one-on-one crisis intervention (although this could occur at any point in the intervention process based upon need). Finally, a few may require referral for more formal mental health assessment with consideration being paid to psychotherapy and perhaps even a combination of psychotherapy and psychotropic medication.

# THE CMB INTERVENTION TEAM

The CMB should be conducted by an intervention team, if possible. The team should consist of an individual who possesses technical credibility in the eyes of the target group in order to best address the "facts" of the incident, as well as a mental health support professional to conduct the reaction and coping phases. If the CMB is done directly with the target group physically aggregated, it is always advisable to have at least one other mental health professional (but preferably a team of several mental health professionals) available in the audience to assess and triage members of the target group who appear to require immediate mental health follow-up.

# MECHANISMS FOR CRISIS REDUCTION IN THE CMB

The assembly phase is designed to combat perceptions of isolation and alienation that may be experienced by victims of critical incidents and traumatic events. A second benefit may be that it allows for formal and informal social and functional support networking to occur.

The information phase of the CMB is designed to provide information that may serve to foster a sense of self-efficacy and a return to feelings of control in those adversely affected or threatened by the critical incident. If, indeed, information is power, this phase fosters such empowerment. Perhaps most importantly, however, this phase of the CMB is designed to control potentially dangerous or dysfunctional rumors.

The reactions phase is designed to normalize, as much as is reasonable, the psychological and behavioral reactions that the majority of individuals will experience. It also serves as an opportunity to point out reactions that may dictate a need for further assessment and perhaps treatment.

Finally, the coping phase is designed to provide practical stress management strategies as well as identify community and organizational resources that may be of assistance in further assessment and treatment, if needed.

It should be noted that the CMB follows a psychological progression which moves from an initial cognitive orientation, through an affective emphasis, and then returns to a cognitive, problem-oriented focus. Experience has taught that this progression is important to maintain.

# SUMMARY

The CMB is a large group crisis intervention technology. As with all other CISM interventions, it is not designed to be a stand-alone intervention. The CMB may represent the most efficient and versatile component within the CISM crisis intervention system. It is applicable in virtually every form of critical incident or traumatic event touching large numbers (20-300) of individuals. The CMB can also be conducted with smaller groups prior to the CISD, if applicable.

The assembly phase would require modification in situations where there is concern over a contagious pathogen. In such cases, mass media and interactive media may be useful.

# Chapter 9

## DEFUSING

### INTRODUCTION

The Critical Incident Stress Debriefing (CISD) is discussed in detail in another chapter of this book. It has been the object of considerable attention in CISM literature and in some news reports. It is therefore a relatively well-known group crisis intervention tactic. CISD is often described as the most complex of all of the interventions by CISM teams. It tends to be time and labor intensive and also somewhat difficult to organize. A CISM team should, therefore, perform a careful assessment of the need for a debriefing before deciding to provide one. One of the tools which helps to assess the need for a CISD is a defusing.

A defusing is a shortened version of a CISD. It is provided on the same day as the incident, preferably within a few hours of the end of the situation. The defusing helps to assess the personnel involved in the incident. Sometimes a defusing is just the right kind of help at the right time. It might eliminate the need to do a CISD. If a determination is made that the CISD is still necessary, the CISD is usually enhanced by having had the defusing first. Even in situations in which a debriefing was still necessary because the event was so powerful, the defusing was an effective intervention. It calmed the reactions of the organization's personnel sufficiently to allow the necessary time to properly set up a full debriefing. This chapter will discuss the defusing process which has been widely used by CISM teams around the world.

### DEFUSING DEFINED

The word defusing means to render something harmless before it can do damage. That is the essence of the support service which a CISM team provides when it deploys a defusing team after an incident. The overall objective is to render the situation harmless to those who were exposed to it. If the situation cannot be made totally harmless, then at least every effort is made to reduce its potential for harm.

A defusing is a small group process which is instituted after any traumatic event (critical incident) powerful enough to overwhelm the coping mechanisms of the people exposed to it. The events which necessitate a defusing have the same or very close to the same intensity as events which would trigger a debriefing. The difference is not to be found in the type of incident, but in the timing of the response and the type of response to the incident.

The defusing is a shortened version of the debriefing, but it is more immediate in its application. The defusing team does not have to wait the usual twenty four hours to intervene with a CISD. Instead, they attempt to intervene with a defusing as soon as possible after the critical incident. Because it is provided so soon, it does not delve as deeply into the emotional material as a debriefing does. It offers an opportunity for people involved in a horrible event to talk briefly about that experience before they have time to rethink the experience and possibly misinterpret its true meaning. There is at least some evidence which suggests that an immediate intervention is more beneficial than waiting until the usual twenty four hours has passed before the debriefing is set up (in the case of emergency personnel).

Although the defusing has some structure, it is much less organized than the formal debriefing. Its structure will be described in the sections to follow. The defusing is less complex than the debriefing. It is easier to organize and manage. It has the advantage of being less costly to provide since it takes people out of service for shorter time frames. The defusing is more immediate than the debriefing and it does not require the services of a full team of debriefers. Most defusings do not require the services of a mental health professional. They can easily be provided by well trained peer support personnel.

There is another significant difference between the debriefing and the defusing. The CISD is usually employed with larger groups of participants. It can bring people together from different emergency professions as long as they worked closely together and had about the same level of emotional distress. The defusing, on the other hand, is generally aimed at much smaller groups. The focus, in the defusing, is on small teams of people who ordinarily work together on the same tasks. The defusing team may have to provide three or four defusings. For example, one may be provided to the nurses, another to the paramedics or emergency medical technicians and another to the police officers who handled a case.

A defusing is certainly not applicable in all situations. It is limited by considerable time constraints which will be explained later in this chapter. But the defusing does have many applications, and CISM teams need to look at it seriously. It is a primary intervention technique following traumatic stress and it has been successfully used not only with emergency personnel, but also with industrial programs, commercial ventures, schools systems and the general public.

# GOALS OF DEFUSING

There are four main goals of the group process called the defusing:

- A rapid reduction in the intense reactions to a traumatic event.

- A "normalizing" of the experience so that people can return to their routine duties as quickly as possible.

- A re-establishment of the social network of the group so that people do not isolate themselves from each other, but instead see that their reactions are similar to one another. In recognizing similarities to others, people are often more willing to help each other in troubled times.

- An assessment of the personnel to determine if a full debriefing is necessary.

There are several other objectives which are also of importance in a defusing. The defusing team is attempting to accomplish:

- Equalization of the information about the incident available to all of the personnel.

- Restoration of cognitive processes which have been disrupted by the incident.

- Provision of practical information for stress survival.

- Affirmation of the value of the personnel.

- Establishment of linkages for additional support.

- Development of expectancies regarding recovery.

# USUAL EFFECTS OF DEFUSING

There are two desirable effects of a defusing which are typical in most cases. The effects depend upon the proper application of the defusing within the time frames described below. A carefully applied and well- managed defusing will usually:

- Eliminate the need to do a debriefing,

**OR**

- It will enhance a debriefing if the debriefing is still necessary.

NOTE: The elimination of the need to provide a CISD is a by-product of a defusing, not a goal. In other words, it may happen naturally, but one is not working to achieve that effect.

# TARGET GROUPS

A defusing is aimed at the core working group that was most seriously affected by the event. Typically, six to eight people from an engine or truck company, an ambulance service, an emergency room staff, a police tactical unit, a business or some specialty team are brought together for a defusing after a particularly bad incident. The defusing team provides as many de-fusings as necessary to accommodate each group which has been affected by the incident. That is, separate defusings are provided for each of the groups.

In some rare instances, all of the various groups are together in the same area. It is then easier to bring them all together and provide one defusing. The defusing team makes that decision only if it appears that a joint defusing is in the best interests of the entire group. Of course, if a joint defusing is held, it is a much more difficult task for the defusing team. It will certainly take them longer to handle a large group defusing. It should be pointed out here that the large group defusing is possible and sometimes beneficial, but it is not the generally recommended course of action.

# PROVIDERS

Only people properly trained in CISM should provide defusings. Those who have experienced a highly distressing event are quite vulnerable to further psychological damage if they are being managed in the crisis state by untrained people.

Defusings may be provided by CISM trained peer support personnel, members of the clergy, chaplains, or mental health professionals. Sometimes the defusing is led by a combined team of peer support and professional support personnel. Even if only peer support personnel or only mental health professionals are leading a defusing, it is best that a defusing team be made up of at least two individuals because it eases the burden that would be faced by a person working alone. But in some circumstances, only one CISM team member is available. Since the defusing is dependent for success on its relatively immediate application, the single trained team member might then have to proceed with the defusing. The management of a defusing by only one helper is to be considered a rare exception to the rule and should generally be avoided. There is considerable danger in attempting to provide a defusing with only one helper. If a participant leaves the group, there is no one else who can go out after that person to check on his or her welfare and to coax the person back into the defusing.

It should be noted that, although it is a desirable course of action, it is not necessary for mental health professionals to be present at the defusing. The defusing is provided so soon following the incident that people have not had sufficient time to process the experience and have not yet formed deep emotional reactions to it. They are often in a state of shock or denial and postpone the processing of their emotions until later. Most of what they are experiencing after the incident, at the time of the defusing, can be managed relatively easily by a team of well trained peer support personnel.

Although mental health professionals may not be present at a defusing, it would be foolish for peer support personnel to provide defusings without contacting a mental health professional later for supervision and additional instructions regarding their intervention. In some CISM teams, peer support personnel have the authority to provide defusing services, but they also have the obligation to contact one of the mental health professionals on the team within 8 to 12 hours after the defusing. The mental health professional goes over the defusing with the peer support person(s) and offers praise for a job well-done and advice on even more effective interventions in the future.

## TIMING

It has been mentioned several times so far in this chapter that a defusing must be provided within certain time limitations to be maximally effective. Defusings are designed to be given within 8 to 12 hours of the conclusion of an incident. The first three hours after an incident is the ideal time frame. Some exceptions to the 8 to 12 hour rule do apply in certain circumstances. For instance, in a situation in which a gruesome crime has been committed and law enforcement personnel are engaged in a search for the suspect, it might not be possible to bring the officers together until more than twelve hours have passed. The fact that the incident does not end until the suspect is arrested, combined with the shocking nature of the event itself, may extend the time in which a defusing is effective to as many as 16-20 hours after the incident. Please keep in mind, however, that a team providing a defusing so delayed will have to contend with a substantial human fatigue factor. If fatigue is a serious disruptive factor, it would probably be better to provide some one-on-one support and set up a CISD for a day or two later.

The rationale for such a tight time frame in providing a defusing has to do with the process of traumatization following traumatic events. During the incident, those exposed to it are in a state of shock. They are very vulnerable to further damage. Coincidentally, they are also very open to help. But over the next few hours, people attempt to re-establish their defense systems. They shut down their connections with the world around them. They begin to "put their guards up." Even though help is waiting outside to assist them, the shock of the incident causes traumatized people to defend themselves from friend and foe alike. They seem to seek no stimuli at all. Traumatized people, within a few hours of the traumatic event, shut off most outside influences without distinguishing between friend or enemy. All influences are interpreted as dangerous until they can stabilize themselves.

It is during the early hours after the trauma, when people are more open to help and before they have begun their "shut down" that the defusing is most helpful. Once the "shut down" has occurred, the defusing is relatively ineffective. After about 24 hours, the person has been able to stabilize and reorient themselves. They have also begun to emotionally process the experience. They may misinterpret aspects of the situation and blame themselves for a failed mission. Later they will gradually open up again and are more ready to accept help. At this point the debriefing is the intervention of choice rather than the defusing. By the time the first 24 hours have passed, the defusing is not powerful enough to make much of an impact. The debriefing is a more powerful tool and therefore more appropriate after the first day.

If the defusing is delayed beyond the 8 to 12 hour time frame, it is usually best for the CISM team to skip the defusing. Instead the CISM team should rely on one-on-one interventions until a debriefing can be organized.

## DISASTER: A SPECIAL CASE

A defusing may be used as an immediate support service after a disaster. It has been used effectively on several disasters. There is, in addition, another intervention called a "demobilization." The only time a demobilization is ever used is in a large scale incident such as a disaster. In a disaster, a demobilization may be provided instead of a defusing, but not in addition to the defusing. One substitutes for the other in a disaster. They both have advantages and disadvantages. Sometimes one is easier to apply than the other. There is no harm in using one technique over the other. The choice of whether to use a defusing or a demobilization depends on the circumstances of the event, the support of the supervisors and administrators of the involved organizations, the CISM staffing and the logistics associated with the situation. Again, human fatigue is of considerable concern. A demobilization may be chosen over a defusing because the demobilization is much shorter and more passive for the participants. A defusing is chosen for selected groups who have encountered severe trauma during the disaster. But, the group members should not be so exhausted that they cannot discuss the event. The demobilization has been described in an earlier chapter. For now, it is important to recognize the existence of an alternate intervention to the defusing for disasters.

# DEFUSING PROCESS

## Location

The defusing is held in a neutral environment, free of distractions. A defusing is never held at the scene of an incident. The room in which the defusing is held should be adequate to accommodate the small group. It should be comfortable, well-lit, and air conditioned or heated as necessary for the weather. The seats should be as comfortable as possible and arranged in a circle or around a conference table or a coffee table. Defusings have been held in meeting rooms, living rooms, church basements, classrooms and hotel meeting rooms. As long as the requirements of quiet and privacy are fulfilled, there are very few places in which a defusing could not be held.

## Most Useful Times

When a particularly bad incident occurs at the very beginning of a shift and the personnel must work through the remainder of that shift, it is very helpful to bring the group together and provide a defusing. This enables them to talk about the event, lower their level of distress and return to their normal duties without the distractions which go along with distress over a disruptive event.

Likewise, when a bad incident occurs at the very end of a shift, it is better to provide a defusing before the group goes home. In this way, they will not be carrying the distress associated with the incident to their homes and families. As a matter of practicality, it is very difficult to bring a group together when they are in the middle of their shift and when they have been deployed to important duties in the field. That is why the beginning or end of a shift is the best time to engage a group in a defusing.

## Time Commitment

The defusing usually takes between twenty minutes and one hour to complete. Sometimes they go on for slightly more than an hour. If they continue much longer than an hour, it is a signal that either the group is highly traumatized or the defusing team leadership is not in control of the defusing. The average defusing lasts about 45 minutes. It is generally best to keep the time of the defusing to within twenty minutes and one hour. If it appears that much longer time periods will be necessary, consideration should be given to providing only minimal stabilization immediately, following with a full debriefing later.

## Preparation

Since notice for the defusing is short, it is rare that a defusing team will have very much time to prepare for the defusing. A brief description of the incident is often all the defusing team has to go on. They will have to do their best with the information available. There is also no time to arrange for refreshments, so the defusing team does not have the luxury of an anchor to hold the group together for any length of time after the defusing.

## OVERVIEW

The defusing has three main segments which are linked to each other in a free flowing conversation about the traumatic event. The segments are:

- Introduction
- Exploration
- Information

The introduction usually takes five to seven minutes. Then the defusing team guides the participants into the exploration segment. Exploration goes on for ten to thirty minutes before the final segment, the information segment, is initiated. The information segment lasts from five to fifteen minutes.

## Introduction

The defusing begins as soon as the group sits down with the team. Team members briefly introduce themselves and then begin to accomplish several necessary tasks. The defusing team is attempting to accomplish many of the same tasks required in a debriefing. One of the main differences between the debriefing and the defusing usually shows up at this time. The defusing is much shorter so the defusing team does not have very much leeway in accomplishing the introductory tasks. The defusing team:

- Introduces itself

- Tells the group why they have gathered

- Describes the defusing

- Motivates the participants

- Summarizes the main guidelines of a defusing

- Encourages mutual support

- Encourages their participation

- Instills the need for confidentiality

- Accepts any questions before beginning

- Alleviates group anxiety about the defusing process

- Assures the group that the defusing is not investigative

- Offers additional support if it should be needed after the defusing

Many of the introductory remarks for the defusing are very similar or identical to those made in the debriefing. It is a good idea to read over the "introduction" portion of the "Debriefing Process" in the CISD chapter before conducting a defusing, especially if it has been a long time since the last defusing or debriefing.

## Exploration

In the second phase of the defusing the participants are asked to discuss the experience they just had. This segment of the defusing would equate to a combination of the fact, thought, reaction and symptom phases of the debriefing. The tone set by the defusing team is conversational, not investigative. Anyone in the group who wishes to speak is invited to do so. There is no order in the defusing process. Anyone may remain silent if they wish, although it is not in his / her best interest. Throughout the defusing process the team members make several gentle efforts to involve everyone in the group by inviting them to speak. The participants are not accompanied by any sense of pressure, just concern for the members of the group.

There is a broad range of questions which team members can ask during a defusing. They begin by asking the group to tell the team what happened. Then there are many clarifying questions which can be asked about the incident and their roles in it. The range of questions goes from asking for additional detail to asking about interactions with people who are not even present at the defusing. Sometimes the defusing team asks about signs and symptoms of distress which are already being experienced by the group members.

It is impossible to list the questions which are asked by the team members during the defusing. They vary from defusing to defusing. They can be fairly straight forward or more complex. Sometimes the group does a good deal of the talking and there is very little need for the team to ask questions. As a group relaxes and begins to trust the defusing team, they tend to talk in more detail about the traumatic experience.

When the conversation about the incident begins to lag or when the side topics begin to take on more importance than the main issues, the team should start wrapping things up so that they can move into the final phase of the defusing. Remember, the entire defusing should last only twenty minutes to an hour in most cases, so there is little time in which to bring the process to a conclusion.

## Information

The information phase of the defusing is equivalent to a combination of the teaching and re-entry phases in the debriefing. There is a considerable amount of information to cover and it must be covered quickly. In this phase the defusing team is trying to provide as much useful information as possible to ensure that the group members are prepared to manage their stress. The defusing team will need to:

- Accept and summarize the information provided by the group in the exploration phase.

- Answer any questions the group members may ask.

- Normalize the experiences and reactions of the group.

- Teach practical stress survival skills to the group.

- Organize a debriefing if it appears that one is necessary.

- Make summary comments which will send the group on their way.

- Make themselves available to the group once the defusing is complete.

# AVERAGE LENGTH OF A DEFUSING

When a defusing team is listening to the defusing participants, it is easy to get caught up in the discussion and forget that the defusing needs to be limited to one hour or less. Anything significantly beyond the hour limit indicates that the group probably would benefit from a full debriefing which should only be provided by a trained debriefing team. In 20 to 45 minutes the average defusing team has completed its work and is ready to release the group.

# CONTRAINDICATIONS

Any tool which is designed for a specific purpose can usually perform that specific job, but over-use or inappropriate uses of the tool can be ineffective and possibly harmful. The same is true for use of CISM interventions, which were developed with specific purposes in mind. Over-use or inappropriate uses can be ineffective at best and damaging at worst.

The defusing was designed as a small group, rapid intervention for distressed people. In most cases, it is applied within eight hours of a traumatic incident. Using the defusing after many days have passed is an abuse of the technique. Using the defusing process at the end of every twelve hour shift is another misuse which will dilute its power and render its use ineffective. Attempting to substitute a defusing for a referral for psychotherapy is a dangerous abuse of the technique. Abuse of that type has a great deal of potential to cause permanent, possibly life threatening, harm to people who need serious help from skilled professionals.

The defusing should only be used by CISM trained individuals and in the manner in which it was designed to be used. Violations of the basic principles of defusing, or any CISM intervention for that matter, should not be tolerated by CISM teams. Allowing team members to use any of the CISM techniques when they are contraindicated, as in the descriptions above, is a dangerous and unprofessional behavior.

# FOLLOW-UP SERVICES

As in debriefings, the follow-up for defusings begins immediately after the session is complete. The team members attempt to contact each of the group members to make sure that they are okay. If there are some particular concerns about one person or another, the team members will attempt to obtain that person's phone number so that a call can be made in the next 24 hours or so to determine if the person needs any additional assistance.

One-on-one consultations are very common after a defusing. Many people have questions which they did not wish to discuss in the presence of other group members. Many of the people who seek an individual consultation have very private concerns which they would be embarrassed to discuss openly.

A full CISD is the most desirable follow-up service if it appears that the defusing was ineffective in resolving the main issues for the majority of the group. It is also the most logical step for an entire group which is seriously affected by the power of a extremely traumatic event.

Other types of follow-up services may be identified during the defusing and these should be applied as necessary.

# SUMMARY

This chapter explored the defusing process, which is one of the main intervention strategies employed by a CISM team immediately after a traumatic stress. It was described as a small group process that can eliminate the need for a full CISD or will enhance the debriefing if one is still necessary. The steps involved in providing a defusing - *introduction, exploration and information*- were discussed in detail.

In the case of disasters or other large scale events, the reader is reminded that there is another CISM intervention, called the Demobilization. Although it is a limited group information process, the demobilization can be very helpful in the aftermath of a disaster and it, like the defusing, "buys time" in which a CISD can be properly arranged. Please see the chapter entitled, "Demobilization."

# Chapter 10

## THE CRITICAL INCIDENT STRESS DEBRIEFING (CISD): Important considerations and preparations

### INTRODUCTION

The Critical Incident Stress Debriefing (CISD) is the most complex of all of the Critical Incident Stress Management (CISM) interventions. This is so whether the process is employed by CISM teams in their work with emergency personnel, or Community Response Teams (CRT) which work with the citizens of various communities, schools and other organizations after traumatic events. The Critical Incident Stress Debriefing was originally designed to reduce stress in emergency personnel after extremely traumatic experiences. More recently it has found application in schools, industries, commercial operations and community groups. It was originally designed with the most resistant and difficult populations in mind. When it is applied to people who are not in the emergency services professions, a CISD generally appears to run more easily. This may be true because the average non-emergency services person does not have the "image armor" that emergency operations personnel have. In other words, the average victim of a traumatic experience does not have to keep up a good "front" before his or her colleagues as a police officer or fire fighter or other rescuer might have to do. The non-emergency services person is more free to express him or herself.

The debriefing was not designed to be applied in the so called "routine" cases. CISD is a useful tool for stress mitigation when applied properly. The overuse of the procedure on relatively minor events is not a proper application of the process. Nor is it a proper application for organizations to to use too broadly for events that are not truly critical incidents in nature, such as mediating management - employee conflicts or investigating employee behaviors. Other procedures would be more applicable in those situations.

The basic concepts of CISD are easy to understand and are clear on paper. The complexities enter the picture when a debriefer is faced with the problem of applying those concepts in "real world" circumstances. When a group of people in distress is before the CISD team, there are many variables which can present a challenge to the team. This chapter will help both experienced and newly trained CISM or Community Response Team members provide a most valuable service to the emergency personnel or to their community in an efficient and effective manner.

# DEBRIEFING DEFINED

A CISD is a group process. It can best be defined as a group meeting or discussion, employing both crisis intervention and educational processes, targeted toward mitigating or resolving the psychological distress associated with a critical incident (a traumatic event). The CISD team consists of one mental health professional and one, two or three peer support personnel when a CISD is applied to emergency services personnel or disaster workers. The structure of the team often is modified when a debriefing is applied to community groups, schools, industries or other populations. In the "Community Response Team" (CRT) mode, a debriefing team may be made up of only mental health professionals. In any event, traumatic stress interventions should only be applied by trained individuals who are familiar with both traumatic stress and its effects on people and the broad range of crisis intervention services available to contend with the traumatic experience.

The CISD has seven phases. The structure allows participants in the groups to discuss a traumatic incident in a controlled manner which does not leave them feeling out of control of themselves. The CISD uses some techniques common to counseling, but it is not counseling nor psychotherapy nor a substitute for psychotherapy. One of the main components, which makes a debriefing different than psychotherapy, is the fact that a substantial portion of the debriefing process is dedicated to teaching the participants about their stress reactions. Stress survival techniques to manage traumatic stress are also taught.

In its applications to emergency personnel, a debriefing is a peer managed and peer driven process which uses mental health professionals for oversight and guidance. In its general community (CRT) applications, a team of traumatic stress trained mental health professionals runs the debriefing without the assistance of peer support personnel unless they request assistance from trained CISD peers from the fire, police, nursing or emergency medical services agencies. When a CISD is applied to non-emergency populations, certain structural and process modifications may be necessary to accommodate ethnic, cultural and traditional issues within those groups. It is also important that all CISD related interventions be appropriate to the age of the participants. In sum, it is important that team members have expertise in dealing with the special needs of the populations they serve. If this is not the case, the ability of the CISD team to achieve the primary goals of the debriefing will be severely jeopardized.

Generally the process of the debriefing and its goals and objectives are essentially the same whether it is being applied to emergency services groups or to citizen groups from the community.

# GOALS AND OBJECTIVES OF DEBRIEFING

There are three main goals of a Critical Incident Stress Debriefing. The process has been designed to:

1. Mitigate the impact of the critical incident on those who were victims of the event, be they:

    a. primary victims, (those directly traumatized by the event)

    b. secondary victims, (emergency services personnel who witnessed or managed the traumatic event)

    c. tertiary victims, (family, friends, and those to whom the traumatic event may be indirectly communicated)

2. Accelerate normal recovery processes in normal people who are experiencing normal stress reactions to abnormal traumatic events.

3. Facilitate the identification of individuals within the group who might be in need of additional CISM services or a referral for therapy.

As described earlier, the CISD process is considered one of the most important mechanisms to reduce the potential of Posttraumatic Stress Disorder (PTSD). It allows people to verbalize their distress and form appropriate concepts about stress reaction before false interpretations of the experience are fixed in their minds.

The core focus of CISD is the relief of stress in normal, emotionally healthy people who have experienced traumatic events. The debriefing has not been developed to resolve degenerative stress, psychopathologies or personal problems which existed before the disaster or traumatic event which is the subject of the debriefing.

There are some sporadic anecdotal records in which clinicians have reported some success in using the debriefing process with clinical subjects. We are happy to hear of those reported successes, but they are beyond the original design of the debriefing process; and formal studies of those unusual applications of CISD are encouraged.

There are several secondary goals and objectives of a CISD. They may not always be achieved in every CISD but they should always be goals. It makes no difference whether the debriefing is provided to emergency personnel by a CISM team or to community groups by a CRT team. The objectives of the CISD are identical. Secondary objectives of the process are:

- Education about stress, stress reactions and survival techniques

- Emotional ventilation

- Reassurance that the stress response is controllable and that recovery is likely

- Forewarning of signs and symptoms which might show up in the near future

- Reduction of the fallacy of uniqueness (or the feeling that one has been singled out to be a victim)

- Reduction of the fallacy of abnormality

- Establishment of a positive contact with mental health professionals

- Enhancement of group cohesiveness

- Enhancement of interagency cooperation

- Prevention or mitigation of post trauma syndromes and PTSD

- Screening for people who need additional assessment or therapy

- Referral for counseling or other services as necessary

# CRITICAL INCIDENTS

A critical incident is defined as any event with sufficient impact to produce significant emotional reactions in people now or later. It is an event which is, in general, considered to be extremely unusual in the range of ordinary human experiences. The incident may be the foundation for Post Traumatic Stress Disorder if it is not resolved effectively and quickly.

The CISD has been developed to help people cope with the most stressful of events. It was never designed with the routine in mind. CISD should be applied only to those events which are extraordinary. Overuse of the process will dilute its potency and cause it to be far less helpful on more serious events. If mildly distressing events occur, other types of interventions should be applied by the CISM team or the Community Response Team.

**TABLE 10.1**

**CRITICAL INCIDENTS FOR EMERGENCY SERVICE PERSONNEL**

| | |
|---|---|
| • Line of duty death | • Serious line of duty injury |
| • Suicide of an emergency worker | • Police shooting |
| • Multi-casualty incident / disaster | • Excessive media interest |
| • Significant event involving children | • Prolonged incident with loss |
| • Knowing the victim of the event | • Any significant event |

# GENERAL ORGANIZATION OF A CISD TEAM

A brief description of the organization of a CISM team will be helpful in understanding the procedures and functions of the CISM team once it is called into action to provide a CISD.

The typical CISM team is made up of 20 to 40 people from a large jurisdiction or a region made up of smaller jurisdictions. Roughly one third of the membership of a CISM team is made up of mental health professionals and two thirds are peer support personnel. Peer support personnel are members of the military, law enforcement, nursing, fire suppression, and emergency medical services personnel, as well as those from corrections, search and rescue groups, life guard services, dispatch centers and other specialty "first response groups." As noted earlier, some industries and school systems are training teams of peers to work with mental health resources for their organizations.

Each team has a basic organizational structure which includes at least the following roles:

CLINICAL DIRECTOR - A mental health professional who provides oversight and consultation to other team members on matters relating to mental health.

SENIOR TEAM COORDINATOR - A peer who serves as the day-to-day manager of the team. The senior team coordinator deploys the three or four team members to provide the debriefing. The senior team coordinator also arranges team meetings and maintains any team related records. The senior coordinator guides the efforts of the assistant coordinators and other team members and provides stress education programs to emergency personnel.

ASSISTANT TEAM COORDINATORS - There may be more than one assistant coordinator depending on the size and activity level of the CISM team. Assistant coordinators take over the responsibilities of the senior coordinator when he or she is away or occupied with other functions.

MENTAL HEALTH PROFESSIONALS - These people share the leadership with the two to four member team assigned to provide a formal debriefing. Frequently the mental health professional is the primary leader in the group, but this is not always the case. It is important to note, however, that mental health professionals on the team have the final say on matters of significant psychological importance. They also provide brief consultation to individuals who have been identified during a debriefing as people who may need additional support services. The mental health professionals provide advice and back up to peers who are doing the bulk of the day-to-day work of the CISM team. Mental health professionals also assist in providing stress education programs to the various organizations the team serves.

PEER SUPPORT PERSONNEL - The majority of team members on a CISM team which serves emergency personnel are emergency workers themselves. They provide stress education to their fellow emergency workers. They handle most of the one-on-one contacts as well as defusings and follow up contacts. Peer support team members work actively in concert with the mental health team leader in a formal debriefing.

# COMMUNITY RESPONSE TEAMS

These team members may be part of a CISM team or they may function in a manner that is separate from the CISM team. The basic structure of a CRT may be quite different from a CISM which is designed to serve emergency personnel. Those teams which serve school systems, the general community or industrial settings may or may not need peer support personnel. They may solely utilize the services of mental health professionals or they may incorporate the services of the medical team which serves the organization. In one company, for example, the CRT team has trained the medical staff of the company in CISM so that they may assist the mental health professionals in providing CISD to the population they serve. The CISM services for the community do not change substantially. Only the team organization needs to be altered.

# CALL OUT PROCEDURES: ACTIVATING THE CISD TEAM

A CISD is a time and labor intensive function which requires a team of between two and four team members. It takes approximately two to three hours to complete a CISD, so debriefings should only be provided when they are necessary. There are other techniques such as defusings and individual consultations which might be more applicable and more effective than the debriefing under certain circumstances. CISM teams should carefully evaluate the true need for a debriefing before setting one up.

Once an incident occurs a set of pre-arranged procedures will be initiated. Someone makes the first call for help. The caller may be a CISM team member or one of the emergency personnel or a representative of the Red Cross or a community official who recognizes the need for assistance for the affected group. Typically the first call comes from someone who is somewhat familiar with the CISM process and the need to apply it. Sometimes the request for assistance is made while the incident is in progress. At other times, the call may not come in for several days because there is no apparent perceived need, or, in some instances, it is not known that help is available. There have been cases in which no request for assistance was made for several weeks.

Regardless of when the call is made, the call out process begins when the first contact is made for help. Some calls are made directly to the team coordinator. This practice is to be discouraged, however, because the coordinator is frequently not in the office when a call comes in through the routine phone system. A far better way for the system to work is to educate all potential callers to contact a 24 hour communications center where a trained communications operator or dispatcher answers the call. The dispatcher attempts to gather pertinent information which will be handed off to a team coordinator:

- What is the nature of the call?

- Is the situation considered an emergency or is the caller asking for information of a routine nature?

- Is there a need for an immediate deployment of a CISM team or Community Response Team?

- Is the incident complete or ongoing?

- Where is the caller now?

- What are the call back numbers?

- Is there someone else to call if the caller is unavailable for the call from the team coordinator?

**FIGURE 10.1**

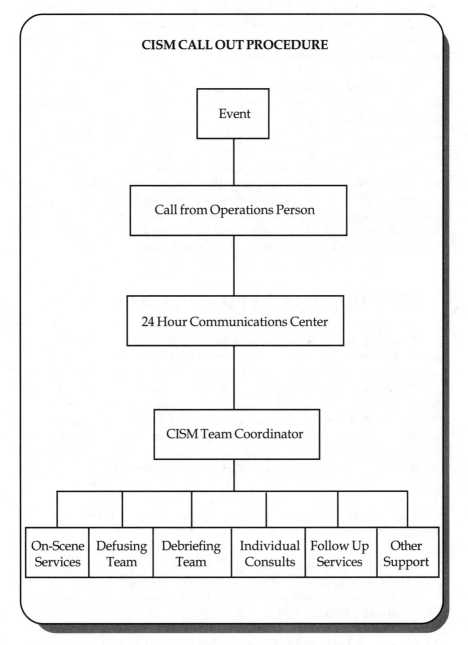

When preliminary information is collected the dispatcher calls or pages the team coordinator or a backup coordinator. The dispatcher advises the coordinator that the services of the CISM team or community response team are being requested. The information the dispatcher has been able to gather is passed off to the team coordinator.

At that point, the dispatcher drops out of the system unless further assistance is needed with communications. The coordinator must then make an immediate call to the original caller to determine what CISM or CRT services, if any, are necessary. The coordinator has the responsibility to assess the need for a debriefing or any other type of service. When the coordinator completes the assessment task and a determination has been made that one form of service or another is necessary, the coordinator then begins the team assignment procedures. Calls are made to team members on the call down list which every team coordinator has readily available. Mental health professionals, chaplains, clergy and peers are chosen according to the needs identified by the requesting party and the coordinator.

# ASSESSING THE NEED FOR CISD

Since CISM and CRT teams want to do debriefings only when they are necessary, they should be careful to properly assess the need for doing a debriefing when a traumatic incident occurs. The following questions and comments should be helpful in determining if a debriefing is necessary or if some other form of intervention would be more appropriate. The team coordinator should use these questions as a guideline for assessment of the situation which needs either a CISM or a CRT response. Some of the questions will be asked directly of those requesting a debriefing service. The answers to other questions may be self-evident or may be determined through other means.

Here are the questions which can help a team coordinator assess the need for a CISD:

1. What is the nature of the critical incident?
2. How long ago did it occur? Is the event ongoing?
3. Is the event of sufficient magnitude as to cause significant emotional distress among those involved?
4. Does the event fit within the definition of a critical incident?
5. How many individuals are involved in the incident?

6. If more than three, think CISD! If less, perhaps a defusing or a individual consult would suffice.
7. Are there several distinct groups of people involved or is there only one? For example, are the targets of CISD operations personnel, victims, witnesses or community members? If so, more than one CISD will be required.
8. What is the status of the involved individuals? Where are they and how are they reacting? Some incidents may need a more immediate defusing rather than waiting for a debriefing.
9. What signs and symptoms of distress are being displayed by the participants or the witnesses of the incident?
10. How long have the reactions or signs and symptoms of distress been going on? Significant symptoms which have continued longer than a few days are a good sign that a debriefing may be necessary. If symptoms of distress are going on longer than one week after the incident, a debriefing is definitely necessary.
11. Are symptoms growing worse as time passes? Worsening symptoms in a group may indicate a need for debriefing.
12. Is the distressed group unusually fearful or anxious?
13. Is the distressed group suffering sleep disturbance?
14. Are members of the group avoiding certain activities?
15. Has the behavior of the group changed significantly?
16. Is the group preoccupied with death or fear of death?
17. Are members of the group suffering from mental confusion?
18. Is there anyone who seems so distressed that they may be contemplating suicide?
19. Are any of the following key indicators of a need for a debriefing present :
    - behavioral change
    - continued symptoms
    - new symptoms arising
    - regression
    - intensifying symptoms
    - group symptoms
20. Is the formal debriefing process necessary or are group members requesting information on stress and stress management?
21. Is the group willing to come to the debriefing or are they being ordered to come?
22. Are there other concurrent stressors going on?
23. Has the place and time of the debriefing been chosen?
24. Are there any other issues which should be discussed?

The questioning process goes along like a conversation. Remember, these questions are only a guide. Not every question needs to be asked. Other questions could be asked by the coordinator and other bits of information can be offered by the people requesting the debriefing.

Based on the answers given to the above sample questions, the coordinator makes a decision to deploy a team for on-scene support services, a demobilization (in the event of a major disaster), a Crisis Management Briefing, defusing, a debriefing, an individual consultation or an educational program. Operational procedures for debriefings will be discussed in the paragraphs to follow. Other interventions will be given special attention in other chapters of this book.

If, after asking these and other questions, the coordinator is still unsure if a debriefing is necessary, one should be provided anyway. If the team arrives to provide the debriefing and realizes, by circulating around and talking to the participants before the debriefing starts, that the event is really not all that bad and the people only wanted a stress education program, the CISD can always resort to teaching an extemporaneous stress education class. Nothing has been lost under those circumstances and the group may benefit form the stress education. Be cautious never to substitute an education process if there is any chance that a debriefing is really necessary.

## PREPARING FOR A CISD

When the decision to hold a debriefing is made, a series of important preparations must be made to enhance the potential that the debriefing will run smoothly and be beneficial to the participants. The coordinator stays busy making phone calls to confirm each aspect of the preparations to be made.

### Essential Considerations for CISD Decision Making

There are three points that must be carefully considered before a decision is made to provide a CISD. Disregarding these important points will set the stage for a failure in a debriefing.

1. **HOMOGENEOUS GROUPS.** The group (s) to be debriefed must be the same. Group members should have similar backgrounds and belong to the same organization. If they come from different backgrounds and do not usually work closely together on a regular basis, provide separate CISDs. *Never* mix victims with rescuers or community members with police officers.

2. **MISSION COMPLETION.** When people are actively engaged in their work or when they are still experiencing the traumatic event, they either will not attend the CISD or will be frustrated and angry if they are required to attend. They will see the CISD as a huge interference when they still have a mission to complete. If the event is still ongoing for them they will be distracted and upset by the debriefing. They will consider efforts to engage them in a debriefing as silly, useless, insensitive, and inappropriate. Police, for example, who are actively searching for a criminal after a colleague has been killed are not ready for a CISD until the subject is found or until several weeks have passed and the search mission is suspended. Citizens who are tacking tar paper to their roofs are not in the mood for a CISD. In hurricane Andrew, it was six to eight weeks after the event when people finally felt safe enough or "finished" enough with the disaster to agree to come to the CISDs that were being offered for them.

3. **ROUGHLY EQUAL TRAUMATIZATION.** Even though people may be from the same organization, their experience of the same event may be very different. Separate debriefings or different types of interventions may be necessary for the subgroups within the same organization. For example, students in a high school where there is a shooting experience the same event from many different perspectives. Some will be close to the site of the shooting and will be very distraught by their wounded friends or the personal threat they encountered. Others may have encountered the shooter, but escaped unharmed. Still others will have only heard about it from their friends, but would have had no direct experience of the event. Some groups need only information and guidance. Other groups will benefit from a CISD. Only people who experienced the same or nearly the same traumatic experience should be put together for a CISD.

## Date and Time

The ideal debriefing in response to acute, well-defined critical incidents takes place between 24 and 72 hours after the incident. It is only in a rare case that everything will work out so well that it can actually be held within the 24 to 72 hour time frame, but that is the ideal target time. The average time frame in which a CISD is actually provided is about five days after the event because scheduling or other considerations get in the way. There are a few important points which need to be made here regarding the time of the debriefing from the conclusion of the incident.

Emergency personnel are cognitively defended. That means that they use their intellectual abilities to suppress their emotions. They do this because emotions can disrupt their operational functions. It often takes about 24 hours for them to be ready to discuss the details of their reactions to the event or to review their emotional responses. There are certainly exceptions, such as line of duty death or a mass disaster, where the shock, numbing or denial mechanisms may last for days or weeks. The CISD will not realize its full potential unless the recipients are psychologically receptive, or ready, for the intervention. In some circumstances, therefore, the CISD may be applied literally weeks after the traumatic event.

The average non-emergency trained individual tends to be less cognitively defended. They are ready earlier to let their emotions and other reactions come to the surface. Debriefings with the average citizens (non-emergency trained) may be held earlier than 24 hours after the event. In some circumstances there are some benefits which are associated with providing a debriefing with the non-emergency groups as soon as possible after the traumatic event. A distraught group of uninjured elderly citizens who have been forced out of their assisted living center because of a fire will need a crisis management briefing after they have been gathered together in a safe area. Then there will be a need for some of them to be supported on an individual basis. They will usually benefit from a CISD provided within about twelve hours or so. The CISD helps to put the event in perspective and guides the group members toward recovery from a frightening experience.

In some cases a debriefing may actually be necessary before a CISD team can be organized. No one should "throw" a debriefing together without a full team of trained CISM personnel. Under those rushed circumstances the CISD has substantial potential to fail. Instead a defusing will be helpful initially (as long as it is done within about 8-12 hours) and a debriefing can be provided later if it is still required.

While intervening too soon can be a problem, waiting more than several months to do a CISD can be potentially harmful to the participants. Victims' defense systems are often reintegrated by that time. A poorly thought out and carelessly presented debriefing may break up some natural defenses and re-traumatize the whole group or some individuals within the group if done after the occurrence of the event.

There is a segment in the chapter entitled "Advanced Concepts in CISM" on managing significantly delayed interventions. It is mentioned that a CISD may be one of many CISM services that are required when there is a long delay in providing CISM support. The provision of a CISD after a long delay is a very complicated situation. It takes proper planning and a skilled and experienced team to handle the set of interventions which are necessary in this circumstance.

If too much time has passed since the incident (three to four months) one might consider not holding a debriefing, but seeing people on an individual basis and seeing if they have left-over reactions to the incident. In some cases, referrals to mental health professionals may be required. In other cases, an educational program on critical incident (or traumatic) stress may be helpful.

There has been no evidence developed to date which indicates that one time of the day is better for a debriefing than another. Debriefings have been held successfully at any time of the day or night. Of course, what is of importance is to have the debriefing at a time which is mutually convenient to the CISD team and the participants in the debriefing. Most importantly, debriefings should be held at a time when the participants are emotionally "ready" to accept and benefit from the debriefing. The right kind of help at the right place will not be useful if the recipients of the help are not ready to accept it. Psychological readiness in response to acute critical incidents often occurs within the 24 to 72 hour "window" previously mentioned, but some critical incidents, especially disasters, require a far longer waiting period.

## Place

Debriefings can take place in practically any private, quiet location. They have been provided with the group gathered under a tree. This is certainly not the most ideal setting, but it emphasizes the point that a debriefing is not limited to one site or another. Debriefings have been held in living rooms, libraries, meeting halls, hotel conference rooms, union halls and many other facilities.

It is usually not possible to obtain a perfect facility, but if an ideal debriefing room did exist, it could be described as follows:

- Private

- Quiet

- Moveable furniture

- Well-lighted but with adjustable lights

- Comfortable seats

- Suitable for the size of the group, not too large or small

- A single door

- Air conditioned or heated

- Well-ventilated

- No windows which allow a view in from the outside

- Available for the full length of the debriefing

- With one or more small private rooms for individual consultations

## Debriefing Room Arrangement

Having an ideal room will not be helpful to the CISD team if the room is not arranged properly. If the group is small (4 - 12 people) the debriefing can be carried out in the living room of a home or in a small conference room. It does not matter if the group participants are seated around a table or if a coffee table is in the middle of the group. In some countries the local culture prefers this arrangement. Local customs and cultural differences should be adhered to whenever possible. If the group is larger than twelve, this arrangement may not be possible. Choose a larger room and arrange the chairs in a circle large enough to accommodate the group. Tables and other furniture may have to be moved to the side of the room to assure that each person in the group has a good view of most of the others.

Avoid placing the chairs so close that the participants grow uncomfortable with the close proximity to one another. Enough chairs should be in the circle to accommodate the CISD team as well as the participants. Sometimes people arrive late for the debriefing and so a few extra chairs should be placed into the circle before the debriefing starts. Having the chairs in place produces less disruption if someone does come in late. The CISD team is spaced more or less equally among the group members. The CISD team does not sit all together on one side of the circle. If they do, the arrangement might set up an "us and them" impression. It is also easier for the team members to see each person in the group if they are spread through the group. The following diagrams provide samples of the typical debriefing seating arrangements. Figure 10.2 shows a typical two-member team debriefing team placement. Figures 10.3 and 10.4 show typical three-member CISD team placements. Figures 10.5 and 10.6 show four-member placements.

The door to the debriefing room should be closed, but not locked. A sign may be placed on the door which notifies anyone who would come to the door that a debriefing is in progress and personnel from the emergency organizations or other groups who were involved in the event are welcome to enter. Late arrivals should be instructed to enter without knocking. If there is fear that news media representatives or other people who are not to be involved in the debriefing might show up, an extra peer support person is brought to the debriefing room and stationed outside of the door. If unwanted people show up, that peer does not permit them to enter the room.

In cases in which only one or two mental health professionals are working as part of a Community Response Team with non-emergency groups, it would probably be better to lock the door to maintain better control of the group without fear of interruption (as long as the locked door causes none of the participants to become distressed). The team leader might simply inquire among participants as to whether the door should be locked to keep unin-

**FIGURE 10.2**

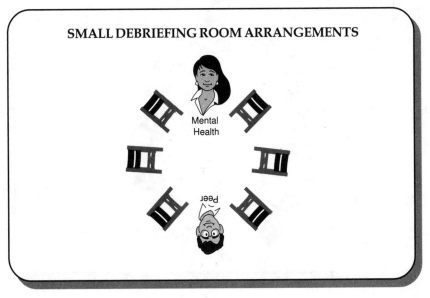

SMALL DEBRIEFING ROOM ARRANGEMENTS

Mental Health

Peer

**FIGURE 10.3**

**FIGURE 10.4**

vited people out of the room. Late arrivals in such a group would have to knock to gain entry into the debriefing. They should be instructed by means of a sign to knock in order to get into the room.

The team leader should be positioned in such a manner that the door is not behind him or her. The management of the door is the responsibility of one of the peers (see "doorkeeper" role below), not the mental health person who is the team leader. A position as far away from the door as possible is usually best for the mental health professional who holds the team leader role. (See the section below entitled, "Team member debriefing roles").

Sometimes the team leaders may use eyes, head nods, or slight hand motions to communicate with one or more of the peers. So it is important that the leader be able to see the peers who are serving on the debriefing team.

## Food

Whenever possible, refreshments should be served after the debriefing. It helps to keep those who attended the debriefing together a little longer.

**FIGURE 10.5**

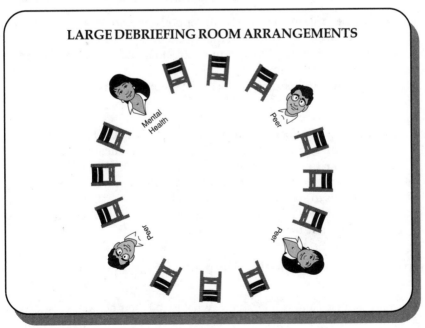

LARGE DEBRIEFING ROOM ARRANGEMENTS

**FIGURE 10.6**

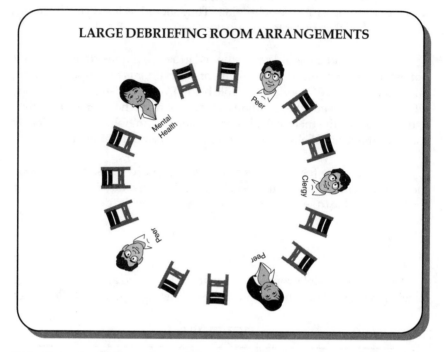

**LARGE DEBRIEFING ROOM ARRANGEMENTS**

This allows the CISD team members the opportunity to contact every person on an individual basis. Words of support, encouragement and understanding can be offered by the CISD team members to individuals who participated in the debriefing. Some people like to speak to a team member personally and privately rather than to talk about their reactions to an event in the group setting.

The best types of food are those which are not likely to enhance stress such as fresh fruits, fruit juices and the like. The practical realities are that what people like to eat may not be the very best for them. Having some refreshments available is better than not having any at all. Sometimes a CISD team needs to arrange for cookies or cake to "entice" the participants to stay nearby for a brief period of time after the debriefing. All food arrangements must be made in advance of the debriefing.

## Instructions to the Participants' Supervisors

Many supervisors want to know what to tell their personnel before the debriefing team arrives. If the CISD team is cognizant of the fact that the supervisor is in the position to either enhance the debriefing or destroy its potential benefit, the question will be taken seriously and answered appropriately.

Supervisors need to have an explanation of what a debriefing is and what it is not. They need to know that it is not psychotherapy, nor is it investigative. The supervisor should know that it is his or her job to encourage the personnel to attend the debriefing session for the good of the entire organization as well as the individuals in the group. Supervisors should be told about the team and the major role played by peer support personnel should be emphasized. The supervisor also needs to assure the personnel that no one has to speak if they choose not to. The fact that no notes are taken and that the information is strictly confidential is of significant importance. The supervisor should be advised to tell the personnel that their attendance and participation is very important because each of them experienced the incident from a different perspective and each has a part of the event to add during the debriefing to make sure that all of the others have the same information. Supervisors can serve as useful role models when they are honest and candid about their own reactions to the critical incident.

Supervisors should be informed as to the CISD team requirements, for example, requirements for the size of the room and what is needed in the room; that the chairs are set in a circle; that personnel should have their pagers and radios turned off during the debriefing; and that the food should be provided after the debriefing.

The supervisors have another responsibility which can directly affect the CISD team's performance. For a team to work well during a debriefing they need to be well aware of the incident. They need to see the pictures and diagrams of the incident and listen to tapes of the call. The supervisor should make sure that the CISD team gets the opportunity to review the incident report or at least that some member of the department gives the team a brief overview of the incident which is to be debriefed.

## Helping the Organization Prepare for the Debriefing

Besides the instructions given to the supervisors, which are described in the previous section, the organization hosting the CISD should be helped to prepare for the debriefing in several other ways. The command staff should invite every member who was involved in the incident. Field command personnel should be part of the debriefing. Only in very unusual cases are the commanders split out from the rank and file personnel for debriefings. This might be appropriate for example, when a commander is the target of extreme anger or resentment by rank and file personnel, or when the rank and file feel they can't trust the command staff. In those cases, a separate debriefing is probably necessary. It may be helpful, somewhat later, to bring both groups together for a discussion of the event in an effort to resolve outstanding difficulties.

Sometimes it is necessary for the CISD team to hold an additional meeting with the commanders, who may have special needs which they would like to discuss with the CISD team members without having their personnel listening in.

The organization should be advised to keep a low profile with the media regarding the debriefing. If the media representatives are asking questions about the debriefing, they should be referred to the local CISM team or to the International Critical Incident Stress Foundation to obtain further information about the debriefing process.

The team members should listen carefully to the questions and concerns of the organization and attempt to alleviate those concerns. The team coordinator usually has numerous telephone contacts with the organization before the debriefing actually occurs. Communications with the organization is of paramount importance during the crisis period. Sometimes the coordinator is able to help the organization find some local resources before the CISD can be deployed. Sometimes a trained CISM peer lives nearby the organization and can be sent in as an advance stabilizing force before the full team arrives.

## Incident Review

CISM team members who are going to provide the CISD arrive at the site of the debriefing about an hour before the debriefing starts. One of the first tasks they have is to perform an incident review to familiarize themselves with the event they are going to be addressing in the debriefing.

The more a team knows about the incident before starting the debriefing, the better they will be able to do their job. Significant surprises during the debriefing usually cause discomfort in the team members and possibly in the debriefing participants as well. Surprises also cause disruption in the flow of the CISD process.

Most teams like to review the written information regarding the event. They like to read the newspaper clippings and the incident report. If a preliminary report has been worked up by the time of the debriefing, it, too, is read by the CISD team. The team members also listen to the audio tapes of the incident, view slides or video tapes, look at charts and diagrams and review any other materials which can give them a good working knowledge of the incident.

Sometimes the reports or newspaper accounts of the incident are incomplete or inaccurate. CISM team members should then ask pertinent operational questions of training officers, commanders, supervisors and or some members of the organization. It is important to avoid questions which lead people into discussions of their reactions to the event. Those will be brought out in the debriefing. What is important during the review is that the team become familiar with the operational aspects of the case.

## Circulation with the Group

The incident review is seldom sufficient to fully prepare the team to process the debriefing. There are two other steps which may be taken before the debriefing begins. Once the incident review is complete, the CISM team splits up and each member begins to circulate among the group members and meet the participants who are coming into the debriefing room. Conversations are a mix of questions with a serious purpose and casual conversation designed to take the edge off the tension and let the participants know a little about the team members. The minimal familiarity between the CISM team and the debriefing's participants usually helps the introduction to the debriefing progress smoothly. It helps the group relax a little and begin to trust the team members.

The questions which are more task-oriented are listed below. Other questions can easily be added to the list and some can be modified or eliminated if the team member decides that they are not important or need to be revamped. The CISM team must use an enormous amount of sensitivity as they ask these questions. They should also be ready to drop any question which would not be handled well by the participants for any reason. It is also important the team not have a memorized set of questions. They should have a free flowing question pattern which gives them some good information but does not come across as artificial or contrived. It is important that people use their own words when working with a distressed group. The wording of the questions below is only a guide and not to be taken as some unchangeable absolute. Common sense needs to be the guide of CISM team members.

1. How well do the people in this organization work together?
2. How well do you get along with the boss?
3. What is the relationship between the staff and the supervisors?
4. Is there anything about the situation that you folks believe might not come out during the debriefing, but which you think we ought to be aware of?
5. Is there anything really unusual or bizarre about this situation which the CISM team should know before we start the debriefing?
6. Are there any relationships going on between people in this organization which either affected the situation or are now being affected by the situation?
7. Anything else which we might be interested in?
8. Has anything similar to this critical incident ever occurred before?
9. Any other pertinent information.

Once the team has had sufficient time to circulate with participants, (10 - 20 minutes) it excuses itself from the group and holds a brief meeting in a separate room. They should encourage the debriefing participants to take care of their personal needs by utilizing the rest rooms before the debriefing begins. The CISD strategy meeting is the last opportunity for the team to make a plan for the debriefing intervention before it actually begins. When possible, the CISD should start on time to reduce anticipatory anxiety.

## Strategy Meeting with CISM Team Members

During the strategy meeting the CISM team privately discusses its approach to the debriefing. Team members are assigned to specific roles - door keeper, co-leader, teaching team and so forth (see below for details). The mental health professional encourages the peer support personnel to actively participate in the debriefing by making statements or introducing questions as necessary for the good of the group. The exact seating position of the team is discussed and agreed upon. The CISM team briefly discusses the event and any points which are considered unusual are brought out so that each of the team members has a good idea of what to expect in the debriefing. If more than the ordinary group resistance is expected, the team members are forewarned about it and a decision to have a slightly longer and more carefully worded introduction is made. Special teaching topics are assigned to the team members. If CISM team members have any clarifications or questions, they are handled during the strategy meeting. Special instructions for this particular debriefing are given by the team leader. When every member of the team feels that he or she has been well informed about the incident and the strategy to be followed in the CISD, the team ends its brief strategy meeting and enters the debriefing room.

## TEAM MEMBER DEBRIEFING ROLES

The CISM team must perform numerous functions during and after the CISD. No person can perform all of the functions single-handedly and expect to do an excellent job with all of them. The tasks of the debriefing must be divided up among the team members. Peer support and mental health professionals need to blend their talents and abilities for the benefit of the entire group.

## Team Leader

The team leader is the person who is assigned to be the primary leader in the group. In many cases it is the mental health professional who is assigned to the CISD. In some cases it is an experienced peer support person and the mental health professional is used as a teaching expert during the teaching phase. In any case, a CISD should have one primary leader to avoid confusing the participants. The team leader's role is to use his or her communication skills to tactfully invite and encourage the group participants to discuss the traumatic event. Usually the team leader starts the questions for each segment of the CISD. The mental health professional , whether he or she is in the team leader role, needs to keep a careful eye on the overall psychological well-being of the group and especially on any one in the group who may be experiencing more distress than the others.

The team leader should be very involved in the teaching aspects of the debriefing and attempt to help people clarify their own perspectives of the incident. The team leader frequently has to weave the various aspects of the group experience into a coordinated pattern so that people can recognize their own part of the experience as a part of a bigger picture. The team leader asks occasional questions, or makes occasional comments when it is appropriate, and listens intently throughout the debriefing. If the discussion becomes too intense for the other team members to manage effectively, the mental health professional may need to enter the discussion to balance it, to explain certain issues or to help people see their own parts of the experience more clearly. The team leader and the mental health professional attempt to bring the group out of the debriefing on as positive a level as possible in light of the tragedy they have experienced.

As can be seen in this discussion, the team leader and mental health professional, as well as the other peer support personnel, must have an interactive leadership style. There is one clear leader in the CISD, but the other team members should be able to ask appropriate questions and contribute appropriate information during the teaching phase. Running an effective debriefing requires a very interactive leadership style which recognizes the abilities of each team member.

Good team leaders develop their skills over time and with a variety of experiences. They would be far more effective if they were to come to the debriefing with a background of exposure to the emergency services professions or to whatever profession they are working with. If the team leader is a mental health professional, it would be wise for that person to have familiarized him or her self with the emergency services professions long before being designated as a team leader in a particular CISD. Ride-along programs, visits to the emergency room or the communications center and spending time at the fire, police and emergency medical service stations are crucial to developing a proper understanding of the emergency services personality and their jobs. In fact, we urge all mental health professionals to become familiar with the emergency services "culture" before providing any service to those personnel.

Mental health professionals who function as team leaders with non-emergency populations such as banks or businesses or who are solely working on Community Response Teams with non-emergency populations in the community do not require such exposure to emergency services personnel. In fact, it is typical for them to work with a second mental health professional in the co-lead position during a CISD with a business or community based group.

## Co-Leader

If the debriefing is with the emergency services professions, the co-leader is one of the peers. The peer who is chosen for this role typically has the most experience as a peer debriefer. If the debriefing is for a community group not associated with the emergency services, the co-leader is usually another mental health professional.

The co-leader's main role is to share and support the leadership of the group with the team leader. The co-leader will bring up any items in the introductory remarks which the team leader did not mention and will add several important comments of his or her own. The co-leader watches the group members for signs of distress and questions, clarifies and makes statements whenever they are appropriate. The co-leader plays a significant role in the teaching phase of the debriefing. The co-leader helps the leader to summarize the debriefing and remains available to the participants after the debriefing to make contacts with those who need a few extra words of support or perhaps a referral.

The co-leader usually has a considerable role in providing for follow- up contacts. In many cases, especially with emergency personnel, it is the peer support personnel, more than the mental health professionals, who have the primary responsibility for the initial contacts within a few days of the debriefing. The peers usually encourage emergency workers who need more help to contact mental health professionals.

The co-leader assigns specific follow up tasks to appropriate CISD team members. For example, one peer may be assigned the task of advising the unit supervisor. Another may be given the task of calling two people who attended the debriefing and are obviously more troubled about the critical incident than the others.

# Doorkeeper

The doorkeeper has a key role in debriefings. The doorkeeper will prevent any unauthorized or inappropriate individuals from entering the room where the debriefing is taking place. This includes people in the organization who were not involved at the scene, family members of participants in the debriefing who are not part of the organization, spectators, media personnel and citizens who just happened to be at the scene of the incident. The doorkeeper allows into the room any appropriate person who is a member of one of the organizations being debriefed and who was involved in the incident and arrives late. If there are only two CISM team members running a CISD, the co-leader must also play the role of doorkeeper.

The doorkeeper has another vital role. If someone leaves the debriefing, it is the doorkeeper's job to go out after that person and encourage that person to return. This task is easy if the person is only going to the men's or ladies' room to take care of personal needs. The doorkeeper simply has to remind the person to come back into the debriefing as soon as possible. If, however, the person is distressed and is leaving the debriefing because of that distress, then it is important for the doorkeeper to gently question, listen intently, and give as much support as possible to the distressed person. It is very important to encourage the person to return to the debriefing as soon as possible. Sometimes the person needs reassurance that they will not be called upon nor will they have to speak if they do not want to. Occasionally, they need to be told that they are needed by the other participants inside the debriefing and that they can be of great help to some of the people in the debriefing room but they have to be inside the room to be helpful. Almost everyone will return to the debriefing when encouraged to do so by the peer support person who is the doorkeeper.

Only in rare instances do people leave the debriefing and refuse to return to it. In those cases, it is important that the doorkeeper try to engage the person on a one-on-one basis. If the person refuses any effort to assist them, then an attempt is made to get the person's name and phone number or at least to give them one's card and a verbal invitation to call if they would like to go back over something related to the incident. Efforts to outreach to that person should be made by a CISM team member after the CISD.

# Clergy

If clergy, who are trained in the CISD process, are part of the CISD team, they play a significant role as listener and guide. Preaching and praying are discouraged during the actual debriefing process because not all participants may share similar religious beliefs. In addition, the CISD is not the proper time for preaching and praying by a clergy person because the distress of the incident mentally blocks people from hearing the important spiritual messages. It would be better if clergy members deal with spiritual issues after the debriefing when the participants' emotional distress has calmed down and the participants are more open to spiritual discussions.

The clergy, during a CISD, may make appropriate comments or ask questions that guide the discussion. Clergy on the CISM team function to support the leadership of the team leader. They participate actively in the teaching phase. They also listen carefully and try to see which people might need a little extra support after the debriefing is concluded. They are very active in checking with people after the debriefing to see that people are coping adequately or if they need help with any aspects of the event or their return to normal functions (especially from a spiritual perspective). Spiritual interventions such as praying or preaching are generally best implemented after the CISD, and preferably on a one-to-one basis.

# Peers

Community Response Teams can work without peers. They may utilize only mental health professionals. But CISM teams doing debriefings with emergency personnel, military personnel, airlines, railroad workers and certain other businesses absolutely need peer support personnel. The keys to success in working with emergency personnel appear to be:

1.  Familiarity with the nature and culture of emergency services

2.  Rapid intervention

3.  An emphasis on pragmatic stress management techniques

4.  Emergency service "peer" support personnel are the embodiment of these characteristics and are therefore an integral pact of the CISD team

During the debriefing, the peer support personnel who are not assigned to specific tasks such as co-leader and doorkeeper do not just sit back. They have important roles to fulfill. They must listen carefully to the discussion, observe the participants, pick out those who they think might need additional help and teach some of the stress reduction techniques during the teaching phase. There is no room in a debriefing for someone to just watch. There are too many things which must be done. All of the peers on a CISD team are part of the process.

The peer support personnel help to make the introductory remarks, ask questions and make statements when it is appropriate and they help to bring the debriefing to a close by participating actively in the summary remarks. When one of the participants is speaking, the team leader might be listening intently to that person and looking at the person as he or she speaks. In that case, the peer support personnel should be looking at the other group members in an effort to read their facial expression and their body language.

When a second participant leaves the room and the doorkeeper is already outside of the room with the first one who left, one of the remaining peers must play a back-up doorkeeper role. If the team leader or co-leader is ready to move ahead into another phase in the debriefing, but one of the peers recognizes that a participant wants to say something else, the peer gives that person the opportunity to speak.

The peers and mental health professionals work together during the entire debriefing. Each has an important job to do and assists the others in doing their jobs. The debriefing process is a team effort.

## SUMMARY

This chapter covered a broad range of topics that are extremely important in deciding upon, planning and preparing for a Critical Incident Stress Debriefing (CISD). The reader should get the correct impression from this chapter that a CISD is a complex crisis intervention tactic that requires careful planning and preparation. Group interventions under any circumstances are complicated. The additional fact that a traumatic event triggered the need for group interaction in a CISD setting makes preparation all the more important. Haphazard group interventions increases the chance that harm could be done to people who are already vulnerable because of the traumatic incident that they have just experienced.

# Chapter 11

## THE CRITICAL INCIDENT STRESS DEBRIEFING:
## Conducting the Group Process

It is important that no CISD is provided unless appropriate planning and preparations have been made. The previous chapter covers many points that are essential to the success of a CISD. Please read it before reading this chapter. Failure to do so may set a CISD up for a failure and it may harm the participants. CISM teams should be aiming for the successful presentation of a CISD with the maximum benefits for the participants. All of the preparations which have been made before the CISD help to ensure its success. Teams should take the time necessary to set up the debriefing properly because the debriefing is the most difficult of the CISM interventions to apply. Efforts made to arrange it properly and to choose the right team members increase the potential that the debriefing will be a success. Since the objective of the debriefing is to mitigate the impact of stress and restore the personnel to normal functions as quickly as possible, a carefully planned approach to the distressed individuals is essential.

It is very tempting for the person who is untrained in the CISD process to read the sections below and believe they are fully trained and ready to manage debriefings. That, of course, is a false belief. Reading about debriefings is not considered training. There are many subtle issues and techniques which cannot be adequately described here. Only appropriate training by qualified and experienced trainers will provide adequate preparation for conducting CISDs. Anything less would be unprofessional and could prove to be dangerous to distressed people who expect quality and trained services from debriefing team members. It is easy to negatively affect distressed individuals by attempting CISD services without the proper training.

The formal CISD intervention has seven phases. Figure 11.1 will be of assistance as the reader goes through the sections to follow.

The overall strategy for a CISD team during a debriefing is to start at the point which is easiest to discuss and then move gradually into more emotionally intense discussions. After handling the intense materials the group is gradually brought back out of the intense discussions to the less intense until the discussion finally concludes.

We will now examine the CISD process step by step.

**FIGURE 11.1**

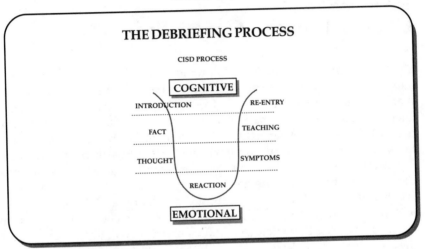

## 1. INTRODUCTION

The introduction to the CISD is crucial. It sets the stage for all of the other phases of the debriefing. If the introduction is not handled well, it is likely that the remainder of the debriefing will be difficult. When debriefing teams have examined debriefings which they believe did not run as smoothly as they would have liked, they can almost always trace the problems to the introduction. This section of the debriefing should help a debriefing team to set a good base for the remainder of the CISD process.

There are several objectives to be achieved during the introduction. The CISD team must:

- Point out the team members

- Introduce the team leader

- Establish the leadership of the team

- Explain the purpose of the meeting

- Explain the process

- Motivate the participants

- Reduce resistance

- Explain the guidelines of the CISD

- Gain the cooperation of the participants

- Answer primary concerns and limit anxiety

- Announce the first set of questions to come

- Encourage mutual help

Although the peer team members are pointed out in the introductory phase, their actual introductions are held off until the fact phase. Peer introductions can be used to help the group get past the discomfort which can occur if there is any significant display of powerful emotions early on in the debriefing process. More information will be presented on peer introductions in the section to follow on the "Fact" phase.

The entire CISD team must show itself to be confident, and as relaxed as the horrible circumstances of an event will allow. They will need to demonstrate by their mood and words that they are sympathetic and concerned with the plight of the distressed personnel. The team needs to believe that they have the proper training and experience to help. They do not, however, want to appear overconfident or arrogant. The team can avoid arrogance by realizing that they could easily be in the same position as the participants if the incident had happened to themselves instead of the distressed group before them. It also helps to recognize that a debriefing team is in the very privileged position of hearing the thoughts and emotions of emergency personnel, a position which few other people will have in their lives.

The rules or guidelines for a CISD which must be discussed in the introduction are:

- Participants are asked to look around the room and point out anyone who, for any reason, might not belong in the group. A few minutes might be spent confirming people's suitability for participation in the debriefing session. (Remember, in a line-of-duty death situation, the entire organization is affected and all members are invited to a debriefing, not only those at the scene).

- Strict confidentiality. Whatever is stated in the room should stay in the room. This rule applies to the team as well as to the participants. After a debriefing, people may discuss their own feelings and reactions or the things that the team taught, but they may not discuss what they have heard from another person in the debriefing.

- The participants should speak for themselves. People may describe others' reactions as they saw them ("I saw John running"), but they may not interpret those observations ("He was afraid"). Each person has the right to speak for themselves ("I was afraid") and not have someone else do that for them.

- Participants in the debriefing do not have to speak if they do not want to. Everyone has a right to refuse to speak. It may not be in their best interests, but they do have that right. Participants are told that they merely have to shake their heads in a "no" pattern and the team will leave them alone.

- Participants are asked not to leave the room without returning. It is important that they complete the entire process. The participants should be forewarned that leaving the CISD may actually cause them to feel worse later. If they must leave to use a rest room, they should be instructed to return immediately.

- No cameras, recorders or note taking of any type is ever permitted in a debriefing. There is never a reason for taking notes in a debriefing. If a team member is concerned about following up on an individual they can get the name and phone number after the debriefing is over.

- CISD is not psychotherapy nor is it a substitute for psychotherapy.

It is simply a discussion of a traumatic event which is led by a team of specially trained people who are attempting to mitigate the impact of a traumatic event and restore people to normal function as soon as possible.

- CISD is not an investigation. Participants are instructed not to disclose any information which would jeopardize an investigation, or would constitute an admission of criminal activity or deliberate violations of usual policies and procedures. Participants are given permission to filter out any information which they feel is inappropriate to discuss in a large group. They are urged to save such information for the investigative team.

- Participants are urged to temporarily forget their rank or station in life and just be a person who is affected by a tragedy.

- Participants are urged to turn off pagers, radios and other distracting devices.

- Participants are informed that the CISD team is there for them and that the team will be available after the debriefing is complete.

- Participants are urged to help one another by participating actively in the debriefing. They are instructed that even if they do not feel that they need a debriefing, others in the group might benefit from it. They can be helpful to those people by discussing their role in the incident.

- CISD is not a critique of the operational aspects of the incident.

- The participants are told that the only reason the debriefing is held is to help people to recover as quickly as possible and return to normal aspects of their lives. Experience shows that people who talk about traumatic events sleep and eat better and generally resume normal aspects of their lives more quickly.

- People in the debriefing need to be informed that reports are not made about the individuals in the debriefing to their supervisors.

- Participants are informed that within a few minutes the team will be asking them to state who they are, what their role in the incident was and what happened from their own perspective.

- No breaks will be taken during the debriefing. If participants need to take care of personal needs, they may leave, but they are requested to return immediately.

- Participants are informed that the team has many important pieces of information to teach to the group. The teaching aspects of the session will occur toward the end of the debriefing.

- Reminders of the need for confidentiality are made several times during the introductory remarks.

- Participants are urged to ask questions any time they need to.

The items in the introductory remarks phase of a CISD may change somewhat from debriefing to debriefing. At times, it is necessary to elaborate on many of the guidelines. This is especially true when a debriefing is being provided to a new group which has never had one before. In a group which has a number of experiences with debriefings, the participants usually know the rules and only need a reminder.

Throughout the introductory remarks the team should be speaking with confidence and concern. The CISD team members need to be relaxed as they speak so that they do not raise unnecessary anxieties in the group of participants. The team members need to be very alert to the verbal and non- verbal emotional cues which will be displayed by the participants in the debriefing. They must likewise be prepared to manage the resistance expressed by individuals in the group. If they ignore the resistance during the introductory remarks phase, it will not go away. It will show up again later in the debriefing. Unresolved resistance usually damages the debriefing when it emerges in more delicate phases of the process.

## 2. FACT

The easiest portion of the discussion for emergency service personnel is usually a description of the facts of an incident. Facts are a collection of items outside of oneself. Facts are impersonal. Discussions of facts are not as distressing as attempting to talk about how one feels, which is a very personal discussion. This is especially so for emergency personnel who are highly cognitively defended and who cautiously avoid almost any discussions of emotions. They sometimes fear that they will be overcome and incapacitated by those emotions and, therefore, unable to perform their jobs adequately. They are often comfortable when someone asks them to describe what happened. They understand facts; they use facts all the time in their work. They almost cling to facts during discussions about a situation. The fact phase is the most logical place to begin a discussion about a tragic event.

To get people talking about a situation in the fact phase, the team leader simply needs to state something like this: "The CISD team wasn't present during the incident. We only know some bits and pieces of the incident. It would be very helpful if we could get some understanding of what happened by having you tell us about the incident. So, we would like you to tell us who you are, what your role was during the incident and, briefly, what happened from your perspective. We just need a thumbnail sketch or a broad overview of the event. We are not seeking a lot of details, just an overview. It doesn't matter if what you experienced is different from what everyone else experienced. You all had an important part to play in the situation and it would help everyone to have a big picture built by putting all your pieces of the incident together. If you choose not to speak that is okay. Just shake your head and we will pass right over you. During this phase of the debriefing, we would like to give everyone an opportunity to tell us a little about their own experience. For the sake of organization we are going to start over here on my left (right) and go around the room. Again, what we need to know is:

- Who are you?

- What was your job or role during the incident?

- A brief description of what happened from your point of view."

The participants in the group will begin to tell their stories. The exact order of the telling does not really matter. The last to arrive at the scene might be the first to speak. All of the pieces will come together as everyone gets their chance to speak. The sorting out of the story comes naturally to an alert CISD team which has done its homework before the debriefing.

If the group is larger than about 20 people, or if there is some unavoidable and arbitrarily mandated short time frame, it may be too time consuming for each person in the group to tell their part of the incident. An alternative fact phase is then employed. The questions differ a bit from the ones outlined above, but they still cause the group to discuss the facts. The alternate fact phase questions are:

• Who arrived first on scene?

• Which units came in after them?

• What happened as additional units arrived?

Usually a "spokesperson" from each unit will describe their unit's role in the operation in a shortened version. Perhaps only six or seven people out of 20 will speak. That is perfectly fine. There is no need to be alarmed if some do not get an opportunity to speak during a debriefing. It is a mistake to think that people derive no benefit unless they speak. Many people choose only to listen during a debriefing, even when they have ample opportunities to speak. Yet they report that simply listening to others was beneficial. Often during the fact phase, participants will spontaneously begin to display emotions.

When participants in a debriefing are asked to describe the *facts* of the situation and they begin to express their *emotions*, it is a sign of how badly they have been affected by the incident. But it does not signal an invitation for the debriefing team to probe further. Personnel who have been probed feel angry. They feel that they may be expressing far more than they had intended. They usually feel surprised by their own emotional reaction to the situation. They prefer to be left alone and not encouraged to let more of their emotions show. The CISD team needs to remember that emergency personnel in particular have a great deal of difficulty losing control in the presence of their fellow workers. They are very embarrassed by an unexpected show of their own emotions. They will have to face their fellow workers long after the debriefing team has left. The very best actions which can be taken by the CISD team are to:

• Acknowledge the emotion.

• Validate that the emotion is appropriate.

• Reassure the individual and the group that the emotion is expected and that any person in a similar circumstance would have the same or a similar emotional reaction.

• Shift focus from that person to someone else unless that person signals that they wish to continue talking.

In addition, the other participants may become very unnerved by this early show of emotion. They do not know what to do. They begin to fear that the CISD team is losing control of the debriefing. It is usually this kind of circumstance which causes a great deal of anxiety for the other participants in the debriefing. The next few participants to speak will hold back much of what they would have said had they not seen the emotional reaction in their fellow worker, or they may not speak at all. This is where the peers, who have not yet had the chance to introduce themselves will be very helpful.

As each participant completes his or her answer to the fact phase questions, the team listens carefully and notices the change in the discussion which has occurred from the beginning of the fact phase until the emotions have shown up. If a strong emotion has been expressed and the group has become anxious, the next *peer* to speak will introduce him- or herself. The introduction of that particular peer is a bit longer (by perhaps a few sentences) than usual. The extra time it takes the peer to make this introduction is usually all the time it takes to calm the entire group. The peer's introduction, coming as it does in the middle of the fact phase, adds a degree of control to the debriefing. The introduction allows a little breathing space before the next participant begins to discuss his answers to the fact phase questions. When the discussion of who they are, their roles and what happened continues, the discussion lacks much of the uncomfortable anxiety which had been stirred by the emotions generated by one of the previous participants.

The fact phase may take between five and twenty five minutes depending on how many people are present and the depth of information. Team members may have to clarify certain responses. They do so whenever it appears appropriate. Sometimes the participants bring up elements of the thoughts or reactions phases even though those questions were not yet presented to them. The team members listen carefully to those items but do not usually react to them in the fact phase. They may use those comments from the participants as material to be presented later in the debriefing, during the teaching or re-entry phases.

When the fact phase is complete, the thought phase begins immediately.

# 3. THOUGHT

The thought phase begins when the team leader asks the participants to state what their first thought or most prominent thought was once they got off an "auto pilot" mode of operating. Since many emergency personnel are predominantly cognitive in their defense system, most of their answers will orient somewhat toward the operational aspects of the incident. Many say things such as, "I thought the suspect wouldn't jump out the window" or "My first thought was, 'God, don't let this one be a kid.'" But the emotional aspects of the case cannot be eliminated or blocked altogether. Some will say things like this: "I was afraid that we would lose the whole street," or "I was really angry that one human being could do something like this to another."

The thought phase is a transitional phase between the factual world and the world that is close and personal. The facts are outside of a person; the thoughts are internal and part of the person. It is impossible to respond to the questions about thoughts without some feelings entering into the discussion. CISD teams should expect this as a part of the CISD process. *The thought phase represents a transitional phase from the cognitive domain to the affective (emotional) domain.* The CISD team should welcome the emotion-related comments of the thought phase as a sign that the process is working and on schedule.

If, however, the emotional content becomes too intense too quickly, the group being debriefed may experience more anxiety and a desire to resist any efforts to bring them any closer to their own emotions. Sometimes the participants express diffuse anger at the team members by claiming that the process is bad. Sometimes, they try to stick only to further discussions of facts and operational procedures. Occasionally they show powerful emotions and look for immediate rescue from the team. Sometimes they will walk out of the debriefing.

No one can predict all of the possible responses from the participants in a debriefing during the transition phase. The participants are testing themselves as well as the CISD team. The team has to be ready for anything. If someone leaves, the "doorkeeper" team member goes after them and attempts to bring them back. If the emotions grow intense, acknowledgment, validation and / or reassurance may be required by the team members. If defuse anger is expressed, some of it may need to be absorbed. Some of it may need to be redirected. The CISD team must stay very alert during this phase. They must react after only a few seconds of thought. They usually make the right choices because they are calm and thinking more rationally than the people in the debriefing, who are distressed.

# 4. REACTION

The reaction phase is typically the most emotionally powerful of all. If the introduction, fact phase and the thought phase have been managed carefully by the CISD team, the reaction phase will flow relatively easily from the thought phase. The CISD team will find that its interactions in the group will quiet substantially during the reaction phase. In fact, most of the talking is done by the participants, not by the CISD team. This is as it should be. The CISD team members should commit themselves to speak only if their remarks are truly necessary and only if they will not interfere with the flow of discussion from the participants.

The question which triggers most of the discussion in the reaction phase is:

- What was the worse thing about this situation for you personally?

There are numerous variations on the question which will elicit a discussion of the emotions associated with the event. They are:

- What part of this event bothers you the most?

- If you could erase one part of the situation, what part would you choose to erase?

- What aspect of the situation causes you the most pain?

- What do you think will stick with you most?

The discussion at this point is free-lance. The team no longer goes around the room with the discussion. Whoever wants to speak may speak. Those who choose to be silent are silent. There is no order in the discussion. Going around the room is only done in the fact phase and in the thought phase. Now the whole group is given the opportunity to speak if and when they choose.

Initially the discussion may be slow. The participants are wrestling with the emotions that they have begun to connect to the incident. One participant will eventually say something and admit a feeling. Another will typically acknowledge fear, anger or grief. After a short period of time, most of the participants have said something.

Some of the comments may cause the entire group to go momentarily silent as another emotion crashes into their consciousness. Some comments will trigger a strong verbal group response. There may be shifting in the chairs, wringing of hands and many other non-verbal signals. Eyes may drop to the floor. Sometimes there are blank stares, sometimes tears or a voice that trembles with every painful word.

There are also many debriefings in which the emotions are very subtle. Tears may not be shown. There may be no significant observable emotions displayed. The words, however, may carry a great deal of emotional content. Every debriefing has its own character which depends on the magnitude of the event, the trust established in the group and the group's willingness to openly discuss their experiences and their reactions to it. Another factor which ties into how a group functions in the debriefing is the skill of the CISD team and how well they have established rapport with the group.

The reactions phase may last between 10 and 40 minutes (sometimes a bit longer) depending on the size of the group and the intensity of the incident. When the discussion drops off and several attempts by the team members to bring out more discussion from the group end with little or no response, it is a signal that the reaction phase has come to an end. The team should now move the group into the next phase of the debriefing, the symptom phase.

# 5. SYMPTOMS

The symptom phase is another transitional phase. The objective in this phase is to begin to move the group back from the emotionally laden content of the reaction phase toward more cognitively oriented material. The symptom phase is a natural part of the overall process from the cognitive domain to the emotional and then back to the cognitive domain. Stopping the debriefing at this point in the process would leave people in a charged emotional state which could possibly be detrimental. The debriefing is always continued to the end in order to complete the process and restore people to the cognitive level so that they can resume the normal responsibilities of their lives, armed with their customary set of psychological defenses intact.

The symptom phase is initiated when the team asks the participants to describe any cognitive, physical, emotional or behavioral experiences they may have encountered while they were working at the scene of the incident. The debriefing team may need to give several examples of stress related symptoms such as trembling hands, inability to make a decision, excessive silence or feelings of anger. Then the group spends several minutes talking about the various ways in which they experienced symptoms of distress while working at the scene.

The CISD team then asks the group what it was like for them during the next few days after the incident but before the debriefing. Again the participants begin to discuss the symptoms or signals of distress they encountered over the next few days.

Finally the CISD team asks the group if they have any leftover symptoms of distress from the time of the incident right up to and during the debriefing. The group may describe a variety of symptoms which they have carried into the debriefing.

Occasionally, the participants are reluctant to mention their symptoms because they fear that they are the only ones and that their symptoms may be abnormal. If the CISD team suspects that the group is reluctant to open up because of such a fear, the team may approach the question in a different manner. For example, the team may ask the entire group to answer by a show of hands how many had one type of symptom or another. Usually the team member asking the question picks a very common stress reaction and presents that symptom to the group and asks for a show of hands. Since it is more than likely that several members of the group would have experienced that very reaction, several hands typically go up. A few questions in a similar manner leaves the group feeling more relaxed and then the CISD team can generally ask the participants to add more information without a show of hands.

The symptoms phase is typically five to ten minutes long. Once the number of people pointing out symptoms decreases dramatically, the team makes a decision to move into the next phase of the debriefing, the teaching phase.

# 6. TEACHING

The teaching phase comes naturally after the symptoms phase. One connects very well with the other. It is easy to begin the teaching phase by pointing out several of the symptoms just described in the symptoms phase and letting the group know that those symptoms are normal, typical or to be expected after the type of critical incident they experienced. A skillful and experienced team can make the transition so smoothly that the participants in the debriefing do not even know that a new phase has begun.

All of the team members are very active in teaching the group. Some of the team members describe the typical symptoms of distress that are usually encountered. Other team members forewarn the group about symptoms which might not have shown up yet but might in the future. Other points made by the team members include comments that the group could not have done anything different during the operation because they had been trained to perform the operation in the manner in which they did. The team spends a good deal of time teaching the group a variety of stress survival strategies. Instructions are given on diet, exercise, rest, talking to one's family, working with the supervisors to initiate necessary procedural changes and a wide range of topics.

The teaching phase is very cognitive in approach. It is designed to bring the participants further away from the emotional content they had worked through in the reaction phase. Some of the information presented in this phase may be "earmarked" for specific participants, but the message is delivered to the group as a whole.

The teaching phase continues until the topics which are most important for this particular group of participants are exhausted. It is important not to drag this phase on to an extreme, however. The group being debriefed is likely to be quite tired by this time and so will the CISD team. Teaching more than is really necessary will only infuriate the group and cause them to miss some of the most important messages from the team.

It is also important for the team to recognize that there are serious limitations to what can be taught in the teaching phase of a debriefing. Teaching somewhat complex techniques like meditation, progressive muscle relaxation and academically oriented cognitive restructuring strategies can be inappropriate at this point. It takes about five exposures to most stress management skills before they can be learned adequately. This type of teaching and learning cannot take place during a debriefing. Those learning experiences should be saved for other stress education opportunities. The teaching of less complex stress management techniques is encouraged, however.

Many times, at the end of the teaching phase, one of the CISD team members asks the group if there is anything that happened during the incident which makes them feel just a bit positive, even if the overall event was one of the worst things they could have encountered. The question, if it is to be asked, must be asked with a great deal of sensitivity and concern. People may have a hard time seeing anything positive about the situation.

The question may be asked in the following manner.

- "Was there any small thing that happened during this incident that makes it just a little less chaotic or painful? Is there anything which gives you a little hope in the midst of all this pain?"

- "Is there something you have learned about yourself or about life from this experience that you might apply to some other aspect of your life or to something in the future?"

The teaching phase leads quite naturally into the re-entry phase.

# 7. RE-ENTRY

The last phase of the formal debriefing, the re-entry phase, is the final opportunity to clarify issues, answer questions, make summary statements and return the group to their normal functions. This phase puts closure on the discussions which have just occurred in the debriefing. Like most things which are human, debriefings have a beginning, a middle and an ending. No part stands alone without the others. Only when an experience has an ending can the beginning and middle make any sense.

The re-entry, which ends the debriefing, has several segments and several tasks which need to be performed. The participants in the debriefing have several tasks which they need to work through and the CISD team also has several tasks which it must work through. The *participants* in a debriefing will need to:

- Introduce any new material they wish to discuss.

- Review old material already discussed.

- Ask any questions they might have.

- Discuss anything they wish which would help them to bring closure to the debriefing.

The *debriefing team* will need to:

- Answer any questions posed to it.

- Reassure and inform as needed.

- State any feelings which are suspected to be there, but which have not been brought up by the participant.

- Provide appropriate handouts.

- Make summary comments.

The summary comments made by the CISD team members are drawn from their hearts. They are usually words of respect, encouragement, appreciation, support, gratitude and direction. Every CISD team member must make a summary comment in the last few minutes of the debriefing. The participants are welcome to comment if they wish, but they are not called upon to do so.

As soon as the debriefing draws to a close the team begins its post-debriefing activities. The team comes to its feet and begins to make contact with those people who seem to need something more than the debriefing provided.

## <u>POST-DEBRIEFING ACTIVITIES</u>

## One-on-One Follow-Up

It was stated earlier in this chapter that one of the most common mistakes for a debriefing team is to believe that all of the work to be done can be done in the debriefing. The debriefing is used more as a preventative than a cure. It is more of an assessment or screening tool than a treatment. There is much more which is left undone at the end of a debriefing. Teams which are not alert to that fact will make the mistake of thinking that the work is complete once the debriefing is finished. Follow-up is an essential component of any CISD. That follow-up can be in the form of, but not limited to, one-on-ones, work site visits, phone calls, and post-CISD education programs.

As the group breaks up, the debriefing team may begin to shake hands with the participants in the group and to move toward those who showed significant signs of distress during the debriefing. Another target will be those individuals who were too silent during the debriefing. The objective is to reach out to those who seem to need more. The debriefing may only have served as an opportunity for screening. Some participants may only need a few supportive words from peers. For some that will be enough. For others, however, they will need a referral for individual therapy. (Referrals for individual psychotherapy are rare. A good guess would be one to three percent need referrals, slightly more under extraordinary circumstances. Non emergency services workers may need more referrals than emergency services personnel.)

Frequently, peer support personnel can manage the distressed person by a brief supportive visit or phone call. If a CISD team member believes that such a contact will be helpful to one of the personnel, arrangements are made between the distressed person and the peer support person and phone numbers or addresses are exchanged.

Refreshments are usually served immediately after the CISD. The refreshments facilitate the interactions between the CISM team members and the participants in the debriefing. The refreshments make it easier to keep the group together in one place and make the contacts between team members and the participants much more natural.

The mental health professional is frequently called upon to see one or another of the participants in a one-on-one session in another room. The extra session may be enough for most people, but others may need a referral for therapy.

The contacts continue until the participants in the debriefing begin to drift away. When it becomes clear that no one is left to make a personal contact with, the CISD team prepares to leave. The team needs to hold its post -CISD meeting before leaving, or it might decide to hold its post -debriefing meeting right in the car on the way home or at some stop-off point before returning home.

## Post-Debriefing Meeting

The post -CISD meeting is a must.

The post -debriefing meeting is one of the most important protections for the team against distressing the team members. There are several important tasks which should be accomplished during the post -debriefing meeting, including:

- Explorations of what was done during the CISD so that the team members can learn more about the process and why certain decisions were made at one point or another, or why certain questions were asked.

- Assignment of specific follow-up tasks to individual team members. There should be no confusion as to who is going to provide follow-up services for whom.

- Assurance that the CISMteam members who just worked the CISD are "okay." This is a time to "debrief" the debriefers. If this is not done after every debriefing, people may return home distressed. Allow that to happen too often and a CISD team will lose good members.

The most important element of the post -debriefing meeting, then, is the debriefing of the debriefers. That process is not formal and structured. It is spontaneous and free flowing

## Post-Action Report

The post-action report is *optional*. It is kept as a mechanism by which the incident can be discussed at the next CISM team meeting during the case review segment. The post-action report should not contain any information which can be used to identify an individual who was in the CISD. It is recommended that the post-action report be simple and short. If one is written, it should consist of a single page with three paragraphs. Each paragraph has a specific function. They are:

- Brief description of the incident

- General themes discussed in the debriefing

- Summary of the instruction given to the participants of the debriefing by the CISD team

The names of the CISD team members, date of the debriefing and overall number of people debriefed may be useful information if the CISM team is trying to keep statistics on each of its team members. Those same statistics can be kept in a much more efficient manner if all the names of CISM team members are listed in one column and the types of CISM services such as CISD, defusing, one-on-one intervention and so on are listed across the tops of other columns. When a team member provides a type of service the date of the intervention is recorded on the tally sheet. There is no need then to put this type of information on the post action report.

# OTHER IMPORTANT CONSIDERATIONS IN DEBRIEFING

## Group Size

- The ideal debriefing group size is between 4 and 20 people.

- A group of between 20 and 30 is okay, but it does take more time and certain other adjustments must be made in the debriefing.

- A group larger than 30 is obviously more difficult to work with.

- A larger group requires that the debriefing team use the alternative fact phase format (Which units arrived first? Who came in after them? What happened?) and allow fewer people to speak. It is also a good idea in the thought phase to ask, "What did you think when you got involved in the incident? Anyone who wants to speak feel free."

- Any group larger than 40 should prompt the team to consider breaking the group into smaller subgroups if that is possible.

# Targeting Groups

When there are many people who need a debriefing, logical groups have to be targeted. Those most affected by an incident are the primary targets of a debriefing. Those directly involved are the next most logical target. Then the supervisory staff. Then those only involved in an indirect sense. Finally those who are affected but who were not involved.

Groups can be broken down according to several logical categories, such as:

- Geographical location of the groups

- Time of arrival

- Specialty function

- Usual working group

- Common profession (law enforcement, fire, EMS)

# Participants

Any emergency personnel who were involved in the incident should be invited to attend the debriefing. This includes supervisory staff. To exclude them produces an "us and them" atmosphere within the organization.

Bystanders, media personnel and other non-emergency people who might need support services should be handled separately from the emergency personnel. Mixing the groups is seldom wise since the non-emergency service workers might hear information that could be stressful in and of itself.

Family members of emergency personnel should also be handled separately. They may be distressed by hearing too much detail from their emergency services loved ones and the emergency services personnel may then shut down their discussions to protect their families. Keep in mind the principles of homogeneity of group, mission completion and roughly equal traumatization that were discussed earlier.

# Breaks

No breaks are taken during a debriefing. Breaks in the flow of the debriefing disrupt the entire process and destroy the emotional momentum in the group.

# Not on Duty

Personnel in a debriefing must be relieved of all response duties. It is harmful for them to leave a debriefing in the middle to handle emergency calls or routine situations. They are brought out of their cognitive defense system during a debriefing and having them respond on an emergency call could jeopardize their safety because they will be functioning more at the emotional level than at the cognitive level.

# Not a Critique

The CISD is not an operations critique. Ideally the operation critique would follow the CISD. But since that is frequently not possible, it would be a good second choice to have the operations critique complete when the debriefing is set up. It is never a good idea to mix the operations critique and the CISD together.

# Confidentiality

Confidentiality is a must. When confidentiality is destroyed, the CISD team's effectiveness can be destroyed. CISD team members must take this commitment seriously.

# Follow-Up Services

Follow-up services are crucial to completing the work begun in the debriefing. In fact, follow-up services are an inherent part of the CISD process. To provide a CISD without appropriate follow-up services is a violation of the standards of practice in the CISM field. CISD without follow-up changes the nature of the CISD. Be very clear about it. A CISD is not a stand-alone process and it should never be provided outside the context of a comprehensive, systematic and multi-component CISM program. No one should assume that simply because the debriefing was provided, the entire work of supporting the personnel has been accomplished. There is much more left to do. Without follow-up services, the symptoms may return to some of the participants even more forcefully than they had before. People without follow-up may feel abandoned and uncared for. They often feel that the help was incomplete.

Follow-up services begin with the one-on-one contacts made with the participants of the debriefing immediately after the debriefing is complete. Within 24 hours, follow-up services will intensify for those who have been identified as needing it most.

There are many types of follow-up services which can be provided. They include but are not limited to:

- Station visits
- Telephone calls
- Chaplain visits
- Individual consultations
- Referrals for therapy
- Additional meeting with a subgroup
- Ride along programs
- Family sessions
- Follow-up meeting with whole group one week after the debriefing
- Others as required

## SUMMARY

This chapter has described the CISD process in detail. It should be seen as the most complex of intervention strategies for CISM teams. In fact, CISM teams are urged to assess carefully the real need for a debriefing and determine if there are other interventions which might be more suitable before committing the team to a CISD.

The chapter includes numerous specific guidelines which have been developed by many teams throughout the world over a 25 year period of time and many thousands of experiences with CISDs.

The reader is again cautioned that the debriefing process cannot be learned adequately by simply reading about the process. One who expects to do debriefings well should have appropriate training to assure excellence in the provision of services.

The reader is further cautioned that the CISD process is not a stand-alone process and must be provided within the context of a systematic CISM program.

# Chapter 12

## TROUBLESHOOTING THE COMMON PROBLEMS IN DEFUSINGS AND DEBRIEFINGS

With more than twenty-five years of experience and nearly fifty thousand actual defusings and CISDs, a formidable body of "lessons learned" has accrued. In this chapter, we shall highlight the most common problems encountered in leading a successful defusing or debriefing.

The most common problems arise, interestingly enough, from the failure of the individuals leading the defusing or CISD to fully understand the dynamic processes inherent in these interventions and the consequential failure to adapt effectively to these challenges. While there are certainly numerous problems that can arise during a debriefing, the vast majority will fall into one of five categories. These are listed in Table 12.1.

Let us now take a brief look at each of these categories.

## OVERLY RIGID APPLICATION

This volume is intended to be an operations manual; a "how to" for CISD, defusings, demobilizations, Crisis Management Briefings and related interventions. The guidelines contained herein are designed to be general prescriptions and reflections on strategies and tactics that have proven useful in the past. New traumas present new challenges, and often there is a need to adopt a dynamic flexibility in the face of crisis or chaos. The guidelines offered in the text are thought to be valuable in the vast  majority of cases but one needs to understand that, occasionally, unique situations will arise that dictate adaptation.

Common variables that may dictate adaptation would include challenging or unique geographical settings; cultural, ethnic or racial diversities; unique intensity or unusual chronicity of the traumatic event; and often, the sheer magnitude of the traumatic event. When in doubt as to how to adjust to a new and challenging CISD simply remember to practice some common sense tactics: 1) listen effectively, 2) employ crisis intervention concepts, 3) do not open any emotional issues that you cannot bring to a closure and 4) depend on peer support personnel who can often obtain a much clearer understanding of the needs of the group.

**TABLE 12.1**

---

### COMMON PROBLEMS IN CISD

1. Overly rigid adherence to general CISD guideline with no sensitivity for unique situational, personal, cultural or social circumstances.

2. Overzealous application of interventions without appropriate assessment of the state of psychological functions and receptivity of the individuals to be briefed.

3. Failure to conduct the defusing or debriefing in a discrete psychological structure that progresses from the cognitive domain, to the affective domain and back to the cognitive domain for termination.

4. The team members' dysfunctional counter transference, that is, over identification with the trauma experience and / or failure to maintain an objective perspective on the debriefing process as it progresses.

5. Failure to comply with basic defusing and debriefing principles and techniques which have been developed and practiced by CISD teams throughout the world and are now commonly accepted as the standard for applying CISD techniques to emergency personnel and disaster workers.

---

# OVERZEALOUS APPLICATION OF THE INTERVENTIONS

The advent of defusings, debriefings, demobilizations, Crisis Management Briefings, and disaster mental health services has the potential to do a great service to society, but we must use care in our application of these powerful interventions. Overzealous or excessive application of crisis intervention or therapeutic strategies can be as harmful as under utilization of the same services.

Any psychological intervention is going to produce its greatest benefit if the person receiving the intervention is psychologically receptive to the process itself. For example, earlier in the text we offered general guidelines in terms of the timing of when interventions should be applied. That which ultimately dictates appropriateness is not how many hours/days have passed since the trauma, but rather is how psychologically receptive the victim is to the help being offered.

Every reader can probably recall a difficult time in their lives when he/ she just wanted to be left alone. Similarly, one can just as easily recall a difficult time when companionship was considered healing. What makes the difference? Answer: the state of psychological receptivity, that is, one's readiness and willingness to accept the form of help or assistance. Forced companionship is as potentially traumatizing as the original trauma to some victims who need isolation and solitude at that particular point in time.

In concert with this discussion of psychological receptivity is the issue of psychological defenses. Perhaps the most commonly used initial defense mechanism in trauma and disaster is *DENIAL*, that is, insistence that everything is okay or that it's really not that bad despite objective evidence to the contrary. Some refer to this as a "shock" phase.

A common mistake made by trauma intervention personnel is to overzealously challenge or confront defense mechanisms. If one recalls the goal of crisis intervention as being the re-establishment of psychological homeostasis, or baseline functioning, we see that defense mechanisms can play a useful role in coping with an otherwise overwhelming psychological challenge. Remember, don't attempt to remove a defense mechanism unless you can replace it with something else that the victim can rely upon for emotional protection until the crisis passes or resolves.

A good example of overzealous intervention can usually be found immediately after large scale disasters. Helpers flock to the scene in record numbers. Many are not sure what they will do when they arrive at the disaster site, but they are irresistibly drawn to the tragedy. Without an organized approach to disaster relief, they may only add to the chaos.

Some CISM teams and CISM trained individuals have unfortunately contributed to the chaos in disaster by arriving at the scene even though they have not been called. They usually have not developed a plan of action in coordination with the local CISM resources. Some have attempted to provide debriefing services when the rescuers and disaster workers were still involved in search and rescue operations or when they were in a state of shock and denial.

CISM teams should slow their overzealous response to disasters. Outside of some brief on-scene support services or some one-on-one contacts with individuals needing assistance (which is provided by locally based CISM teams), CISD work in disasters does not begin until three to six weeks after the event. The best response of a CISM team to another community is to coordinate those efforts with that community and with the efforts of the International Critical Incident Stress Foundation, Inc. An unrequested presence at a disaster is an overzealous and inappropriate response which may produce harm for CISM teams everywhere as well as for the people who need their help.

# FAILURE TO UTILIZE THE NECESSARY PSYCHOLOGICAL STRUCTURE

The CISD process was carefully designed to follow the natural psychological structure of cognitively (intellectual) processing information first and then formulating an affective (emotional) evaluation of their experience. To jump immediately to a discussion of the affective factors and skip the normal cognitive factors is disruptive to psychological processes. In emergency personnel, such a movement will cause anger and rejection. Some emergency workers could actually be harmed psychologically by such a dramatic violation of their normal psychological process for handling traumatic experiences.

Table 12.2 outlines the debriefing process and the psychological structure which should be followed during each phase.

Note that the thought phase and the symptom phase are transitional phases which allow for movement which is as smooth as possible from one psychological process to another. Too rapid a transition produces discomfort in people who are dealing with traumatic material.

**TABLE 12.2**

| _CISD Phases_ | _Psychological Process_ | |
|---|---|---|
| Introduction | Cognitive | |
| Fact | Cognitive | |
| Thought | Cognitive ⟶ | Affective |
| Reaction | Affective | |
| Symptom | Affective ⟶ | Cognitive |
| Teaching | Cognitive | |
| Re-Entry | Cognitive | |

Failure to follow this structure during a CISD will generally lead to a series of problems including but not limited to: 1) participants feeling pressure to discuss affective factors before adequate trust of the team and the process has been established, 2) participants feeling cut off once they begin their affective discussions and 3) participants feeling that the CISD team is incompetent and out of control.

# LEADER COUNTERTRANSFERENCE

Countertransference develops when the CISD team begins to over- identify, on a personal or professional basis, with the personnel being debriefed. CISD personnel must be careful to walk a difficult course, showing sufficient caring, understanding and empathy without becoming immersed or overwhelmed with the intensity or familiarity of any given critical incident. It is not an easy task, but debriefing teams need to keep an objective view of the critical incident and the people they are helping.

One of the best ways to assure an objective CISD is for the team members to keep the experience a cognitive one. For example, instead of looking for similarities between the current event which is being debriefed and one's own past painful experiences, debriefing team members should focus on the current debriefing. They may ask themselves for instance, "What questions do I need to ask, what steps do I need to perform, what do I need to teach to bring these people the maximum benefit from this debriefing?"

# FAILURE TO COMPLY WITH BASIC CISD PRINCIPLES

The vast majority of CISM teams have provided high quality defusing and debriefing services and have helped many thousands of emergency personnel. Their work has been consistently positive during the last twenty-five years. These dedicated people deserve a great deal of respect and admiration for their work.

A small number of teams, however, have made serious mistakes during defusings or CISDs. And virtually every team has made some minor mistakes as they provided services. The paragraphs to follow should not be perceived as finger-pointing accusations. Rather, they should be seen as opportunities to learn from others and remind ourselves of the limitations of CISM services and the pitfalls to be avoided while providing those services.

One of the most serious problems encountered in the debriefing work is the attempt to turn a debriefing into psychotherapy. A CISD is not psychotherapy nor is it a substitute for psychotherapy. A CISD is a stress prevention oriented group discussion of a traumatic event. Psychotherapy, on the other hand, has been developed to "cure" or "fix" an already existing problem or disorder. CISD work should avoid taking on traditional psychotherapeutic roles and stick to its primary goals of: 1) reducing the impact of a traumatic event, 2) accelerating the normal recovery process for normal people who are experiencing normal reactions to totally abnormal events and 3) identifying those in the group who might need additional support.

The second most serious problem faced by CISM teams is associated with and often the root cause of the first. It is the fact that some teams falsely believe that some of their members can serve without appropriate CISM training. As it has been pointed out elsewhere in this book, the lack of training for professional and peer support personnel is a formula for potential disaster.

Another serious mistake made by a team providing a CISD is the false belief that every person in a debriefing must speak during the debriefing or they will not receive any benefit from the session. The very few CISD teams which believe this myth have, on occasion, come close to violating the absolute right each person has to maintain one's privacy.

CISM teams which believe that all the supportive work of the team must be accomplished during the actual debriefing are also making a serious mistake. The CISD is more of a screening tool than a recovery tool. After the debriefing much work remains. The team members need to follow up by means of phone calls, station visits and other methods. The belief that a single two or three hour contact is going to complete all of the work necessary for resolving the thoughts and feelings associated with the traumatic experience is indicative of a team that misunderstands the limitations of the debriefing process.

Yet another serious problem is the misapplication of the CISD to events outside the power of the process. To attempt, for example, to resolve long standing social problems by applying CISD is a prescription for failure.

Debriefings fail for many other reasons. Here is a list of some of the more common pitfalls to be avoided:

- Using untrained CISM team members or a team with no experience.

- Not using mental health professionals in a debriefing.

- Insufficient use of appropriate, well trained peers from the same professions.

- Not preparing adequately for debriefing (e.g. not doing an adequate case review.)

- Not having a CISD team strategy meeting before the debriefing.

- Not following the CISD model, altering the CISD model, or misunderstanding the CISD process which progresses from strongly cognitive, (**Introduction** and **Fact** phases) to a transition phase from cognition to affect (**Thought** phase) to a strongly affective phase

(**Reaction**) and finally back through a transition phase (**Symptoms**) to cognition phases again (**Teaching** and **Re-entry**).

- Providing too much advice or trying to argue with the participants.

- Attempting to turn CISD into psychotherapy or a substitute for psychotherapy.

- Writing anything during a debriefing.

- Inadequate knowledge of the incident before starting a CISD.

- Providing CISD services to close relatives or friends or to people whom team members supervise or work with very closely.

- Choosing debriefers who were directly involved in the incident to be debriefed or who have a currant serious personal problem.

- Interrupting a person who is expressing his or her emotions during a debriefing.

- Inadequate introductory remarks.

- Allowing the CISD to turn into "war stories".

- Inadequate teaching and summary remarks.

- Public discussions of the debriefing by CISD team members once it is concluded (breaking confidentiality).

- Not providing appropriate follow-up services for CISD.

- Underutilizing (not handling serious events) or overutilizing (using it for minor incidents) the CISD process.

- Not meeting after a debriefing to make sure the CISD team is okay.

# SUMMARY

This chapter explored the five main problems which can jeopardize the effectiveness of CISD teams. Readers were cautioned about too rigid an application of CISD guidelines as well as overzealous use of the CISD process. One of the most significant problems is the failure to utilize the proper psychological structure for the debriefing. The issue of losing one's objectivity was also presented as was the failure to comply with a standard set of operating procedures in debriefings.

The chapter concluded with a list of pitfalls to avoid to ensure the most effective and efficient performance of CISD teams.

# Chapter 13

## ADVANCED CONCEPTS IN CISM

### INTRODUCTION

As described in previous chapters of this book, Critical Incident Stress Management concepts, in general, have undergone a phenomenal development during the last two decades. Likewise, the group crisis intervention technique called Critical Incident Stress Debriefing (CISD) has developed substantially and has had to adapt to a variety of challenging situations. Although the core of the debriefing process has remained the same since 1984, applications of the process have been made, with relatively minor adjustments, to accommodate complex situations. The core CISD model stays the same but the prompts for the different phases are changed to facilitate the process in more challenging circumstances. Some applications of CISD to complex situations will be described in this chapter.

The advanced concepts of the field of CISM and specific applications of the CISD technique that are described in this chapter are intended for use by experienced CISM teams which have had the advanced CISM course provided by the International Critical Incident Stress Foundation, Inc. The applications of CISM concepts and CISD procedures to complex situations should not be attempted by teams without specific training. Reading about special applications alone does not equate to specific training.

### TIME LINE FOR CISM INTERVENTIONS INCLUDING THE CISD

Some confusion exists as to the best time to provide certain CISM processes to distressed individuals and / or groups. The following chart and the paragraphs which follow should be helpful in determining an overall CISM strategy. One caveat to be kept in mind is that *people generally accept help when they are most ready for it.* No chart will be capable of providing all of the information necessary to make all of the decisions about the applications of specific interventions to all situations. Providers of services must think their way through situations. They should start by assessing the circumstances of the situation first and then determining the status of the people in need of support. Once they have that information, CISM team members can then decide which applications of CISM will be necessary to achieve the goals of the intervention.

## CISM TIME LINE

| Time | Circumstance | Intervention |
|------|--------------|--------------|
| Minus zero | Pre-incident status | • Plan<br>• Educate<br>• Prepare<br>• Brief<br>• Practice<br>• Evaluate<br>• Write protocols<br>• Assess potentials<br>• Choose staff<br>• Train |
| Zero | Event | • Deploy assessment team<br>• Assess<br>• On-scene support services<br>• Advise command<br>• Brief individual support<br>• Care for primary victims and family members and witnesses<br>• Plan next steps |
| First 8 hours | Ongoing operations | • Continue on-scene support as necessary<br>• Establish nearby demobilization center if warranted (First one or two shifts only) |

| Time | Circumstance | Intervention |
|------|-------------|--------------|
| | | • Call in additional CISM support if necessary<br>• Provide one-on-one services as required<br>• Set up defusings |
| First 24 hours | Operations wrapping up | • Continue one-on-one or completed contacts<br>• Continue on-scene if necessary<br>• Arrange debriefing(s)<br>• Plan other possible interventions |
| 24 - 72 hours<br>*(May be weeks longer if disaster work is prolonged)* | System returning to normal (ideal time for CISD(s)) | • CISD(s)<br>• One-on-ones follow-up for all previous CISM interventions<br>• Significant other support to start as necessary<br>• Community outreach programs to start<br>• Informal discussions encouraged<br>• Follow up on all previous CISM interventions |
| 72 hours to one month<br>*(May be longer if disaster work is prolonged)* | System restored to normal or near normal conditions | • Continue follow-up conditions<br>• Continue one-on-one contacts<br>• Make referrals as necessary<br>• Evaluate<br>• Plan<br>• Educate<br>• Practice |

**FIGURE 13.1**

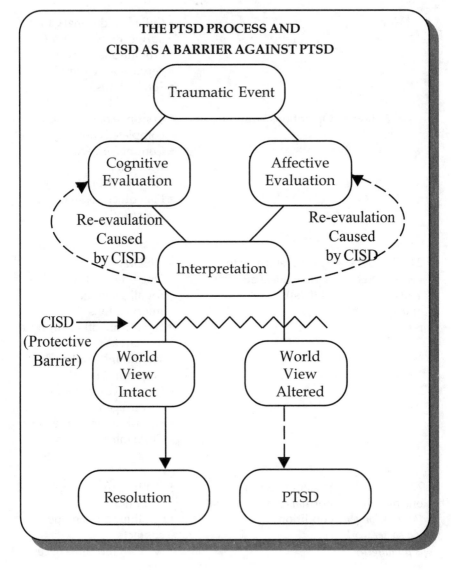

THE PTSD PROCESS AND
CISD AS A BARRIER AGAINST PTSD

Traumatic Event

Cognitive
Evaluation

Affective
Evaluation

Re-evaulation
Caused
by CISD

Re-evaluation
Caused
by CISD

Interpretation

CISD
(Protective
Barrier)

World
View
Intact

World
View
Altered

Resolution

PTSD

# CISM: A PROTECTIVE BARRIER

When CISM services are applied properly and in a timely fashion, they can act as a protective barrier which may help to prevent the development of Posttraumatic Stress Disorder (PTSD). The development of PTSD depends on several factors converging. First, there must be a traumatic event which is beyond the usual experience of everyday life. Then there must be a reaction to the traumatic event. This reaction is usually made up of cognitive and affective evaluations of the traumatic event which produced a state of physical and emotional arousal. The cognitive and affective evaluations of the event lead to an overall interpretation of the trauma experience. If the interpretation is one that can produce a significantly changed view of the world, PTSD can result. The diagram (Figure 13.1) depicts this process.

If CISD is applied to a group before the altered worldview which leads to PTSD can be established, it may, in many circumstances, help to prevent PTSD. CISD may have this positive effect by providing an enhanced knowledge base about the traumatic experience. With a broader knowledge base about the event, which has been contributed to by everyone in the group, individuals may be able to reprocess the experience and develop an interpretation which is less likely to lead them toward PTSD. For example, if a person goes through a traumatic event and then begins to cognitively and effectively evaluate the incident and concludes (even if it is a false conclusion) that he is at fault because he should have been able to prevent an injury to a colleague during the operations at the incident, he is more likely to develop PTSD.

If, on the other hand, that same person participates in a CISD and learns that the injury to his friend was produced by his colleague's own failure to follow proper procedures, it is far less likely that he will interpret the event in a manner which leads to PTSD. The diagram in Figure 13.1 demonstrates how a CISD may act as a protective barrier against PTSD by causing people to re-evaluate cognitive and affective factors. The broken line leading to PTSD indicates that some traumatic events are so severe that they may produce PTSD despite CISD services. In general however, the chances of developing PTSD are lessened when CISD services have been properly provided.

# DIFFICULT INTERVENTIONS

When one considers the amount of information in this text, no one should have the idea that CISDs are easy processes which anyone can provide even when they have no training. Nothing could be further from the truth. Debriefings, in the best of circumstances, can be a challenge which demands well trained and experienced team members whether they be peers, clergy or mental health professionals.

Adequate training in the advanced CISM course is essential if a CISM team is going to be involved in any of the following interventions. These types of situations are very complex and things can go wrong quickly. CISM teams managing the following types of events must be resourceful and capable of altering their approach rapidly while maintaining the core elements of the debriefing process.

# COMPLICATED CISM INTERVENTIONS: THE BIG FIVE

Advance CISM tactics are required in a number of situations. The following five are the most challenging circumstances for a CISM team.

## 1. SIGNIFICANTLY DELAYED INTERVENTIONS

There are situations in which those who were involved do not call for assistance from a CISM team for several months. Many factors can contribute to a failure to call for help in a timely manner. Some supervisors do not want to call for help because they fear that their ability to lead others will be called into question. On occasion, the personnel themselves may not realize that they would benefit from CISM services. In other situations people may not know that help is available or how to call for it if it. Sometimes pride gets in the way.

When a set of interventions are delayed longer than three months or when inadequate services were provided originally and remedial services are now necessary, a CISM team will be facing a complex problem. Significantly delayed interventions must be carefully planned out. Many CISM interventions will need to be utilized in combination. The steps to an effective program of delayed interventions are outlined below.

1. Carefully assess the situation and its history. The more that the CISM team knows and understands about the situation and people's reactions to it, the better.

2. Make sure that the team is responding to an official request by people within the organization who have the authority to make such a request. It is never a good idea to enter an organization without proper invitation and authorization. If only one or two individuals need help instead of the majority of the group, provide one-on-one services only to those in need.

3. Develop a comprehensive but flexible plan of action. Determine which combination of CISM services are likely to have the most positive results.

4. Go over the plan with officials of the organization and gain their approval and feedback.

5. Choose the response team from the CISM members.

6. Schedule the interventions with the group requesting assistance.

7. Start with whatever services appear to be most logical.

8. The usual list of interventions for a significantly delayed intervention include, but are not limited to:

- one-on-one services

- education programs

- family support programs

- CISD

- spouse support

- organizational support

- follow-up meetings

- referrals for therapy

- identification of additional resources

- other innovative interventions as required

The key to success in applying CISM interventions to significantly delayed interventions is to not rely too heavily on one single tactic. The interventions must be carefully tied together. Team members should work exceptionally hard to assure that appropriate follow-up is instituted and carried out.

## 2. MULTIPLE INCIDENT DEBRIEFING

The multiple incident debriefing or multiple events debriefing is used when the same personnel in an organization experience several horrible events in a brief period of time. A maximum of four events can be debriefed simultaneously in the same session. More than four events would overburden the CISD team and they would likely fail in their attempts to help the group. If there are more than four events the CISD team should choose the four worst ones. The group receiving the support service can usually tell the team members which of the incidents are the worst four for them.

None of the other four of the "Big Five" are ever included in the list of events to be debriefed in a multiple incident debriefing. Each one is so complex in its own right that their presence in a multiple incident debriefing would make it nearly impossible for a team to successfully complete the CISD. A line-of-duty death is especially to be avoided and never be a part of a multiple incident debriefing. It is so powerful that it would overshadow any other event. Line-of-duty deaths should be handled completely separately.

The events to be debriefed may be very similar to one another or they may be quite different but may have just occurred in a brief time frame. The usual time frame is between one shift and no longer than fourteen days. Picking events older than fourteen days can produce additional complexity for the team managing a multiple event CISD.

The CISD team assesses the situation and makes a conscious decision to utilize the multiple incident debriefing format. The team providing the CISD should never be surprised and have a multiple incident debriefing spontaneously begin within a regular debriefing. In other words, a multiple incident debriefing is a planned process not a haphazard or surprise occurrence.

To assess the potential for a multiple incident debriefing, a CISD team should ask the following question in their initial assessment of a request for debriefing:

- Besides this incident for which you are requesting a debriefing, are there any other significant events which have occurred within the last fourteen days? If the answer is "no," make preparations for a standard single incident debriefing. If the answer is "yes," then ask for the following information:

    * How many events have there been?
    * What types of events have occurred?
    * Are any of the events very similar?
    * What is the exact time frame for the events?
    * Were the crews the same for each event or were some of them only on one or two of the events but not all of them?
    * Is each of the events serious enough to be debriefed by itself even without having had the others?
    * Is there one event which people seem to be focusing most upon?
    * How are the crews from these events right now?
    * Are there any unusual reactions or symptoms noticeable among crew members?
    * Any other pertinent information?

Once an assessment is made and the CISD team decides to provide a multiple incident debriefing, it should begin to organize the members of the team who will actually do the debriefing. It will be necessary to have at least one extra team member for the team. If it would only take two team members to do a standard single incident CISD then three are chosen for the multiple incident debriefing. If it would take three to do a standard debriefing, then four are chosen for the multiple incident CISD, and so on. More time must also be planned. Most multiple incident debriefings require one half hour to one hour extra time to complete.

The CISD team must know about each of the events as if each one of them was the only event to be debriefed. This means that the team has to do some "homework" before they go to the multiple incident debriefing.

A team member should be assigned a "specialist" role. Each team member is instructed to pay close attention whenever the incident to which he or she has been assigned is mentioned in the debriefing. During the teaching phase the team member who is assigned to a specific event teaches on that event. Any team member can teach on any of the incidents, but the "specialist" has to teach on the incident to which he or she has been assigned. This spreads the team work load out so that one team member does not have to do all of the work.

It is okay to mix in people who only worked on one of the incidents with others who have worked more of them. More than likely they have already heard of the event through the organization in which they work. There is little chance it will negatively affect emergency personnel because they are usually unaffected by events in which they did not participate.

It should be noted, however, that the multiple incident CISD was never designed with the average citizen in mind. The procedure should only be employed when the group is either emergency services, military or some very close industrial group. Community members are not offered multiple incident CISD services because one member of the community might upset another member of the community. That does not happen with emergency operations personnel.

The events are debriefed simultaneously. The various events are blended into the discussion randomly and no attempt is made to organize the discussion into blocks. The sorting out of the various events is accomplished in the teaching phase of the debriefing. This is a real challenge for a CISD team. The team members try to follow each situation as it is expressed and intermixed. It is essential that each event be discussed in the teaching phase. If not, the participants will get the impression that one of the events is considered unimportant by the CISD team. That could cause a person to be distressed if they just happened to be upset by the one event which was not discussed in the teaching.

To begin the multiple incident debriefing, the CISD team asks, "Tell us who you are, your regular job, the incidents you were involved with and the one which was the worst for you. A very brief description of what happened in each event will be helpful. You do not have to discuss them in any particular order."

In the thought phase the question is asked, "What thoughts came to mind on each of the events? Are there any thoughts which stand out overall as you look back on these events? You may speak about your thoughts about any one or more or all of the events if you so choose."

Likewise, in the reaction phase the question is modified from the standard CISD in the following way, "What is the worst thing about any of these events for you personally? You may wish to state something about each of the events or just pick the overall worst thing about any one of them."

In the symptoms phase the participants are asked if any signals of distress showed up in them in any of the events.

The teaching phase of the multiple incident debriefing process is just like the teaching which goes on in any CISD. The difference is that each event must be discussed in the teaching phase. Another difference is that the team makes considerable effort to link the events together and point out any themes which seem to exist.

# 3. SUICIDE OF COLLEAGUE

There are few critical incidents that can produce the disruption to unit cohesion and performance that suicide can. Even when responded to early, it is a complex circumstance and demands a wide range of intervention tactics. The first of the tactics is a day-one debriefing. This CISD takes place within a few hours of the incident and replaces the defusing. The defusing is the wrong tool for the intensity of a suicide of a colleague. It does not have as much power to assist the personnel as a CISD. The CISD is adjusted to accomodate the specific needs of a group suffering the loss of a co-worker. Its primary purpose is to equalize the information the group has regarding the suicide death. A second goal is to assist the shocked group in preparing to handle to funeral and the initial stages of mourning.

Instead of being the usual seven phases in length, the CISD provided on the same day as the death of a colleague is only five phases in length. Both the thought phase and the symptoms phase are left out. The reason the thought and symptoms phases are eliminated is because they would generate intense anger if someone asked about those phases on the same day as the death of a friend. The only realistic responses to the question, "What were your thoughts when you first heard about your colleagues' suicide" would be shock, denial, mental confusion and feelings of being emotionally overwhelmed. The same answers would apply if the group were asked about symptoms they were encountering after learning of the death by suicide of a colleague just a few hours earlier. Those answers should be relatively obvious to CISM team members during the day -one debriefing. When people ask questions which have obvious answers they are considered insensitive and irresponsible.

Once the five-phase CISD is complete there will be many tasks to keep the CISM team busy for days, weeks and sometimes even months to come. Here are some of the CISM interventions that are recommended for implementation after the suicide of a colleague.

1. Be prepared for the provision of many one-on-one interventions

2. Hold a second CISD after the funeral. This is usually held between 3 and 10 days after the burial. This particular CISD is a full seven phase CISD. The post-funeral CISD helps to put the group on the track to recovery. It is a beginning of the long range grief reactions.

3. More one-on-ones will be necessary in the weeks and months to come.

4. Family support services will definitely be needed for the person's family. They may be required for the families of other operations personnel who lost their colleague.

5. A post CISD educational program on suicide prevention may be helpful. It is recommended that some time be allowed to pass prior to this educa tional program. If it is too early, it can produce very intense feelings in the group.

6. Referrals for therapy may be necessary if the symptoms of distress do not subside in a reasonable time (about a month or two) despite the support that has already been offered.

# 4. LINE-OF-DUTY DEATH

Line-of-duty death is, without doubt, one of the most difficult of all debriefings to manage. The death produces intense levels of shock, denial, anxiety and grief for the participants in the debriefing. Great tact and sensitivity must be displayed to the individuals in the group. There is a considerable need for individuals to receive one-on-one services before and after the CISD. A CISM team managing a line-of-duty death will have a formidable amount of work to accomplish from the time the death is announced until several weeks after the funeral. The early stages of grief are difficult times for an organization and for the individuals in that organization. Emotions will remain high although they will be changing as the group and the individuals pass through the grief stages. Individuals will continue to need assistance for many months after a line-of-duty death. They occasionally seek out individual peer support services for depression, mental confusion, physical complaints, feelings of guilt, grief and anger.

These feelings are frequently transmitted to the CISD team members. The team members may endure vicarious traumatization from the experience of the debriefing. They need detailed briefings before they provide the CISD. The team members will also need a more intense post-debriefing meeting at the conclusion of each CISD and the other CISM services.

Line-of-duty death requires a broad range of CISM services. Once the team is notified of the death, it goes into action. The team may assist the organization in developing a quick plan for death notifications to family members. Many CISM teams have actively participated in providing death notifications to the deceased's family according to contingency plans. When this occurs, a team approach is recommended. Usually a department chaplain, a high ranking officer of the department, a mental health professional from the CISM team and a peer support person are brought together to make the death announcement. If it is not possible to bring such a joint team together quickly, then a high ranking official of the organization should make the announcement. In any case, the announcement to family members is always the worst experience. No amount or type of training can adequately prepare anyone to present such bad news to the loved ones of a deceased member of the group.

Once the death announcement has been made, the team turns its attention to the organization of the first group contact with the members of the group. On the day of the death the first debriefing is held. It should be noted, however, that this debriefing does not follow the same format as the seven phase debriefing which is used after the funeral. It is also much shorter in length than a seven phase debriefing. In fact, the first debriefing is more like a defusing than it is like a debriefing. The two major goals of this first debriefing are:

- To establish a baseline of facts about the situation

- To assist the group members in preparing for the funeral

In the first debriefing the CISD team asks the group if they could briefly explain what happened so everyone will have the same information. The comments usually come slowly and with great pain. People are very shocked and have trouble sorting out some of the details. The thought phase is skipped since no one has had adequate time to sort out their thoughts. When the reaction phase is brought out, the CISD team has to emphasize specifically that it wants to know if people can identify the aspect of the situation which is giving them the most pain at the time of the debriefing. Do not expect that they will be able to give much coherent information during the debriefing. Only a few people usually speak at this time. The symptoms phase is usually skipped since they have had little time to experience any symptoms except shock and denial. The teaching phase gives a very brief overview of the early stages of grief and some time is spent preparing the personnel to cope with the intensity of the next few days and especially the funeral.

CISM team members provide one-on-one services on request and whenever necessary during the next few days as funeral preparations are made. A small delegation representing the CISM team may attend the funeral out of respect to the organization and its membership. No specific CISM functions are outlined for this delegation. There is usually no need for specific services. The funeral tends to preoccupy everyone's thoughts and few seek direct assistance at this time. Immediately after the funeral, some individuals do seek out team members for an opportunity to ventilate. Team members may assist as requested but they should not "push" themselves on anyone. *Grief is a natural process and too much help can actually interfere with natural coping and recovery processes.* So CISM team members generally take on a watch and see approach to this stage in the grief and mourning process. Help when requested to do so, but do not overdo efforts to help. The funeral delegation from the CISM team should not be expected to conduct the debriefings after the funeral. It will be too hard for them to do both the funeral and the debriefings.

The second debriefing occurs usually three to seven days after the funeral. This debriefing is designed to round out the details of the loss and to set the path forward through the long range grief process. The standard seven stages are followed unlike the debriefing done on the day of death which was previously described. Issues which may trigger painful reactions at this point are associated with events which occurred during the funeral, or the fact that the organization is making efforts to return to normal. For example, the administration may have arranged to have the person's locker emptied and that triggered anger in other personnel. The team needs to process all of the various issues which are brought out in the debriefing. As part of the reaction phase of the CISD, the team asks the participants how they would most like to remember the deceased. Then they must discuss in detail the grief process and present realistic estimates about how long it will take for the group to work through grief. Often the team provides advice on how to keep the memory of the deceased alive within the organization by plaques, live tree plantings, scholarship funds and other activities.

Follow-up over the next few weeks is important. Some individuals will need to talk to CISM team members. There may be a need for a brief group meeting to find out how they are doing since the funeral and the last CISD. Administrators and supervisors may seek advice on how to handle one or another aspect of the recovery process. The family of the deceased may need additional support or recommendations on finding grief counselors to help them if they are getting stuck in the grief process. The CISM team usually provides debriefings and other services as required to the department's spouses and significant others. They are usually terrified by the loss and need help in re-balancing their lives after a death which could have just as easily been their own loved one. Sometimes debriefing support may need to be provided to the children of operations personnel.

One month, three months, six months and one year anniversaries are rough times which tend to trigger additional reactions. CISM teams should be aware of these time frames and be prepared to provide individual services if they should be requested.

## MULTIPLE LINE OF DUTY DEATHS

If the effects of one line-of-duty death are devastating to the organization then the word to describe the impact of a multiple line of duty death on an organization is "catastrophic." Recovery from multiple line of duty deaths is a grueling task. CISM teams will certainly work very hard if they are brought in to assist after a multiple line of duty death. The experience is very emotionally draining on the team members and replacements may be required to prevent the team members from "burning out" as they render assistance.

The previous paragraphs on the issue of line-of-duty death certainly apply here. There are, however, some specific items which should be mentioned here since multiple line-of-duty deaths are so out of the ordinary.

First, it is important to treat each of the affected families in an individual manner. Never group all of the bereaved families together. Each family has different needs. They generally pull together and depend on family members, not outsiders, to assist them with their immediate needs. Putting all of the bereaved families together may stir unusually intense grief feelings which can get out of control. Also, if one family perceives (even if it is completely false) that the deceased person in another family caused the death of their loved one, there will be an explosive situation established if the families are put together. They may choose to get together on their own, but the department does not attempt to put the families together before, during or immediately after the funeral. Months later the families may choose to get together or they may be brought together for some special ceremony. By that time the facts of the loss of their loved ones will have been established and the individuals will have had time to deal with the early stages of grief. Each family should initially be given crisis intervention support. Later they may benefit from grief counseling when they are ready for it.

Significant other support services including debriefings and one-on-one support are essential for all of the families associated with the organization. Many times children's groups and teen groups have to be established to calm the fears generated in the children by the dramatic loss of personnel. This is a CISM team function since these services are not provided by any other program in the organization or the community.

The CISM team may have to assist the organization in buffering the media. Making statements approved by the organization can alleviate some of the distress caused by intense public interest.

The CISM team must remember the people who work in support functions for the organization. Such groups might include those who are clerks, secretaries, computer operators, supply personnel and many others. These people will feel the loss even if they were not regularly working around those who were killed.

Many who survived experience "survivor guilt" and may need brief counseling or even therapy to overcome the impact of the losses. Others may be angry that one person was killed and not another. This is called "survivor resentment" and is a natural, although uncomfortable, reaction to loss. If it becomes severe, those who suffer from it may also need support.

# 5. DISASTER OR MULTI-CASUALTY INCIDENT

The material in this section has special applicability for both emergency services and disaster workers on Community Response Teams (CRT).

Disasters, in one sense, are great learning opportunities. This is especially so if one hopes to learn how to manage the operations of the disaster. Being present at a disaster can teach a person a great deal about what to expect about those large scale incidents. In another sense, disasters are horrible learning environments. This is so if a person is trying to learn how to provide crisis intervention services and Critical Incident Stress Management. Sending inexperienced people to a disaster to learn the skills of crisis intervention can be a dangerous process which can cause harm to the people to be served and which often teaches all the wrong things. Disasters are so unusual and so overwhelming that unprepared people are shocked by the situation and have a hard time learning anything more than personal survival skills to help them to get through the experience.

Crisis intervention skills and CISM should be learned gradually in smaller events and then the experienced person is exposed to the disaster where he or she can apply their well developed skills. What is learned in a disaster is so different than what is experienced in day to day life that it is hard to apply the lessons from the disaster to what a person does every day in CISM.

The best way to approach disaster support services is to train, practice and pre-plan. Small events and drills gradually expose a person to the crisis concepts which can be employed in providing support at a disaster. The people in need of help are given the very best services by trained and experienced personnel and not mediocre services by personnel who are struggling to orient themselves to a highly unusual circumstance.

Here are some general CISM rules which can be useful in a disaster situation.

1. Avoid the urge to bring too many CISM personnel to the scene. Too many people might be exposed to the gore of the scene and may not be able to help others when they have been traumatized. Also, timing is a very important consideration. See the section of this chapter entitled "Too much too fast" for additional information.

2. Never interfere with people who are performing their jobs adequately. The display of emotions is less important as an indicator of how well a person is doing than the ability to continue to function.

3. Expect emotional suppression on the part of emergency operations personnel at the scene. It may take days before operations personnel have any reactions to the situation. The victims and the survivors will be more likely to have immediate reactions.

4. Never provide group service in the midst of the disaster. Group services of any kind are not utilized until the personnel have completed their work at the disaster and are being released from the scene.

5. Demobilizations are used after a disaster. These are then followed in a week to ten days with a full CISD.

6. Any decisions made by CISM teams which affect staffing or operations must be approved by operations field supervisors.

7. Those who provide disaster support services should always follow the same rules for good health that they are promoting for the personnel at the disaster. That includes proper food, rest and time away from the scene.

8. Support personnel should not be physically involved with the operations. To do so risks injuries, and distress so that they might not be able to support the operations personnel well enough.

9. CISM personnel work within the rules established by the operations authorities in the field.

10. Call for additional CISM teams as required.

Debriefings held after disasters may be a little unusual because the events were so intense that people develop many reactions to the experience. They may have ten or more "worst things" to share in the reaction phase. Often people remain silent in the debriefing until the very end and they bring up some item that has not been stated earlier by anyone. When they bring up the item they wish to discuss, the entire group may slip out of the teaching or re-entry phase and go back to the reaction phase. This can be worked through if the CISD team is tactful and confident. When the discussion dies down, a little more teaching from the team will help to bring the group back up to a positive ending of the debriefing.

## TOO MUCH TOO FAST

A string of disasters, which stretch back to the very beginnings of the Critical Incident Stress Management movement, have taught us many valuable lessons and CISM teams have generally been able to apply these lessons effectively to more recent disasters. Unfortunately, there are a few lessons which seem to be harder for some organizations, individuals and even for some CISM teams to learn and apply. In fact, it appears that certain organizations, individuals and teams practically ignore or refuse to accept some very important lessons from past disasters. Perhaps that occurs because they have some inexplicable need to be involved in the drama of the disaster or to be a part of history. Who really knows? Their motivations are unclear. For whatever reasons may apply, serious mistakes are being made in the application of psychological support services in disasters.

The problem is not the presence and use of CISM services. The appropriate application of support services is welcomed and important for the overall management of the disaster. The painful facts are, however, that there is a history of serious overreactions to almost any disaster from the support services point of view. Overreacting to a disaster is a dangerous course of action which deserves some rethinking and considerable alteration.

Timing of appropriate psychological support services appears to be among the most critical problems in disaster management. Despite very clear patterns which have been repeated numerous times in various disasters over the past decade, some people still respond to an internal, almost irresistible urge to dash immediately into a disaster scene with potentially disruptive CISM and other psychological support services. Rushing in ignores an important concept of crisis intervention. People have to be *ready* for help before it becomes useful to them. Providing help too early usually sets the stage for the rejection of the help and failure of the effort.

When emergency services people are involved in the response, rescue, fire suppression, triage, treatment, transport, body recovery and wrap up phases of a disaster they are rarely ready for psychological help. They are caught up in the operations and they suppress their emotions and focus on the cognitive processes which help them to complete their jobs. This is so even if the disaster operations last from several days to a week or more. It is only when they have moved away from the situation sufficiently that they begin to move from the cognitive processes to the emotional processes which might generate their stress reactions. Figure 13.2 based on real disasters and the appearance of significant stress symptoms within the emergency services groups, may help to demonstrate the necessity of providing help when the personnel are most ready for it.

The chart is based upon the experiences of the senior author (J.T.M.) in a variety of major disasters after which he led debriefings. The Amtrak wreck in Baltimore required two days of operations. Although some individuals

**FIGURE 13.2**

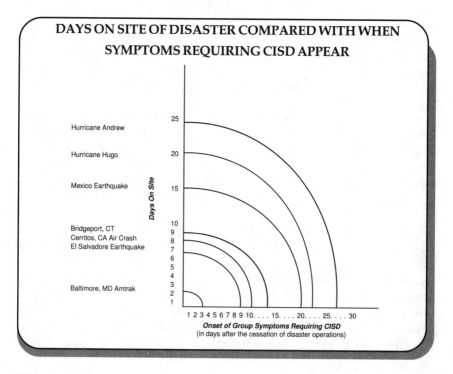

**DAYS ON SITE OF DISASTER COMPARED WITH WHEN SYMPTOMS REQUIRING CISD APPEAR**

Hurricane Andrew

Hurricane Hugo

Mexico Earthquake

Bridgeport, CT
Cerritos, CA Air Crash
El Salvadore Earthquake

Baltimore, MD Amtrak

*Days On Site*

1 2 3 4 5 6 7 8 9 10. . . . 15. . . . 20. . . . 25. . . . 30

*Onset of Group Symptoms Requiring CISD*
(in days after the cessation of disaster operations)

showed symptoms of stress earlier and needed assistance in the form of individual consultations, the majority of emergency personnel did not show stress symptoms significant enough to warrant a group debriefing until three to five days after the operation ended.

Seven days of on-scene services in El Salvador caused emergency workers to suppress their symptoms so much that they did not show up until seven to ten days after the end of the operation. Likewise, in Cerritos, California, after eight days of constant work at the plane crash site the symptoms remained relatively dormant until 10 to 14 days after the end of the incident. Figure 13.2 shows other examples from the author's experience.

Figure 13.2 should help CISM teams to understand that CISDs are usually not required right away. On-scene support services such as one-on-ones with obviously distressed *individuals*, advice giving to command staff, and direct assistance to distressed victims and bystanders at the scene are required. Disaster demobilizations or defusings may be required as units are being released from service. But hold off on the formal debriefings (CISD) until things settle down a little (usually a week to ten days in most disasters). Some disasters last so long that debriefings have to be delayed for six to eight weeks after the incident. There may be exceptions to this general rule under some extraordinary circumstances, but exceptions should be well thought out. Another related problem is asking people how they feel during the operations at the disaster site. Emergency personnel are in a highly defended cognitive state during operations and they resent anyone making efforts to make them concentrate on their emotions. In fact, taking them out of their cognitive defenses and opening up their emotions could literally jeopardize their safety and / or their lives.

In a recent plane crash disaster, some obviously poorly trained mental health professionals who were completely unfamiliar with basic CISM principles, were following emergency workers around with a survey attached to a clipboard on which they were checking off the appropriateness of emergency workers behaviors and whether or not they were showing emotions. They also tried repeatedly, and annoyingly, to get emergency personnel to open up and discuss their emotions related to the event while they were still involved in the most sensitive aspects of the disaster operation. This technique is totally inappropriate. It screams out a complete ignorance of basic crisis intervention principles and demonstrates an incredible insensitivity on the part of those who participated in this absurd procedure. It certainly points to a severe lack of understanding of both the jobs and personalities of emergency workers.

The actual victims of the disaster may respond earlier to their emotional reactions, so various types of help are usually accepted by them much earlier than by the emergency workers. Victims do not have to worry about "image armor" or the need to keep up a good front as the emergency services personnel do. They let go of their cognitive defenses earlier and are therefore ready for help much faster.

Disaster interventions are different than ordinary CISM services. They are a terrible learning experience for inexperienced or inadequately trained CISM team members or representatives of disaster relief agencies because they are so different from the usual CISM and psychological services. Disasters demand the most highly skilled CISM helpers, not the least experienced. Less than that standard opens up an enormous potential to create a situation which does far more harm than good. So, let us all be careful in the management of a disaster support service. Assess first, provide one-on-one help as might be necessary at the scene, and defusings for seriously impacted small groups or demobilizations for larger groups of less impacted disaster workers in a secure zone after personnel are released from the scene. Then carefully design CISD groups to follow up in a week to ten days (or more depending on the situation) after the conclusion of the incident. Some prolonged disasters may necessitate holding off CISD services for several weeks after the event concludes.

With a cautious, well-designed approach, we can assure that the right type and the right amount of help is given at the right time when people are most ready to receive it.

## LESSONS LEARNED

The last twenty-five years of CISM work has taught us many lessons. Mistakes have been made and corrections have occurred. The lessons of the past are important for us now and for the future of CISM services in general and CISD in particular. Some of the lessons learned about CISD have been written in other portions of this book. At the risk of a little repetition, but with the understanding that there is learning in repetition, some of the key lessons learned from the past will be presented here.

1. **CISD is not psychotherapy.** It was never developed to be a therapy nor a substitute for psychotherapy. It was designed to be a team facilitated, organized and structured group discussion of a traumatic event with three main goals: 1) mitigation of the impact of a traumatic event and 2)

acceleration of normal recovery processes in non-pathological populations who are having generally normal reactions to abnormal events 3) identification of those who may need additional assistance. The very general descriptions in the Table 13.1 indicate the main differences between psychotherapy and CISD.

2. **CISD is a team approach.** The most effective approach to the facilitated group process of CISD is a team approach. In the emergency services, corrections facilities, air line industries, hospitals, military organizations, railroads and other front line operations or in companies with large stable work forces, teams made up of mental health professionals *and* peer support personnel drawn from those populations are always utilized. In small companies and community groups which are not associated with emergency operations, a team of two or three mental health professionals are more likely to be the intervention team. It has been found that peers drawn from the same professions are best. That is, police serve police best and nurses serve nurses best. Likewise, every emergency profession gains the best benefits from the CISD when they are served by peers from their own profession.

3. **CISD is more helpful when applied within a brief time after the traumatic event.** In most cases, the debriefing is *ideal* when it is offered within 24-72 hours of the incident. In the majority of situations, a debriefing will lose its effectiveness after four to eight weeks depending on the intensity of the event. It may, however, be provided later and will still be beneficial even several weeks after an event. The more powerful the situation, the more likelihood there is that a CISD will have a positive effect.

There is a caution, however, and that is, if the CISD is offered a very long time after the event, such as more than two months later, it may actually be counterproductive. It could open up the psychological wounds and rip down defensive barriers which the people need to maintain themselves in their work environment. Significantly delayed interventions should be carefully planned out and all possible consequences should be thought of before such interventions are initiated. In some cases of significant delay, the CISD may not be chosen as one of the interventions to be utilized. In other cases it is used because the group has a need to discuss an old traumatic event that has not been previously discussed among the group members.

In some very rare cases it has been necessary to provide debriefings several years after a traumatic incident. This has been done, with considerable success, in circumstances in which no help had been provided to the group at the time of or since the incident. The events stand out as highly traumatizing to the group members and are not easily forgotten. Such events tower over all of the events in the history of the organization. In these situations, CISD alone is typically not effective. One-on-ones, neuro-cognitive or other forms of therapy such as Eye Movement Desensitization and Reprocessing, education programs, significant other support and administrative education and support programs are necessary.

4. **CISDs should be short in length.** The CISD process has been designed to be completed in approximately 2 to 3 hours. It may be done more rapidly when the group is small. It may take a little longer when the group number is higher or when an incident is particularly distressing. It is extremely rare, however, for a CISD to last longer than three hours. Avoid having debriefings which last four or more hours. Marathon CISD sessions indicate one or more of the following problems:

- The incident is extremely powerful.

- The team is allowing too much to be said in the fact and thought phases.

- The team is very inexperienced.

- The team leadership is poor.

- The team is unfamiliar with the CISD process.

5. **Probing is out of place in CISD.** Debriefing teams have to be satisfied with the information they are given by the participants in a debriefing. Every person in the debriefing has a right to refuse to participate actively in the process if they so choose. It is especially important that a CISD team never probe to gain personal information about a person in the debriefing.

6. **Never embarrass a participant in a CISD.** Drawing attention to an individual participant in a debriefing is inappropriate. Avoid mentioning the fact that they are weeping, wringing their hands or showing emotions in any way. Do not pass boxes of tissues around to the distressed participants. Also avoid touching distressed people during the debriefing. Remember emergency personnel have a high need for control and anything which embarrasses them will threaten that control and cause them to react negatively.

**TABLE 13.1**

## CONTRAST OF PSYCHOTHERAPY AND CISD

| *Psychotherapy* | *CISD* |
|---|---|
| Therapeutic model: intervention for an established problem to change defense mechanisms and initiate life style changes or relationship changes | Crisis Intervention model: stabilization, mobilization of resources, normalization, restoration of function |
| Generally long term (12 or more sessions) | Very short term (3-8 total contacts, one of which is a CISD) |
| Emphasis on individual needs | Group emphasis |
| Treatment | Prevention |
| May require change in defenses | Reinforces effective defenses |
| Must deal with transference issues | Transference minimal due to brevity of contacts |
| Treatment continues until problems resolve and symptoms recede or disappear | Referral is made if symptoms persist or worsen |
| An extensive amount of therapy may be required in cases of significant psychopathology | No attempt is made to treat those with significant psychopathology, instead referrals are made to mental health professionals |
| Therapist driven | Peer driven, mental health guidance |
| Skilled therapist(s) | Peer / mental health team |

7. **Maintain the confidentiality of CISDs.** Any violation or perceived violation of the confidentiality of a debriefing threatens the integrity of the CISM team and may cause great harm to the debriefing process itself.

8. **Avoid giving too much advice in CISDs.** The debriefing has been designed to provide the opportunity for ventilation. It is not an opportunity for team members to wax eloquent about their favorite advice. The team obviously needs to give some helpful advice about stress management, but they should not overdo this advice giving.

9. **Never tell personal "war stories."** Team members who tell their own stories in the CISD harm the process by detracting from the incident which is being discussed by the group. "War stories" take the focus off the incident to be discussed and place it instead on the CISD team members.

10. **The CISD team should quiet down in the reaction phase and let the participants talk more.** The CISD team is most active in the introduction, teaching and re-entry phases. The participants, on the other hand, are usually very active in the fact, thought, reaction and symptoms phases. Allow silences to work for very brief periods of time (ten seconds in most cases). If the silence goes on too long, it may be necessary for one of the team members to ask the question again or to encourage someone to speak if that person wants to or looks like they do.

11. **An education session is NEVER a substitute for a debriefing. Although stress education is very important, it can never be used as a** substitute for a debriefing. To do so would deprive the participants of the opportunity to vent their emotions and find out from one another the details of the incident which might help them to resolve the pain they may be experiencing.

12. **There is always a need for follow-up after a CISD.** Sometimes a brief follow-up meeting (**not** another debriefing) is held about a week after the debriefing. People may be asked how it has been since the debriefing has taken place and if they are still having any left over reactions which need to be discussed. Whatever the group members need to discuss is worked through and information which might help them is presented.

Most of the follow-up work is provided in one-on-one sessions. It is important that peer support personnel obtain peer counselor training so that they may be more effective in their individual follow up sessions.

224

# SYMBOLIC DEBRIEFING

On occasion, a debriefing for a single incident will trigger many old memories of past traumatic events. The discussion in the debriefing makes an unexpected shift into a broad range of old events. The CISD team members are usually surprised by the shift from the current event to the old events. It occurs naturally.

The shift from the present event to the older ones is produced because there is something which triggers the old memories. Sometimes the events are very similar, or similar feelings exist in the new event as were present in the old ones. Occasionally the five senses play a role in stimulating the old memories. The current event represents or "symbolizes" the older ones.

To manage a "Symbolic Debriefing" the CISM team must first recognize the possibility of such an occurrence. The possibility is always present. The team needs to listen carefully as the old events start showing up in the debriefing. They need to see how the old and new events are linked. The CISD team, once it becomes aware of the shift, makes one or two gentle attempts to reintroduce the current event. An example of an attempt to reintroduce the current issue would be, "We can see how this situation reminds you of many past events and we appreciate you bringing that out. The connections you make with the past are important, but we would like to ask another question about this current situation." Then a question pertinent to the current event is brought out. If the discussion drifts off to old events again it may be a signal that the old painful experiences have never been worked out and need to be discussed. Efforts to recover the current event are stopped and the team pays close attention to whatever the group discusses.

If the old events have no significant emotional power and the group just seems to be avoiding the current, more painful incident, the drift into old topics is resisted and the group is kept on track in the current event. Under those circumstances, the drift away may be a smoke screen to avoid the pain of the current event.

If the symbolic debriefing is progressing and many old events are being brought in, the CISD team must listen carefully and attempt to find any common themes. These themes will be taught in the teaching phase as the team attempts to tie all the loose ends up and make sense out of the various events which have been discussed. The CISD team has to be flexible in the number and types of questions it asks. The scatter in the events requires such flexibility. A wide range of questions also assures that the old and new events will be properly connected so that at the end of the symbolic debriefing the issues are more resolved for the participants.

## SUMMARY

This chapter presented an overview of some of the core advanced concepts and issues in the CISM field. A time line for CISM interventions was presented along with information on the lessons learned from past CISDs. Considerable space was allocated to a discussion of complex situations and debriefings. Included in this discussion was information on disaster work, multiple line of-duty-deaths, symbolic debriefings and multiple incident debriefings.

It was emphasized that no individuals or team members should attempt to employ these advanced techniques without proper training in Advanced CISM concepts. Newly organized teams in particular are cautioned not to attempt to manage situations which are well beyond their knowledge and experience because it is possible that they might do some harm to the people they are trying to help.

# Chapter 14

## MASS DISASTER CISD INTERVENTIONS AND COMMUNITY RESPONSE TEAMS

Within recent years there has been much discussion of the applicability of the CISD model, as originally developed and promulgated by Mitchell and others, to situations other than the acute critical incident variation of traumatization. Admittedly, the CISD as originally formulated was, indeed, designed to mitigate posttraumatic stress as caused by the acute critical incidents most commonly encountered by emergency service personnel. Herman (1992) and others have described a variation of PTSD referred to as "complex" PTSD. The "complex" variant PTSD is engendered by prolonged chronic traumatization and /or acutely chronic repeated traumatization. With "complex" PTSD in mind, a "mass disaster" CISD model (Everly and Mitchell, 1992) was derived from the original CISD model (Mitchell, 1983).

## DEVELOPMENT

For years, experienced crisis interventionists have utilized the CISD model as originally formulated by Mitchell (1983) to successfully mitigate what has been referred to as "complex" PTSD. A few slight alterations were required to render the original protocol usable.

Recent experiences with Hurricane Iniki, Hurricane Andrew, the Yugoslavian conflict, the on-going Middle East turmoil and finally the interventions in Somalia convinced the authors to formalize the alteration in the original CISD model to create a "mass disaster" CISD model designed to mitigate "complex" PTSD, whether it be engendered by combat, prolonged civil unrest, mass disasters or prolonged community response operations. This model could prove useful in combatting "burnout" or cumulative stress as well.

# COMPARING ACUTE CISD MODEL TO THE MASS DISASTER MODEL

Perhaps the easiest way to introduce the mass disaster CISD model is by way of comparison. Table 14.1 lists the stages of the original acute critical incident CISD model (Mitchell, 1983, 1988). Table 14.2 introduces the "mass disaster" CISD model (Everly and Mitchell, 1992).

Close scrutiny reveals that the mass disaster variation of the CISD places slightly more emphasis on direct ventilation of emotions (stage 4) and also places great emphasis on the importance of the constructive aspects of the experience (stage 5) with the goal being to aim toward rebuilding and "mov-

## TABLE 14.1

| STAGES OF CISD | | |
|---|---|---|
| Stage 1 | Introduction | To introduce intervention team members, explain process, set expectations |
| Stage 2 | Fact | To describe traumatic event from each participant's perspective on a cognitive level |
| Stage 3 | Thought | To allow participant's to describe cognitive reactions and to transition to emotional reactions |
| Stage 4 | Reaction | To identify the most traumatic aspect of the event for the participants |
| Stage 5 | Symptom | To identify personal symptoms of distress and transition back to cognitive level |
| Stage 6 | Teaching | To educate as to normal reactions and adaptive coping mechanisms. (i.e., stress managment) Provide a cognitive anchor |
| Stage 7 | Re-Entry | To clarify ambiguities and prepare for termination |

**TABLE 14.2**

## THE MASS DISASTER / COMMUNITY RESPONSE
## VARIATION OF CISD

| | | |
|---|---|---|
| Stage 1 | Introduction | To introduce intervention team members, explain process, set expectations |
| Stage 2 | Fact | To have each participant describe the nature of their participaion, from a cognitive perspective |
| Stage 3 | Thought Reaction | To solicit cognitive response to: "What aspect held the most negative impact?" or "What aspect was the worst for you?" Then, transition from cognitive to emotional processing |
| Stage 4 | Emotional Reaction | Given the response to stage 3, to solicit emotional reactions or consequences |
| Stage 5 | Reframing | To transition from emotional domain back to cognitive. "What lessons could be learned from this experience?" and "What is something positive that you will take away from this experience?" |
| Stage 6 | Teaching | To educate as to normal reactions and teach basic stress management if applicable |
| Stage 7 | Re-Entry | To summarize experience with emphasis on positive or learning aspects |

ing on" emotionally. In situations where there are no lessons to be learned (hard to believe!) or there is nothing constructive or positive, emphasis can be placed upon shear survival, or the like. Remember, survival itself is often an accomplishment. Obviously different situations will dictate different consideration.

# USES OF MASS DISASTER CISD MODEL

The mass disaster CISD model was designed to be utilized with disaster work crews who have been exposed to multiple traumatic incidents during a disaster. It has also been developed to assist in situations in which disaster workers have experienced work in numerous disasters over time or a single prolonged exposure to one disaster. First-response emergency personnel and Red Cross disaster workers have effectively employed the mass disaster model. The use of the mass disaster CISD model assumes that several important factors have been considered. They are:

- *Work crews have been released from their duties and have been returned to their home bases for rest.*

- *Personnel have been "processed out."* That is, they are not expected to return to that particular disaster for at least one week and preferably not for two to three weeks.

- *They have had time to reconnect with their families and friends.* If this has not occurred, workers will frequently resist any efforts to assist them by means of debriefings or other support services.

# CONDUCTING A MASS DISASTER CISD

The Mass Disaster CISD is conducted in much the same manner as a debriefing for emergency personnel who have experienced a severe but much smaller incident in the course of their normal work. There are, however, some significant differences. The main differences show up in the third, fourth and fifth phases of the debriefing. In fact, the names of the phases have been changed to accommodate the differences in the technique (see Tables 14.1 and 14.2).

In phase number 3, for example, the name of the phase has been changed from the *"thought"* phase (as it is applied to emergency personnel such as paramedics, fire fighters and police officers) to the *"thought reaction"* phase. To assist the group in the transition from the cognitive aspects of an experience to the emotional aspects, the emphasis shifts from a nonspecific question such as "What was your first thought after you got off the auto pilot mode?" to a more direct question such as, "What aspect held the most negative impact for you?"

It is likely that the CISM team will hear more emotionally laden content in this type of debriefing than would ordinarily surface in a debriefing of an emergency services unit. Sometimes the participants are so distraught that they describe their thoughts during the fact phase. If the participants join the two phases, accept it and move on with the emotional reaction phase.

The fourth phase asks very direct questions about the emotional aspects of the situation. For example, it may be asked "What emotional reactions did you experience?" Unlike the debriefings held for police, fire and emergency medical persons in which the discussion of emotions is somewhat covert, disaster workers are asked direct questions about their feelings and reactions to facilitate catharsis.

The "reframing" phase departs from the discussion of symptoms which is traditional in the police, fire and medical debriefings. Instead the participants in the group are asked about what they have learned from the experience. A common question in this phase is, "What lessons have you learned from this experience?" Another common question is, "What is something positive you will take away from this experience?" or "At what moment were you most proud of your involvement?"

The CISM team members play a very active role in attempting to get the participants to view their experience in a positive light. For example, if a person in the group was feeling guilty or cowardly because they ran from the danger while others were being killed or injured, the CISM team helps that person to see how wise it was to save himself in order to be helpful to those who were injured. The whole idea behind reframing is to find a positive in the midst of the chaos and negatives. Again the CISM team efforts are more overt in this form of debriefing than they are in the emergency services debriefing.

The other phases of the debriefing remain essentially the same.

# COMMUNITY RESPONSE TEAMS

Many communities have utilized emergency-based CISM teams to render assistance to community groups which have been seriously traumatized. Other communities are formulating independent teams which only respond to community situations involving citizens but not to emergency organizations.

The needs and responses of community groups will be considerably different than the needs and responses of emergency organizations so some adaptations have to be made to assist the community groups.

It is not always necessary to apply debriefing services to the community. Other interventions will work (perhaps even better than debriefings).

When there are many hundreds of people in a community who have been traumatized, providing full debriefing for all of them is not only a difficult task, it may be a totally unnecessary or counterproductive approach.

Instead of trying to organize time-consuming and complex debriefings for each group or subgroup in a community, it would be more efficient to bring large groups of people together in a meeting facility and present a brief class on traumatic stress and its effects in the community. Information could be given and questions answered. Informative handouts could be distributed. The usual time frame for such an approach is one to one and one half hours. Another useful tactic with non-emergency operations personnel is the Crisis Management Briefing (CMB). The CMB is a large group process in which the employees of a large firm or the citizens from a community are brought together and given roughly a forty-five minute informational program on the crisis situation and the efforts that are being made to resolve that crisis. The Crisis Management Briefing is similar to the demobilization provided for emergency personnel. The CMB is more interactive, however, and questions and comments from the participants are encouraged. The CMB opens up a brief discussion of the experience of the traumatic situation and provides information, guidance and instructions to the participants. It has been very effective in disaster situations involving large numbers of people. The tactic is so important that there is an entire chapter on it in this book.

Those groups which still need special help can be given debriefings conducted by the Community Response Team (CRT). Individuals can also be identified who would benefit from individual brief counseling or referrals for psychotherapy.

Community Response Teams need to ensure that whatever services are provided are:

- Appropriate

- Adapted to the needs of the group

- Carefully coordinated with local resources

- Age-appropriate

- Organized around a follow-up or referral system

- Provided quickly

- Provided with planned follow-up services

# SUMMARY

Critical Incident Stress Debriefing (CISD) and its parallel intervention, posttraumatic stress defusing, are interventions designed by one of the authors (Mitchell, 1983; 1988a; 1988b; 1991) specifically for the prevention of posttraumatic stress and PTSD among high-risk occupational groups such as fire fighters, emergency medical personnel, law enforcement personnel, public safety, nurses, dispatch personnel and disaster and combat personnel. The recently modified CISD appears especially suited for mass disasters and community response applications. It is clear that as trauma preparedness training expands, the CISD model will find its way into ever new and exciting applications. Minor alterations in the CISD process may need to be made to maximize its effectiveness in certain situations. In most cases, the model stays the same but the *prompts* for the various phases of the CISD model are changed. Nevertheless, these modifications are best made, when necessary, by those highly trained in the fundamentals of CISM and the specific group process of CISD as originally designed and field tested for more than a decade.

# Chapter 15

## THE ROLE OF PASTORAL CRISIS INTERVENTION IN DISASTERS, TERRORISM, VIOLENCE, AND OTHER COMMUNITY CRISES

Violence, terrorism, disasters, and even certain types of natural loss can send shock waves through a community, jeopardizing the psychological foundations of that community. It is well known that a common goal of terrorist activities is to threaten the sense of psychological cohesion within a community, but community group cohesion may be threatened by accidents, violence, and natural disasters as well.

It has been commonly observed that in times of crisis and disaster, many individuals seek out religious or spiritual leaders. Individuals in times of crisis will sometimes gather at houses of worship, or locations of religious or spiritual significance. This chapter examines one potential formalized role for pastoral crisis intervention in community crisis and disaster response.

## PASTORAL CRISIS INTERVENTION DEFINED

Given the apparent natural affinity that many individuals show for faith-based support, guidance, and/or reassurance, it is interesting, indeed, to note historically the conspicuous omission of faith-based resources as part of a "formalized" community-wide crisis intervention and disaster response. Such services have traditionally been supplied within the context

From the International Journal of Emergency Mental Health. Reprinted with permission, Chevron Publishing Company.

of chaplaincy services to well-circumscribed groups, but have usually lacked breadth in large-scale community crises. Pastoral counseling services have certainly been used in the wake of community crises and disasters, but these are, by definition, "counseling services" and not "crisis intervention." As noted by Everly (1999a, 1999b, 2000; Everly & Mitchell, 1999) crisis intervention is very different compared with counseling and psychotherapy. As described by Everly (1999b), crisis intervention may be considered a form of psychological "first-aid." The goals of crisis intervention are to: 1) stabilize signs and symptoms of distress and dysfunction, 2) mitigate signs and

**TABLE 15.1**

### ACTIVE MECHANISMS OF CRISIS INTERVENTION (FROM EVERLY, 2000)

#### Traditional Mechanisms:

Early Intervention                     Cathartic Ventilation
Social Support                           Problem-Solving
               Cognitive Reinterpretation

#### Potential Mechanisms Unique to Pastoral Crisis Intervention:

Scriptural Education, Insight, Reinterpretation
Individual and Conjoint Prayer
Belief in Intercessory Prayer
Unifying and Explanatory Worldviews
Ventilative Confession
Faith-Based Social Support Systems
Rituals and Sacraments
Belief in Divine Intervention/Forgiveness
Belief in a Life after Death
Unique Ethos of the Pastoral Crisis Interventionist
Uniquely Confidential/Privileged Communications

Note: Depending upon the faith, more or less of these mechanisms may be active.

---

NOTE: *In the present context, the term community shall be used to refer to any group of individuals who share, or are aggregated around, political, geographic, ethnic, cultural, racial, and/or religious boundaries.*

symptoms of distress and dysfunction, 3) facilitate a return to adaptive functioning, or 4) seek continued care, typically a higher level of care.

Everly (2000) has offered the term "pastoral crisis intervention" as the functional integration of any and all religious, spiritual, and pastoral resources with the assessment and intervention technologies typically thought of as crisis intervention. Thus, pastoral crisis intervention may be seen as a "value added" form of crisis intervention. Table 15.1 enumerates the active ingredients in crisis intervention including pastoral crisis intervention.

The reader will note the considerable degree of "value added" by the addition of the potential mechanisms of pastoral crisis intervention. It is important, however, that the pastoral crisis interventionist views the

**TABLE 15.2**

### INDICATIONS FOR THE UTILIZATION OF THE PASTORAL CRISIS INTERVENTION MECHANISMS

1.  Receptive Expectations, i.e., the expectation/desire on the part of the person(s) in crisis for prayer, scriptural guidance, provision of sacraments, rituals, etc.

2.  Receptive State of Mind, i.e., while not specifically "expecting" such interventions, the person(s) in crisis is "open," or psychologically receptive, to pastoral intervention. It is important that argumentation, or debate, be avoided in the acute crisis state. Such actions tend to make the interventionist part of the "problem" not part of the "solution."

3.  Pastoral crisis intervention can, obviously, be employed with not only primary victims of crisis, but with family members, emergency response personnel, observers, etc., but the same guidelines listed above would be applicable.

effectiveness of the pastoral mechanisms as resting upon a foundation of effective communication skills and differential recognition of patterns of acute stress, as well as the consideration of the more traditional active ingredients of crisis intervention as enumerated in Table 15.1. Table 15.2 enumerates the indications for a more pastoral approach to crisis intervention.

Thus far, pastoral crisis intervention appears to represent considerable added utility when used at the appropriate time and place, with the appropriate individual(s). Pastoral crisis intervention obviously requires significant insight and skill to affect in such a manner as to achieve a positive outcome. It is not without its pitfalls. Table 15.3 enumerates potential problems associated with the application of pastoral crisis intervention.

The preceding section has attempted to review and expand the definition of pastoral crisis intervention as originally proposed by Everly (2000). As defined, pastoral crisis intervention represents a potentially powerful addition to traditional community crisis intervention services. The preceding section has also offered recommendations for the use of pastoral crisis intervention as well as potential concerns associated with its implementation. The next section offers a pastoral crisis intervention within an overarching public health perspective.

# A PUBLIC HEALTH MODEL OF PASTORAL CRISIS INTERVENTION

One goal of this chapter is to encourage the integration of pastoral crisis intervention as a formalized resource within a larger community crisis intervention/emergency mental health model. Figure 15.1 offers one model of the form in which such an integration may be functionally structured. As noted in Figure 15.1, effective use of pastoral crisis intervention as a general community resource is predicated upon integration with traditional community mental health resources.

Subsequent to a community traumatic event, some individuals will seek support directly from ministers, pastors, chaplains, even pastoral counselors, and other spiritual leaders. Many of these individuals will be in need of, and prosper from, acute pastoral crisis intervention services as described above (1) or pastoral counseling services (2) Some, however, will be in greater need of traditional mental health assessment and therapeutic intervention. In cases such as these, it is imperative that the pastoral crisis interventionist be trained in psychological triage and referral to other, more appropriate community resources (3) Subsequent to a traumatic event, there will be other individuals who will seek out or be referred to traditional crisis and therapeutic mental health services (4). Most will benefit from access to those services. However, there will be some who will experience a "crisis of faith" and may derive greater benefit from a cross referral from the community mental health agency to a pastoral crisis intervention facility (5) (keeping in mind that pastoral crisis intervention is different from pastoral counseling).

**TABLE 15.3**

**POTENTIAL PROBLEMS IN THE APPLICATION
OF PASTORAL CRISIS INTERVENTION**

1. Failure to "listen" to the secular needs of the person in crisis.
2. Lack of a structured intervention plan, or approach, to the person in crisis.
3. Arguing or debating spiritual/theological issues with the person in acute crisis.
4. Attempting to explain spiritually/theologically "why" a trauma occurred.
5. Preaching or praying with the "unreceptive" individual.
6. Attempting to "convert" the unreceptive individual.
7. Difficulty in the differentiation of clinical signs/symptoms, for example:
   a. Major depression vs. grief reaction
   b. Brief psychotic reaction vs. intrusive ideation
   c. Brief psychotic reaction vs. dissociation
   d. Dissociation vs. intrusive ideation
   e. State dependent learning sequela vs. personality disorder
   f. Acute transitory cognitive impairment vs. severe incapacitation
   g. Failure to detect suicidal or homicidal cues
   h. Lack of familiarity with guidelines for psychological triage (especially predictors of posttraumatic stress disorder) and referral
   i. Major depression vs. acute dysphoria
   j. Failure to refer for mental health services when indicated.

FIGURE 15.1

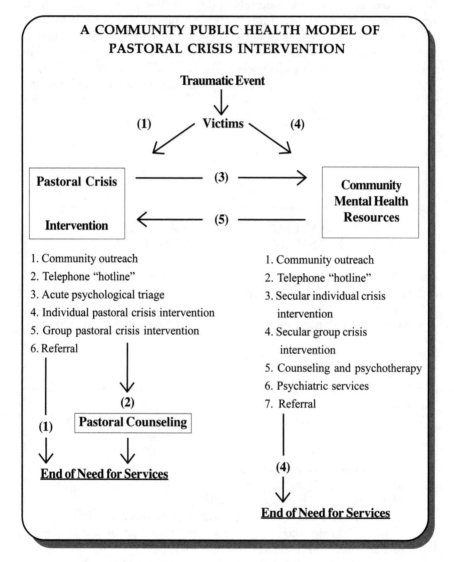

Crisis intervention, whether it be from the traditional perspective or the pastoral, will be enhanced when a community outreach component is provided. Visibility in the eyes of the community may be the greatest predictor of service utilization.

## SUMMARY

Pastoral crisis intervention is not merely crisis intervention services performed by those possessing a spiritual or religious orientation. Pastoral crisis intervention is not pastoral counseling. As crisis intervention is to psychotherapy, pastoral crisis intervention is to pastoral counseling. As described in Figure 15.1, pastoral crisis intervention is the functional integration of pastoral activities with traditional crisis intervention/ emergency mental health services. It represents a rich resource in times of human distress and, as such, should be part of every community mental health/crisis intervention program.

# Appendix A

## COMPONENTS OF AN EMERGENCY SERVICES CRITICAL INCIDENT STRESS MANAGEMENT TEAM

### INTRODUCTION

In this appendix, we will discuss the specific components of a CISM team developed for use specifically with emergency service workers and public safety personnel. In reading this appendix it is important to keep in mind that the comments are made in the context of an emergency services CISM team. Having read this book, some of this material may be redundant but the decision was made to utilize this format so as to provide a complete, discrete compendium within this appendix. Adaptations of much of the material in this appendix can be useful to people in the military, business or industrial settings as well as school systems, non-emergency organizations and communities. The reader should feel free to utilize and adapt the aspects of this material that are most useful to them in the development of their own CISM teams.

Crisis Response Teams (CRT) which serve industrial and commercial settings as well as community groups may need to be structured differently than CISM teams that serve predominantly emergency personnel. CRTs may or may not use "Peer Support" personnel. The use of peers may depend on the existence of a large and stable work force from which to choose peers. CRTs may rely more on mental health professionals and medical staffs than the use of peers. They may also serve only small designated populations such as companies, schools and communities but not the emergency services organizations. Although the teams may be structured differently, the interventions in the field of CISM usually follow the same models that have been described in this text for use with emergency personnel. The crisis intervention models of CISM stay the same. What changes are the prompts that are used to start or maintain the discussions of the traumatic events.

Under certain circumstances, however, some modifications to the intervention strategies may be necessary to suit the needs of particular industrial, commercial or community groups. Any alterations should have specific, supportable rationales and should not be arbitrary.

# OVERVIEW

In most cases, a CISM team is a voluntary (unpaid) partnership between various individuals and groups who work together to achieve common goals — lessening the impact of traumatic stress on emergency personnel, accelerating the recovery from stressful events and the enhancement of the psychological health of the emergency worker. The motivation for their service is a sense of dedication and commitment to people in the helping professions who give so much of themselves to their communities.

Most teams are multi-agency and multi-jurisdictional. They provide services to any emergency personnel who need them. Teams may also serve community groups under certain circumstances or on a case by case basis.

A CISM team is made up of two distinct, but interrelated, groups of members who rely upon one another's expertise to prevent critical incident stress, to reduce it when it is not preventable and to hasten the recovery from it when it occurs. The two groups of members are:

• Professional support personnel

• Peer support personnel

Professional support staff include mental health professionals and clergy personnel. Mental health professionals and clergy have somewhat different roles which will be described later in this appendix. Peer support personnel are police officers, fire fighters, nurses, paramedics, emergency medical technicians, dispatchers, physicians and other primary operations personnel. (see Table A.1)

CISM teams are peer oriented crisis intervention programs that depend on guidance and assistance from mental health professionals. Their main function is to attempt to stabilize chaotic and highly stressful situations before those events can cause damaging stress reactions in emergency personnel. Prevention is far more heavily emphasized than treatment.

There have been attempts to establish critical incident support services for emergency service workers without incorporating all of the essential elements of a Critical Incident Stress Management team. For example, some

**TABLE A.1**

## MEMBERS OF AN EMERGENCY SERVICES CISD TEAM

Professional Support Personnel

1.  Mental health professionals
2.  Clergy

Peer Support Personnel

1.  Firefighters
2.  Police officers
3.  Paramedics
4.  Emergency medical technicians
5.  Nurses, especially critical care and emergency
6.  Dispatch personnel
7.  Search and Rescue personnel
8.  Park Service rangers
9.  Corrections officers
10. Ski patrol
11. Search dog team members
12. Wildland firefighters
13. Disaster workers
14. Professional lifeguard services
15. Physicians
16. Other first response personnel

have tried to establish a stress team without appropriate mental health personnel. Others have tried to develop a team without peers. We believe both alternatives are misdirected. If mental health consultation and guidance are absent, peer support personnel could easily miss significant psychological problems. If peers are not included on the team the emergency workers involved in an incident may suffer long delays in obtaining support services from mental health personnel. In effect, peers may serve a valuable role in the early recognition of unusual or dysfunctional behavior in other peers in the emergency organization. In addition, mental health professionals are frequently resisted by emergency personnel and they may often have difficulties in entering into effective helping relationships with the emergency personnel whose jobs may be "foreign" to them. Peer team members may form a psychological bridge from the emergency service worker to the mental health professional.

Interventions from CISM teams are short term. Anyone who does not show signs of improvement within three to five contacts (maximum 8 contacts) is referred to a mental health professional by the CISM team. The primary functions of a CISM team do not include long term counseling or psychotherapy. Interventions may have therapeutic elements but they are not a substitute for psychotherapy.

# TYPICAL TEAM STRUCTURE

## Lead Agency

CISM teams have a lead agency (police, fire, EMS, hospital, etc.) which serves as an umbrella organization under which the CISM team organizes itself and, at least in its early stages, functions. The lead agency establishes the environment in which the CISM team can be developed and supported. The services of the lead agency may vary somewhat from jurisdiction to jurisdiction and may change as the team evolves. In some cases, the lead agency dissolves its role as the team develops and the steering committee takes over the management of the team. This is especially so when a community decides to have a "combined emergency services steering committee or board of directors" that takes on the general management of the team. In other words, instead of a single lead agency, all of the participating agencies share in the responsibility of team management. There are, however some basic functions of a lead agency regardless of how it is structured. They are:

- Provision of funding or arrangements for the funding of initial team development

- Development of a steering committee or board of directors for the CISM team

- Staffing for meetings during the developmental stages

- Establishment of a team membership committee

- Coordination of initial (basic) team training

- Assistance in recruiting team membership

- Assistance in locating appropriate team leadership

- Provision of general support for the activities of the CISM team

- Assistance in developing research and evaluation methods as well as quality assurance

- Collection of data for statistical reports and research

- Provision of office space when necessary

- Provision of necessary equipment and supplies (phone, communications, stationery, etc.) to adequately manage the team

- Provision of release time for staff members to manage the team

- Arrangement of continuing education for team members

- Adoption and promulgation of rules and policies and procedures for team operation

- Maintenance of an up-to-date call-out list of all team members and a background file on each team member

# Team Coordinator

Each team needs at least one coordinator who is in charge of the day-to-day operations of the team. The best people to place in the coordinator positions are members of one or more of the emergency organizations. Mental health professionals and chaplains are usually less knowledgeable of the inner workings of the first response organizations. They are also not present in the stations, squad rooms, break rooms and other common gathering places for emergency personnel. Therefore, they seldom hear about the tough incidents early enough to maximize intervention effectiveness.

Teams should build in redundancy. That is, they should have back-ups for coordinators. One coordinator, no matter how efficient, can be overwhelmed from time to time and will not work as effectively. Besides, people need to be able to carry out life's other responsibilities. When there is a family gathering or a vacation, or even illness, someone must carry on the coordination functions for the team. Missed calls or delays in responding to the needs of distressed emergency personnel deteriorates trust and incapacitates a CISM team.

Some CISM teams have different coordinators for each of the organizations served by the team. For example, there may be two coordinators for police, two for fire, two for emergency medical services and two for nursing. Almost any combination or number of coordinators is fine as long as the tasks of team coordination are properly managed. The tasks to be handled by coordinators are:

- General managing of the CISM team

- Evaluating the need to dispatch a team or to provide any other services once a call has been received

- Receiving the call from the dispatcher and then calling the necessary team members to respond to the situation

- Assisting in developing team membership

- Representing the team at emergency and community meetings

- Assisting in the selection of appropriate members for the team

- Providing opportunities for continuing education of the team

- Coordinating with the clinical director to assure appropriate support services

- Developing positive relationships with agency administrations, Red Cross and other community groups

- Handling requests from community groups for assistance and dispatching team members if those requests are appropriate for team intervention

- Soliciting support from the emergency services organizations

- Assisting in the writing of the team policies and procedures

- Co-leading team meetings with the clinical director

- Assuring that distressed debriefers are given appropriate help

- Establishing a peer review board to correct problems on the team

- Sponsoring periodic team meetings

- Developing a program of quality assurance for the team

- Maintaining any records of team activities

- Maintaining a referral list

- Arranging for workshops, seminars and for lectures to enhance team education

- Teaching some of the stress management programs to emergency personnel

- Keeping up-to-date on the most current research, findings and theories of emergency services stress, occupational stress, critical incident stress, Posttraumatic Stress Disorder and related topics

- Maintaining association with national and international organizations which foster critical incident stress work

- Maintaining up-to-date call-out list of all team members

# Clinical Director

Teams, as previously mentioned, must have mental health professionals who serve them. Mental health professionals include psychologists, social workers, psychiatrists, psychiatric nurses and certified mental health counselors. Although it is not necessary to have different types of mental health professionals on a team (social workers, psychologists, etc.), it is usually necessary to have more than one mental health professional on a team in order to avoid overworking that one professional. One of those mental health professionals is chosen as the clinical director. The clinical director provides oversight to the intervention activities of the team and ensures that the right kind of service is provided and that all team members work within the limits of their training and experience. The clinical director performs the following tasks:

- Works closely with the team coordinator to assure proper team performance and quality assurance

- Represents the CISM team before the public and before the organizations the team serves

- Monitors the debriefings provided and offers suggestions for future debriefings and suggestions regarding follow up services

- Assists the coordinator in developing appropriate CISM team continuing education

- Provides some of the continuing education training for the team

- Assists the coordinator and team committees in developing written policies and procedures for the team

- Assists the team in developing a cross familiarization program for mental health professionals so that they might observe emergency personnel in action

- Assists in the selection of team members

- Participates in the peer review board to correct team problems

- Conducts periodic reviews of team records and services

- Assists the coordinator in maintaining a comprehensive list of referral sources

- Ensures that follow-up services are provided to those in need

- Offers clinical guidance to coordinator and team members

Note: The issue of insurance is one that is less than clear at this point in time. Nevertheless, it is highly recommended that all mental health members of the CISD team carry malpractice insurance.

## Team Liason

Every team has some business, correspondence and other administrative responsibilities. Every team has to negotiate some necessities such as phone service, a checking account, a desk for its work, meeting space, etc. The team liaison manages all of the team's business while coordinating his or her efforts with the team coordinator and the clinical director. The team liaison serves as the bookkeeper, secretary, treasurer and logistics coordinator for the team. The person who holds this position should have sufficient rank within an emergency services organization to ensure that the team's needs are managed in a timely and efficient manner. It is also important that the person in the liaison position be a firm believer in the team effort and willing to work for the benefit of the team.

## Mental Health Team Members

Mental health professionals are people who hold advanced degrees (master's or doctoral) in a mental health field and work as a mental health services provider in one or more professional settings such as hospitals, crisis centers, community mental health centers or in private practice.

Mental health professionals are obviously vital to the team's functions. They are frequently given the name "professional support personnel." They provide several important services for the team. They are the mental health professionals who work with a Critical Incident Stress Debriefing (CISD) team when a debriefing is being provided. They provide consultation and clinical guidance to the peer support personnel on the team. They may also assist in the education of the team members. They may provide a few counseling sessions when individuals have been overwhelmed by the stressful event and it becomes evident that the debriefing alone will be insufficient to resolve the problem. Mental health professionals frequently serve as referral resources when long-term counseling is required. It should be noted, however, that if a referral for long-term counseling is made, the usual fees and requirements of regular counseling sessions will then apply. It would be unreasonable to expect that a mental health professional would provide free services beyond the very few contacts which fall under the CISM banner. When possible, mental health providers who are members of CISD or CRT teams should refrain from referring victims of trauma and disaster to their own private practices. Mental health professionals perform CISM services under the guidance of the clinical director and those services include:

- Assistance with the education of the team

- Psychological leadership during the CISD

- Assistance in the development of referral services

- Assistance to the coordinator in determining the appropriateness of a debriefing request

- Assistance with follow-up services after the debriefing

- Service, when necessary, on the peer review board

- Acceptance of long-term therapy referrals when appropriate (see above)

- Active participation in cross familiarization training

- Attendance at periodic team meetings

- Representation of the CISM team before emergency organizations and the public

- Providence of clinical guidance to peers who have intervened in traumatic events

- Assistance with the interpretation of data collected by the team

- Assistance in the selection of team members

**TABLE A.2**

## MENTAL HEALTH PROFESSIONALS

The minimum criteria for choosing mental health professionals are:
- At least a Master's degree in one of the following areas:
  - A. Psychology
  - B. Social work
  - C. Psychiatric nursing
  - D. Pastoral counseling
  - E. Mental health counseling
  - F. Training and certification as a physican who specializes in psychiatry
- Regular employment or services in one of the following areas:
  - A. Social services
  - B. Psychological or psychiatric services
  - C. Crisis intervention services
  - D. Pastoral counseling
  - E. Psychiatric nursing
  - F. Other counseling services
- Professional training in the following areas is essential:
  - A. Critical Incident Stress Debrieifing (CISD)
    1. Basic CISD training (required)
    2. Advanced CISD training (required)
    3. Posttraumatic Stress Disorder Training (required)
  - B. Crisis intervention
  - C. General stress
  - D. Group processes
  - E. Human communication skills
  - F. Directive intervention strategies
  - G. Familiarization through "ride-alongs" with emergency personnel in their environments
- Professional training in the following areas is beneficial:
  - A. Substance abuse
  - B. Alcoholism
  - C. Family therapy
  - D. Neuropsychology
  - E. Physiological basis of behavior
- Professional support personnel should have their own professional pursuits insurance.
- Unless some specialized local arrangements are made, professional support staff should be willing to donate their time to the emergency services for CISM activities.

# Clergy

Most of the CISM teams in the United States have clergy personnel who serve as part of the professional support staff. If they have appropriate degrees in the mental health field (see section on mental health team members above), they may take on mental health roles on the team. If, on the other hand, they serve their communities as active emergency personnel, they may take on peer support roles. In rare instances, clergy are both active emergency personnel and certified mental health professionals. Because it is confusing to those they serve to constantly be switching from one role to another, it would be best if they served their teams as mental health professionals if they hold mental health degrees.

Usually they provide their ministry on a CISM team as a concerned presence in which they function as active listeners to the pain of emergency personnel. Clergy may provide spiritual support when it is clear that the emergency worker is seeking such support. Clergy must be careful, however, not to impose a given religious perspective on emergency personnel who may not be ready to hear such a message. This is true for one-on-one interventions as well as in groups. Religion and philosophy are deeply personal issues. Many people like to keep those issues to themselves. The best discussions of these topics will take place when people are voluntarily involved and when they feel ready for those discussions. The clergy can, in the final analysis, reassure those who have encountered a faith crisis as a result of their work in a traumatic event. In that sense, clergy play a uniquely powerful role in CISM.

Upon occasion, the clergy may be asked to lead a group prayer in an especially distressing situation or community wide event. It is obviously a good practice to comply with the requests of the traumatized group. However, this should not be done unless the entire group is seeking such support.

CISM trained clergy will be far more prepared for their role on a CISM team if they go through the familiarization program with emergency workers. They need to know as much as possible about the job and personalities of the operations people they hope to serve. Obviously, the same guideline can be applied to the mental health professionals who serve on a team.

# Peer Support Personnel

In situations involving commercial establishments, industries and educational programs, and communities it is not necessary to utilize "peer support personnel." However, in the emergency services the use of peers is absolutely essential. Nurses understand nurses and, in most cases, are more easily accepted as support personnel than mental health professionals or clergy. Likewise, firefighters prefer to receive help from one of their own and police officers report that they can receive unique insight from other police officers. The list can go on by category of emergency workers, but the reader has the basic idea by now. The use of peers from one's own professional group cannot be overemphasized for emergency personnel. This is especially so in the period shortly after the traumatic event. If the situation is not resolved by the crisis intervention efforts of peers, then referrals to mental health professional and clergy personnel will be necessary. It is important to keep in mind that many Critical Incident Stress Management services are peer oriented and peer driven, but clinically guided by mental health professionals.

Peer support personnel on a team are drawn from all of the organizations which could use the team. Any emergency or specialty service organization can contribute membership to a team. Specialty service groups include ski patrol, corrections, lifeguard services, dive teams, national park service personnel, mountain rescue groups, search dog teams and any groups which are likely to regularly function in a first response mode.

Peer support personnel are chosen because of their maturity (not age), and ability to work with people. They have an understanding of the harmful effects of stress and have a desire to lessen stress in their fellow workers. They are dedicated and caring people who are willing to give of their time and their talents to assist distressed fellow workers. Peers are usually the prime movers on a CISM team. During the last decade their role on CISM teams has been dramatically expanded. They have received more training and now have a wealth of experience. They have proven themselves to be extremely competent in rendering assistance to their fellow workers. They:

- Often initiate the first contacts with those who are showing signs of distress after exposure to a critical incident.

- Assist in assessing the need for defusings, debriefings, individual contacts, family support services, referrals and others.

- Contact the team coordinator to begin the set up process for the services of the CISM team.

- Serve as the eyes and ears of the CISM team and are alert to the signs and symptoms of developing stress problems.

- Perform services such as defusings, under the guidance of mental health professionals on the team.

- Take on a very active role in the debriefings.

- Provide basic on-scene support services to individuals who are showing signs of distress during the incident.

- Call for mental health assistance when their training and resources are exceeded.

- Assist the CISM team in educational programs for their fellow emergency personnel.

- Provide peer counseling if they have been properly trained.

- Serve on the peer review committee when necessary.

- Assist in providing follow-up after defusings, debriefings and other interventions.

- Assist the team coordinator and mental health professionals as required.

- Provide individual consultations as required.

- Report their interventions to the mental health professionals on the CISM team who guide them in their work.

- Assist the team in CISM related projects.

- Function only within the limits of their training.

Table A.3 describes minimum criteria for peer personnel. Figure A.1 illustrates the typical relationships between the main components of a CISM team. The entire team is able to communicate directly and indirectly with any one of its members or the steering committee. It is extremely important that the clinical director and team coordinator work closely together with the support of the steering committee or board of directors and also the team liaison.

# TEAM MEMBER SELECTION

It is crucial for a team's survival and efficient function that the very best people be chosen to serve on the CISM team. "Political" appointments to the team are not only inappropriate, they can be dysfunctional. The wrong kind of help may be more destructive than no help at all. The task of finding and recruiting the best individuals can present some significant challenges to the steering committee or the membership committee.

### TABLE A.3

**PEER SUPPORT PERSONNEL**

The minimum criteria for choosing peer support personnel are:
- Emergency service experience
- Emotional maturity
- Respect of one's peers
- Ability to keep information confidential
- Sensitivity to the needs of other people
- Willingness to work as a team member
- Willingness to learn psychosocial behavior
- Agreement to work within one's limits
- Agreement to follow the established criteria
- Training in Basic CISM (required)
- Training in Advanced CISM (required)
- Training in psychology and / or social work (preferred)
- Training in human communication (preferred)
- Training in traumatic stress and Posttraumatic Stress Disorder (preferred)
- Training in Crisis Intervention (preferred)
- Training in Assisting Individuals in Crisis training (required)
- Training in Advanced Peer Counseling (preferred)

The first task is to choose a membership committee and then determine the best methods to find and recruit the team's membership. The membership committee must be trained themselves in the CISM program or they will be unable to choose the right people to perform the task of helping others. At times, the right talent for the team is readily available and willing to participate. At other times, active recruitment efforts will be necessary to contact the right team members. One way to actively recruit team members is to provide stress education programs and invite a broad range of participants. Frequently, people attending educational stress programs develop sincere interest in the team and wish to join it. Occasionally, potential team members must be approached and asked if they would be willing to assist on the team.

## COMPREHENSIVE APPROACH TO CISM

A team which believes it only has to do debriefings to manage stress in the emergency services is only functioning at less than a fraction of its capacity. In fact, such an attitude may actually be harmful to the people they hope to help. Remember, CISM is a comprehensive, systematic and multi-tactic approach to managing traumatic stress. It takes much more than performing debriefings to be a CISM team. The following programs are vital for a comprehensive approach to CISM:

- Extensive basic stress and continuing education program(s)

- A CISM team in place and ready when needed

- "Significant other" support programs

- Family support and family life programs

- Administrator / supervisor education and support programs

- Peer support (counseling) strategies

- Mutual aid and community outreach programs

- A wide range of flexible intervention techniques such as:

    A.  Mid-action support (on-scene)

B. Individual consults for peers

C. Defusings

D. Demobilizations (disaster only) and Crisis Management Briefings

E. Debriefings

F. Follow-up services

G. Informal discussions

H. Chaplain services

**FIGURE A.1**

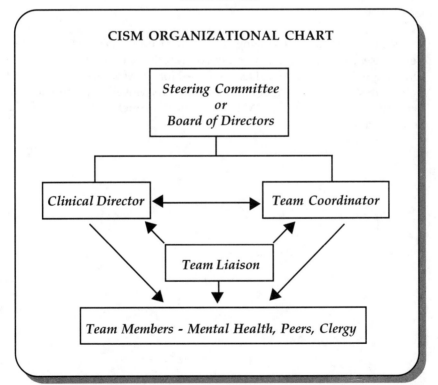

I.   Professional counseling services

J.   Mutual aid programs with other organizations

K.   Community education programs

L.   Other services as required

## SUMMARY

This appendix has described the structure and components of the emergency services CISM team. An overview of the components of a critical incident stress team was presented. Considerable emphasis was given to the criteria for team membership. Also emphasized were the roles and responsibilities of the leadership and general membership positions on the team. The appendix closed with a description of the general functions of a CISM team.

NOTE: Lynn Kennedy-Ewing of Delaware County, Pennsylvania CISM Team deserves special thanks for her contributions to this appendix. The written guidelines which she has developed for CISM team operations and policies has served as a model for this appendix as well as for the policies and procedures of many CISM teams in North America, Europe and the South Pacific.

# Appendix B

## ESTABLISHING AND MAINTAINING A CRITICAL INCIDENT STRESS MANAGEMENT TEAM IN THE EMERGENCY SERVICES

### INTRODUCTION

Some readers of this book will be struggling to establish a brand new CISM team. Others will be trying to recondition a much older team which has lost a considerable amount of its membership. This Appendix (B) has been written to assist those who face the problems of team organization or reorganization. It is designed to serve as a set of guidelines which can help the team organizer reach the goals of team development in the shortest possible time. It has been based on the experiences of many who have struggled through CISM team development or redevelopment during the last decade.

Assistance in developing a CISM team may be obtained by contacting the International Critical Incident Stress Foundation, Inc. (a non-profit organization) at (410) 750-9600, or by contacting established CISM teams.

### FIRST STEPS

CISM teams do not appear overnight. They are always the end result of careful study, planning and a great deal of hard work on the part of many dedicated people. Team development requires effective leadership, a dedicated development committee, clearly stated goals and objectives and a drive for excellence in service to one's fellow workers. Several groups have failed in their efforts to establish a CISM program in their locality because they lacked the essential elements for team development described above.

Experience with CISM team development suggests that one of the most essential elements is a person in the emergency services who is a strong believer in the CISM program and who has an energetic personality. Such a person usually becomes the leader in developing a CISM team. The development of a team can be enhanced and facilitated if the developer has the following characteristics:

- Knowledge of CISM

- A drive to establish a CISM Team

- A dynamic personality

- Persistence

- Positive outlook

- A sense of humor

- Positive interpersonal style

- Incessant care for others

- Some dedicated supporters

- A plan of action

- A guidance from another team or ICISF

- Administrative support

## DETERMINING THE NEED FOR CISM AND CONVINCING ADMINISTRATION

Determining the actual need for a CISM team is important because it makes a person credible when he or she approaches the administration to obtain permission to move ahead with CISM plans. Determining that a need exists usually goes hand in hand with a presentation of the need to the administration. There are several approaches which can be followed. The least desirable is guess work. Rarely does guess work carry any weight with doubting administrators. Other, more beneficial approaches include, but are not limited to the following:

- Bring in experts to address the administration.

- Have experts present at large conferences and thus begin a "grass roots" approach.

- Collect personal accounts of individuals within the jurisdiction and present these to the administration.

- Be careful of confidentiality. Do not name people or use events that are too familiar without permission of the person(s) involved.

- Develop an informal data collection process and find out how many and what types of events have occurred in the last three, five or ten years.

- Develop a formal data collection and/or research project to look at the experiences of the past three, five or ten year periods. Find out what events have occurred, what stress reactions were involved, how long the symptoms lasted, what effects the critical incident(s) had on one's family members, what changes took place in the emergency workers' lives as a result of the incident and so on. Present the data to the administration.

- Bring in senior officers or supervisors from organizations which have used the services of a CISM team.

- Present reading materials to the administrators.

- Develop a cost/benefit analysis for the administration, if possible.

- Collect the accounts of other organizations which have teams and present that information to the administration.

- Utilize the assistance of the International Critical Incident Stress Foundation, Inc. and other teams to guide a new or restructured team development program.

- Utilize any combination of the above techniques.

# IMPORTANT ISSUES IN TEAM DEVELOPMENT

The set of questions which follows has been developed to serve as a guide to the organizers of a CISM team. It is suggested that the questions be reformulated into subdivisions on a check list or survey. Team organizers can use the check lists and survey to assure that they achieve the development of the very best team possible. Local problems and issues may influence the development of a team and those special circumstances can be included in subdivisions of the questions in the list below.

- Does the data collected indicate a need for a CISM in the area?

- Is there already a nearby team in operation?

- Are arrangements made to bring in an existing team when necessary?

- Can existing resources suffice or is it necessary to form a new team?

- How often would a new team be used in an average year?

- Is there a realistic start-up date for the team?

- What are the objectives of the team?

- Have membership criteria been established?

- What is the team member application process?

- Who will choose the team members?

- Will the team incorporate itself?

- Are the mental health professionals self insured?

- Would it be better to develop a new team or join an existing one?

- How large an area will be served?

- Is there an appropriate lead agency?

- Do the emergency personnel want the team?

- Are there sufficient knowledgeable mental health professionals willing to serve on a team?

- Does a good referral system of mental health professionals exist?

- Is one of the mental health professionals willing to serve as the clinical director of the team?

- Are the available mental health professionals willing to train with the peer support personnel to serve on the team?

- Will all of the agencies cooperate in running the team?

- Is there a pool of peer support personnel willing to be trained and to serve on the team?

- Is there an available leader for the team development?

- Is a steering committee or organizing committee being formed?

- Is there a team membership committee and a membership application?

- Is a nearby Basic CISM training available or are arrangements being made to bring in a training consultant or training team?

- Have any attempts been made to educate the potential users of a team about its services?

- What plans exist for familiarization programs for the emergency personnel in the area to be served?

- Is the organizing committee prepared to write a set of team operating protocols based on the basic CISM concepts described within this book and utilized by other well organized teams?

- Are team members willing to meet regularly to assure the best possible development of the team?

- Is there sufficient financial support available to establish a CISM team? (Experience indicates that it costs about $6,000 to $10,000 to train a team to the basic level of CISM).

- Is there a 24-hour communications system willing to handle the incoming calls for a debriefing team or other CISM service?

- Are sufficient team coordinators prepared to screen incoming calls on a 24-hour basis and assign priorities to CISM services, alert team members and deploy teams as required?

- Are team members willing to obtain regular continuing education in at least the following areas:

> Crisis intervention
>
> Human communication skills
>
> General stress
>
> Physiological response to stress
>
> Posttraumatic Stress Disorder
>
> Conflict resolution techniques
>
> Peer support techniques
>
> Directive intervention skills
>
> Incident command
>
> Disaster services
>
> Line-of-duty death
>
> Significant other support

Group dynamics

Knowledge of emergency services

Advanced CISD training

Suicide recognition / intervention

Making referrals

Grief and mourning

Understanding children in stress

Cumulative stress

CISM team protocols

Ethics and confidentiality

Multi-agency support services

Updates on CISM programs and on the group process, CISD

Updates on defusings, one-on-one and so on

# MIDDLE AND FINAL STEPS IN TEAM DEVELOPMENT

Rather than repeat most of the issues presented in the previous section as steps to developing a team only a brief summary will be presented here.

The **FIRST STEPS** are concluded once:

- The need has been determined.

- The program has been approved by the administration.

- Peer and mental health support of the program has been reasonably assured.

- Existing CISM programs have been reviewed.

**MIDDLE STEPS**

- Establish an organization committee.

- Decide on a lead agency.

- Develop team structure.

- Solicit applications from potential team members.

- Schedule training.

**FINAL STEPS**

- Train.

- Select team members.

- Establish effective leadership.

- Establish written protocols.

- Maintain team operations.

- Evaluate team performance.

# TEAM TRAINING

There are many issues which a CISM team must face as it develops and maintains its operations. Training stands out as the most important of all. Without training, the team cannot perform its mission and the chance of causing damage to another person increases sharply. Even the most knowledgeable mental health professionals need to have the CISM training to assure that they are familiar with the terminology utilized in the field. They also need to interact with emergency personnel and other peer support personnel from industries to gain an understanding of their personalities and their jobs. The training program provides an opportunity to begin the necessary interactions with emergency as well as other types of peer support personnel.

Unfortunately, in the great majority of cases, mental health professionals do not receive training in stress, job related stress, critical incident stress and related crisis topics when they are in graduate school. Most pick up that type of information when they are in the work environment. Typical mental health professionals come to the CISM team with a vast array of backgrounds. The Basic CISM training serves to bring everyone to the same level. It confirms the fundamentals of what is known to be successful in working with emergency personnel and with the community at large.

Critical Incident Stress and the intervention programs which have been developed to reduce it and to accelerate a person's recovery is a specialty field. It requires people with specialized training. Mental health professionals, clergy personnel and peers must be well versed in the special problems and interventions which are involved in working with traumatic stress (Critical Incident Stress). They will be providing preventative support services, not psychotherapy. It is also important that they understand that the intervention techniques which have been designed for use with emergency personnel may be used, with only minor adjustments, in the general community as well as in industrial, educational, commercial and community settings. But the techniques which were developed for use specifically with the general population cannot be used with the emergency personnel.

Prior to service in any CISM activity:

- All CISM team members must complete a minimum two-day ICISF approved Basic CISM Training course

As soon as possible after the initial training, all team members should complete both of the following courses:

- The two-day ICISF approved Advanced CISM course.

- The two-day ICISF approved Assisting Individuals in Crisis course.

Proficiency in CISM does not arise from the completion of a single course.

All three courses mentioned above are considered "core" courses in the field of CISM. Please note that the International Critical Incident Stress Foundation now has more than twenty (20) two-day training programs that cover a broad spectrum of crisis intervention topics. These courses are considered electives and CISM team members who want to excel in the CISM field take these courses over time. Each team member should attend at least one continuing education session per year.

# ORGANIZATIONAL STRUCTURE OF A CISM TEAM

Detailed information on the structure and components of a CISM team is contained in Appendix A of this book. The following is an overview of the minimal organizational structure of a CISM team.

Each team shall have the following components:

- Steering committee or a board of directors

- A clinical director

- A senior team coordinator

- As many team coordinators as needed to assure 24-hour coverage

- A sufficient number of mental health professionals to fulfill team requirements

- Numerous peer support personnel from the various agencies. Peers may be currently active or former members of emergency service organizations. Even retirees play an important role on teams. They have a career full of experience which can be very helpful to people still in the emergency services. Every agency served by the team shall have representation on the team when possible. Generally there should be two-thirds or more peer support personnel and one-third or less mental health and clergy personnel.

# TEAM MEMBER SELECTION

The criteria for selecting team members is described in detail in Appendix A. This segment merely describes the process by which members are chosen for the team. The reader is urged to review the team member selection criteria which is presented in Appendix A.

The first step in choosing members is to establish an application for team membership. The applications are collected and then reviewed by the selection committee which is usually made up of two or three mental health professionals or clergy personnel and five or six peer support personnel. The selection committee then makes reference contacts, arranges for interviews when more information is necessary and, finally, selects the candidates who seem to be most suitable for service on the team.

In cases in which the team does not know the candidate or when there is a need for more information or there are doubts about the suitability of a candidate, the membership committee may hold an interview to help resolve the doubts or find the information which may be missing. Typically four or five committee members meet with the candidate, ask questions and try to determine if their doubts are groundless or warranted. An example of when an interview is necessary is when a team candidate has recently experienced a highly traumatic incident and there is some question as to the readiness of the candidate to handle other people's pain when he or she is still struggling with his / her own.

Once the interview is complete the interviewers make recommendations to the remainder of the membership committee. The committee then completes the selection process and writes to inform the candidates of the results of the membership selection process.

# COMPREHENSIVE APPROACH TO CISM

In Appendix A it was suggested that a comprehensive CISM program was extremely important. Organizations which attempt to deal with traumatic stress by utilizing a single focused strategy, such as the development of only an educational program or only the provision of debriefing services are doomed to failure. A more sensible approach to traumatic stress management is a multifocal or comprehensive approach which includes a strategic plan for a wide spectrum of stress control programs.

Building a comprehensive Critical Incident Stress Management program seems like an overwhelming and extremely expensive task. It is not if it is done properly by combining resources with other agencies, services and organizations within the community. It is not necessary for each organization to create its own comprehensive program to manage traumatic stress. A much more efficient and effective approach to managing traumatic stress is to become a part of an extensive system of Critical Incident Stress Management services provided jointly by a number of organizations within a community or shared between several jurisdictions.

At present, in the United States, there are more than 500 Critical Incident Stress Management teams spread out throughout the country. There are about 200 CISM teams in 28 other countries. Practically every CISM team is a "combined emergency services" team which serves hospitals, fire services, law enforcement agencies, paramedic and emergency medical technician programs, communications personnel, corrections officers, search and rescue groups, ski patrols, disaster workers, military services and other primary response organizations. Many are serving school systems and communities.

If the CISM team is properly organized and if sufficient mental health professionals are available to serve on the team, a Community Response Team (CRT) can be developed as a subcategory of the CISM team. The Community Response Team takes on the responsibility of managing support services after crisis events within the community which are affecting the citizens. The victims of traumatic incidents need rapid intervention from mental health professionals who are trained in managing traumatic stress. Emergency personnel have very different needs and responses to traumatic events. In addition, their personalities are very different from the personalities of average non-emergency people. It is usually best to have the CISM component of the team deal with the emergency personnel and the CRT component of the team deal with the victims who are traumatized.

In some areas of the country, the American Red Cross disaster mental health network is joining its resources with the CISM team to develop the Community Response Team. This cooperative arrangement is encouraged. The interventions with emergency personnel should be provided by the peers and professional support staff of the CISM team. The interventions for the community are managed by the CRT with less emphasis on the use of peers.

The combined emergency services teams described in the paragraphs above can work quite well. All of the organizations feed members onto the

CISM team. They all benefit from each other's experiences. They share in training of the team; they utilize the same mental health professionals and can rely on each other in a disaster. Other benefits of working together are that the various groups develop mutual respect and understanding, and they learn that there are many similarities among the various emergency service professions. Most importantly, combined CISM teams have a major advantage of being able to emotionally support one another in the difficult work of traumatic stress management.

This approach can easily be used by any emergency organization. There is no need to duplicate services. Combining one organization's resources with another's in a consortium of support saves money, effectively utilizes resources, improves the breath and depth of the experience and enhances the training efforts. One organization may contribute a member of the clergy to the team. Another may have a mental health professional who would like to serve. Yet another has a physician who joins the CISM team. Nurses, fire service personnel, law enforcement officers and other emergency personnel are usually drawn from the organizations in the area.

## AVOIDING MAJOR PITFALLS

One of the key guidelines for success on a CISM team is never to provide services on a formal debriefing team to people with whom you are very close friends. It is alright to help a friend by means of a one-on-one consultation or an on-scene support service. Those interventions by CISM team members are generally very brief contacts which hold little danger of getting involved too deeply. When no other trained CISM personnel are available in a timely fashion, a peer support person may provide a defusing to his or her fellow workers if he or she was not involved in the incident. Caution is advised in these circumstances, however, because the CISM person is operating in a gray area which could produce some problems. The formal debriefing service is a point of potential problems. When a debriefing is necessary, it is not advisable for the peer to provide support services to his close friends. Debriefings are more complex and emotionally involved and they also allow for more in-depth discussion of traumatic events which can cause an atmosphere of confusion for the peer who is too close to the personnel or to the situation.

There are reasons why a broad spectrum team is more efficient and effective than a CISM team which is developed to serve only one organization. It is generally unsound for the providers of Critical Incident Stress services and for the recipients of those services to know one another too well. Every medically trained person recognizes the inherent psychological dangers of providing medical treatments to seriously ill people who happen to be one's relatives or close friends. Similar dangers exist for those who serve on CISM teams. The same problems arise when supervisors try to provide support services to their subordinates. Too close an association between those who give the help and those who receive it can cause emotional turmoil related to role and boundary distinctions.

It is strongly recommended that a person on a CISM team not provide debriefing services if any of the following conditions exist. Instead, some other peer support personnel should be chosen to work at the debriefing.

Do not serve as a team member chosen to do a debriefing if:

1.  You have played a significant role in the actual event.

2.  You have direct command or supervisory responsibility for the personnel involved in the incident even if you were not there.

3.  You are very close friends with the members of the group involved in the debriefable event.

4.  You are working with the group involved in the incident on a regular basis (as part of a unit or station), even if you were not with them during the incident

5.  You are part of the internal affairs or operations investigation unit and have responsibility or the potential responsibility for investigating the event.

6.  You are a close relative of one of the affected people.

A combined emergency services CISM team is one situation where competition between organizations is decreased and an atmosphere of mutual cooperation and support is enhanced. It is clearly a recommended course of action.

# GUIDELINES FOR EFFECTIVE CISM

Emergency organizations, if they are going to provide the services which will preserve their personnel in their careers, must first make a proactive commitment to the appropriate development of a Critical Incident Stress Management program.

The first commitment is to find an appropriate emergency person to chair the development committee. A major mistake made by emergency organizations and hospitals is the assumption that critical incident stress management is solely a mental health professional's task. No one will deny that mental health professionals play a highly significant role in a comprehensive CISM program. They are vital to the program's success but often they do not have the time to develop, coordinate and administer a CISM program. They also suffer another handicap. They are seldom providers in the emergency operations environment and, therefore, lack an understanding of how to work with the emergency services.

The development committee should coordinate its efforts with CISM teams which may already exist in the area. The fact that there are more than 300 teams in the United States makes it likely that an active CISM team may be already working in the region. Every effort should be made to join their resources rather than to set up a competitive team which serves only one organization. The best interests of a team and the community are usually served when there is a multi-agency and multi-jurisdictional team structure.

The tasks assigned to the steering committee include selection of professional and peer support staff to serve on the team, as well as the establishment of a policy and procedures committee to develop appropriate written operating procedures. Most steering committees have a subgroup which ensures close coordination with the CISD team(s) in the local community and region and with the International Critical Incident Stress Foundation, which serves as an international coordinating, standard-setting and education body for CISM teams. Steering committees also must provide appropriate training and education opportunities for the CISM team members.

The CISM team needs to be a peer focused support service which utilizes mental health professionals and chaplains as consultants. When effectively led and given the freedom to do its work, a CISM team can be a powerful force in maintaining personnel. Therefore, the next commitment the administrator of the emergency organizations have to make is the commitment to trust the members of the CISM team to carry out their mission without threatening the operation of those organizations.

CISM teams can only function if they have an open network of communications. There must exist an effective means for emergency personnel to call for CISM team assistance. In addition, to be consistent, frequent communication with the local, regional and national CISM networks for information exchange and mutual aid is a must.

# REDUCING THE RISK OF LEGAL ACTION

Up to the time of printing of this book the only known lawsuits that occurred involve situations in which CISM services were not provided by an organization for its distressed employees. All of these lawsuits were settled out of court in favor of the plaintiff. That is, when an organization had no support for its personnel, it stood a greater chance of being sued successfully by one or more of its employees. In another case, the defense's suggestion in a murder trial that police officers should testify as to the content of a CISD which they attended was thrown out of court. The judge stated that psychological support for police officers had nothing to do with a review of the facts of the murder case. The record so far, especially in light of the fact that more than 40,000 debriefings have been provided since 1983, is a good one. We believe that the fact that teams have been following the guidelines is the main reason why lawsuits have not occurred involving CISM teams. It is important to function within the widely accepted standards that currently exist when applying CISM services.

No one wants a lawsuit and no one expects one when providing support services to emergency personnel. But clearly there are no guaranteed protections against legal action. There are some steps, however, which may reduce the risk of adverse legal complications. This section will detail some of those protective steps. If there is a need for specific legal advice, that should be sought through attorneys familiar with emergency services operations, disaster relief work and possibly CISM.

- The very best protection against legal action is excellence in the practice of CISM services.

- The next protection is to carefully follow the written policies, protocols and guidelines of local and international organizations associated with CISM. In some jurisdictions such guidelines may become "standards of care."

- CISM teams would be wise to incorporate.

- Any time a person in a debriefing demonstrates a clear and imminent danger to themselves (suicidal threat) or others (homicidal threat or actual or threatened other serious crimes), the team is required to act in the best interests of the individual and / or the person(s) who may be in danger. This might require disclosure of certain pieces of information to the person's family or to the person's supervisor. It might also entail involuntary hospitalization or other actions deemed necessary to save a life. Saving a life has a higher priority than stringent adherence to absolute confidentiality. Team members should follow the guidance of their clinical director or the mental health professional involved in the debriefing. It should be pointed out now that the examples given here are merely theoretical. There is no known case of an emergency worker who disclosed such information in the midst of a debriefing. It is more likely that a civilian (one not involved in the emergency services) would bring such information up in a debriefing. Teams which serve non-emergency populations need to be alert to the fact that they may see this particular situation arise more than teams which serve emergency personnel.

- Laws vary from jurisdiction to jurisdiction. Team members should be familiar with the laws which apply in their own jurisdiction.

- Respect the right of refusal. In some cases personnel are ordered into a debriefing for the good of the individuals and the organization. Since part of the debriefing is an educational session, the mandating of the debriefing can be appropriate. No one can be ordered to talk in a debriefing if they choose not to. If a person's objection to attending the debriefing is extreme, it might be best for the CISM team to allow that person to exclude themselves from the process. The person should be advised that his or her choice for exclusion may not be in his or her own best interests. The individual should be advised that various types of help are available if he or she should decide it is needed at some other time. The names of team members and their telephone numbers and the types of services which could be provided should be given to the person who chooses not to attend the CISD.

- Informed consent is necessary. The process followed in a debriefing should be no surprise to people. They should be told about debriefings in pre-incident stress education programs and as part of the introductory remarks made by the CISD team.

- Advice which is given in a debriefing should be limited to those things which are considered reasonable and prudent and would be the kind of advice given by anyone to people who are coping with stress. The advice given should be backed up by literature in the field of stress mitigation.

- The advice provided in a debriefing should be limited only to the current situation.

- Participants should be advised not to discuss anything which could jeopardize an investigation, cause them to be disciplined or which would cause them to admit deliberate violations of the policies or procedures of their organization.

- Do not turn a debriefing into psychotherapy. It is not psychotherapy, nor is it a substitute for psychotherapy.

- Do not take notes, make recordings or allow cameras at a debriefing.

- When you tell people you will keep the contents of the debriefing confidential, keep it confidential.

- Licensed professionals must always follow the dictates of their professional code of ethics and the law as it may be applicable to their functions within the context of CISM services.

# MAINTAINING A CISM TEAM

There are three primary techniques and several secondary considerations which will keep a CISM team healthy and functioning once it has been established. Ignoring these guidelines for team health, especially the primary techniques, sets the stage for the eventual failure of a team. The primary guidelines for team health are:

> 1. Education
> 2. Cross-familiarization
> 3. Regular team meetings

# EDUCATION

Stress education is one of the primary elements of CISM team health. It is divided into two main areas: 1) education of the personnel in the organizations who will be using the team's services and 2) education of the team itself.

No one will think of calling the CISM team during or after a crisis event if the team is not known. One of the first steps to be taken by a new team is to present an educational program to each emergency services organization. The education programs (typically 2 - 3 hours in length) usually cover the following topics:

- Nature of stress

- Emergency services stress

- Causes of critical incident stress.

- Signs and symptoms of distress

- Survival strategies for stress

- The CISM team

- Accessing the team

It may be necessary to modify the education program into twenty minute or half hour modular presentations to accommodate groups which are on shifts and unable to get together for more than brief periods of time. It is inconvenient to teach the stress material in small segments, but it is effective if organized and coordinated properly.

It is also very important for the team that the leaders of the various organizations are given information on the functions of the team and the reasons for calling upon the team. When supervisory staff understand the functions of the team and how to call upon the team they are more likely to use the team to assist their personnel.

For more information on education in Critical Incident Stress Management see Mitchell, J. T. and Everly, G. S. (1994) *Human Elements Training*, Ellicott City, M.D., Chevron Publishing Corporation. It is also suggested that the International Critical Incident Stress Foundation be contacted for information on CISM training and education. The Foundation can be reached at (410) 750-9600 or by writing to: ICISF, 10176 Baltimore National Pike, unit 201, Ellicott City, MD 21042. The web address is www.icisf.org

## CROSS-FAMILIARIZATION

Cross-familiarization or cross-training of CISM team members is essential for team survival and appropriate team function. Cross-training means that peer support personnel are trained in issues which are usually the domain of the mental health professionals. For example, peers are trained in crisis intervention, human communications, stress management, Posttraumatic Stress Disorder, grief and critical incident stress.

Cross-familiarization also means that mental health professionals and members of the clergy are familiarized with the equipment, personalities, organization and the strategies and tactics of operations personnel. The professional support staff cannot learn this in a classroom. They must spend several hours in an emergency department of a hospital, ride along with fire fighters on the engine, ride with the police on patrol, make runs with the emergency medical crews and visit the communications center. Cross-familiarization takes place over a long period of time. No one can gain all of that exposure in one night. A few hours in one organization and then a few in another will help. Over time the experiences mount up and the professional support staff become more well versed in dealing with emergency personnel.

We believe it is not possible to be truly effective with emergency personnel without this cross-familiarization process. Emergency personnel will tend to have difficulty trusting anyone who does not have a substantial awareness of their jobs and their personalities.

# REGULAR TEAM MEETINGS

Teams which do not meet regularly are likely to develop problems. Lack of contact with the team members isolates the leaders and fragments the team. Teams without meetings lose a sense of direction and purpose. The lack of contact encourages team members to go off in their own directions. The end result is often team disintegration. To survive, a CISM team should meet every four to six weeks. A time frame of every eight weeks is probably a little too long but it is better than none at all.

There are usually three segments to a CISM team meeting. They are:

- Intervention Review

- Team Business

- Education

The intervention review segment is open only to team members since the information discussed relates to the critical incidents managed by the team members during the last four to six weeks. In this segment each situation managed by the team is briefly presented and the team response is discussed and analyzed. Advice may be offered by the team members to ensure that the follow up is provided as necessary. Any points to be learned for the benefit of the team members are discussed as necessary. Team members are reminded that the information discussed in the intervention review segment is confidential.

The second segment of the team meeting is team business. Any correspondence to the team is discussed and decisions are made to respond in one manner or another. Issues related to membership, training, funding, future plans and other elements of team business are openly discussed. All team members should be encouraged to participate in the discussions.

The emphasis in a CISM team meeting should be on a casual, democratic meeting in which everyone feels equal. When a team gets stuck on minute issues of parliamentary procedure, they have lost sight of what they are all about. There are certainly more important issues to be faced by a team than who is to speak and in what order. Keeping the meeting light and functional is the objective. The lighter style will keep people interested in coming to meetings in the future. *Remember, one of the functions of CISM team meetings is team building and development of cohesion.*

The third segment of the team meeting is the educational segment. Continuing education is the objective. A team that does not continuously upgrade itself will stagnate. A suggested list of continuing education topics was presented in the section of this chapter entitled "Important Issues in Team Development." Those topics and a number of others are important for the team education program. The usual education segment of a team meeting is 30 to 45 minutes.

## SECONDARY GUIDELINES FOR TEAM HEALTH: IN-SERVICE EDUCATION FOR TEAM MEMBERS

In addition to the regular educational sessions which take place during team meetings, team members should have at least eight hours of continuing education per year at regional, national or international conferences on stress, crisis intervention or other related topics. Staying within the team's own jurisdiction for additional training does not afford team members the opportunity to network with stress management teams from other areas of the country or the world. People who do not interact with other CISM organizations tend to lack depth and become fixed within a limited number of intervention strategies. As a result they become less effective in rendering assistance to their fellow workers.

## A MECHANISM FOR TEAM RECORD KEEPING

Team members like to be credited with the work they have performed. Some records should be kept for statistical purposes and to determine which team members have the most experience and which have the least. Check-off sheets which show the number of times a person has performed defusings, debriefings or other interventions can help to determine which strategies need to be reviewed at team meetings.

# WRITTEN PROTOCOLS AND PROCEDURES

Few things can be as frustrating for a team as not having written guidelines by which they function. The lack of written guidelines also causes disruption between the CISM team and the operations units during the incidents. Written guidelines, protocols and procedures help to ensure that all team members are functioning according to acceptable standards. It is possible that written protocols and procedures may afford some degree of protection to the team in the unlikely event of a legal contact or a disciplinary action against a team member who has violated the procedures.

# NEW MEMBER RECRUITMENT

There is some attrition on every team. People are busy. They may have family responsibilities as well as professional responsibilities. Since most are not paid to participate on CISM teams, they do not always have the luxury of putting CISM activities at the top of their priority list. Some aspects of their lives are constantly changing. When those circumstances change, team members may take a temporary or permanent leave from the team.

It is necessary to keep the team membership up to near maximal levels to ensure effective response to crisis events and the best use of the team membership. Both peer and professional staff should be interested in adding team members to replace those who have left the team. Sometimes just a suggestion to a friend that they might be very helpful on a team is sufficient enticement for a potential new team member to join. At times it takes announcements and a more active recruitment program to find the right candidates for the team.

Once a new team member decides to join the team, full CISD training should take place as soon as possible. No one should provide CISM services without the proper training. In addition, new team members should be placed on a trainee status until they have had sufficient experience on the team to allow them to move into a full member position.

# IN-SERVICE EDUCATION OF EMERGENCY SERVICES

It is not enough to present a broad educational program one time and expect that it will be sufficient to keep emergency personnel knowledgeable regarding the team's existence and functions. Most CISM teams have found it necessary to go back into the fire and police stations and to the communications centers and into the hospitals to provide periodic updates on the team. One of the main functions of the team is to mitigate stress reactions. Continuing education programs which provide additional insight into stress management for the staffs of the various organizations can do much to help prevent or mitigate stress. Those programs will also keep the team visible to the groups that could best benefit from it.

# COMMUNITY EDUCATION PROGRAMS

In many areas of the country, particularly in areas in which Community Response Teams (CRT) have been established, significant efforts are underway to alert the community to the threat of traumatic stress. Where the CRT program has been attached to the Critical Incident Stress Management team there tends to be greater involvement from the general membership of the CISM team with the community. The prevention of stress through education is a key element of the CRT. And when a major incident occurs in an area, the provision of crisis education programs and debriefing services may be necessary.

Although CISM teams have been developed to assist emergency organizations and personnel, they have a strong record of responding to the community during times of disaster and have proven their benefit on numerous occasions. They should take a leadership role in preparing mental health professionals to assist stricken communities after a crisis event. They should also stand ready to render humanitarian aid to the community when their services are required. A close coordination and cooperation between the CISM team, the Red Cross, the Community Response Team and the local mental health services is necessary if adequate stress reduction services are to be provided to the citizens.

If the Red Cross and the local mental health services have not yet organized a Community Response Team, and if the CISM team is asked to provide services to groups other than emergency personnel, several considerations should be made before committing the CISM team to support services for the community. Those considerations can best be made in the form of the following questions:

1. Are there organizations or agencies which should be managing the psychological needs of the community during the crisis?

2. Are the members of local mental health services adequately trained to manage the psychological trauma produced by this crisis situation?

3. Can the organization respond in a timely fashion to assist the community? The response to a major community disaster must be within hours, NOT days.

4. Do the organizations which have training and responsibility to respond to the psychological needs of the community have sufficient personnel to manage the situation?

5. Are the trained organizations requesting assistance or is the call originating from sources outside of those organizations?

6. If the request for assistance is coming from the organizations which are trained to handle the crisis response, what exactly do they need from the crisis team?

7. Are there adequate lines of communication between the CISM team and the CRT program or the other relief groups?

8. How quickly can the CISM team draw upon its resources to respond to the situation? Where do the team members report and who is in charge of the situation and the CISM teams?

9. Is the intervention being provided for humanitarian reasons only? (Accepting fees for services may be unwise for a CISM team developed for the emergency services.)

10. If the CISM team is deployed to assist community groups, will they be unable to achieve their primary mission of providing support services to emergency personnel or are there sufficient team members to cover both the community and the emergency personnel?

When a CISM team is requested to assist a CRT or provide direct services to the public, the team's clinical director should be notified of the request. Usually there is no negative reaction to the request for help, but occasionally, there are some jurisdictional issues which may need to be addressed before the help can be provided. The decision to render assistance is usually reached within minutes.

See the index of this book for the location of additional information on Community Response Teams.

# SIGNIFICANT OTHER EDUCATION / SUPPORT SERVICES

At this point, it should be obvious that a CISM team has many more tasks than that of just providing debriefings. The CISM team employs a holistic approach. That is, it is concerned with many aspect of the emergency worker's life. CISM teams take a proactive stance not just a reactive position. Providing debriefings after the incident is considered reactive. Providing preventative stress education programs and significant other and family life programs is proactive.

It is not sufficient to support only the person in uniform. Instead, it is necessary to support the entire environment in which the uniformed person operates. That includes the person's family. Also, sufficient evidence already exists which indicates that the families of emergency personnel have frequently been ignored after critical incidents in the past.

To rectify that unfortunate situation, CISM teams have developed support programs which reach out to significant others of the emergency personnel. Support programs include stress prevention education programs and debriefings and follow-up services for significant others after particularly distressing situations have affected their loved ones in the emergency services. Significant others are given information on a number of topics designed to lower their anxiety and prevent the harmful effects of stress. The following is a list of the typical programs presented to significant others by the CISM team. In some cases the emergency personnel are asked to be present during the education programs.

- The personality of the emergency worker

- Communications for couples

- Fair fighting

- Decision making in families

- Financial planning and budgeting for families

- Familiarization with emergency equipment

- Tours of the work place

- Ride along programs

- Spouse support programs

- Meet your loved one's commanders / supervisors

- Understanding grief

- Coping with anxiety

- Child rearing in the emergency services family

- Critical Incident Stress

- Getting help

- Supporting the distressed loved one

- Children in crisis

- Caring enough to confront

- On-going spouse education support groups

After tragic events, which seriously affect not only the emergency workers, but their families as well, several services may need to be provided to help the significant others recover from the stress they experienced because their loved ones encountered critical incident stress. Examples of direct services to significant others include:

- Debriefings to spouses of surviving personnel after a line-of-duty death in an organization

- Bereavement - crisis oriented counseling to the wife, children and parents of the deceased emergency worker

- Grief seminars for the families of deceased emergency personnel approximately six months to a year after the death

- Follow-up contacts with the bereaved family members for several weeks after the death

- Teen groups for children of surviving emergency personnel after a line of duty death in an organization

- Young children's groups for children six to twelve years old after a highly distressing incident which may have affected their parents

- Debriefings for significant others after a particularly distressing incident in a community

- Advice to the significant others about child care during times of distress in the family which is directly associated with the work of the emergency services person

- Follow-up services to significant others of emergency service personnel as the needs may require

# MECHANISMS TO DEBRIEF THE DEBRIEFERS

The old adage, "a little knowledge can be a dangerous thing," may have some applicability for people trained to provide services to others through the CISM team. They seem to develop an idea that they are totally invulnerable to stress reactions themselves since they have some stress knowledge and some stress experience. Obviously that misconception can be the foundation for some serious problems. Debriefing teams are on the cutting edge of services to people with raw human emotions. They can get hurt. They need to take many of the same precautions to protect themselves from becoming as stressed as the people they serve.

Team members stay healthy and functional on a team when they follow the same guidelines for breaks, food, rest and the amount of time on-scene that they teach to others. It is not only a good practice from their own health perspective, it is the very best example they could give to others. As individuals, CISM team members need to ask for relief when they are getting overwhelmed. If there are family problems in their own homes, they might need a break from debriefings for awhile. The same might be true if they have done too many debriefings in a short period of time. Team members should always have a right to go on a temporary leave of absence from the team when their personal health or home life needs more attention.

One extremely important mechanism to preserve the CISM team members is to require that team members meet immediately after a debriefing. This meeting is an opportunity to "debrief the debriefers." At the meeting the team should accomplish the following:

- Quick review of the debriefing / understand what just happened and why it happened.

- Assign tasks for follow up services to specific team members.

- Allow sufficient time for the debriefers to ventilate their own reactions to the debriefing and make sure everyone is okay before releasing the team.

Some incidents are so powerful, requiring such extensive time and energy on the part of the CISD team m embers providing the debriefings and follow-up services, that they may need another team to debrief them. This is likely to occur in line-of-duty deaths and disaster. A neighboring team or a specialty team from another state may be brought in to provide this type of debriefing. At the very least, team members who were not involved in the debriefing are called upon to debrief the debriefers.

The team that is debriefing the debriefers must realize that the debriefing team already knows many of the basic techniques of debriefing and may resist a debriefing which is too close to the exact seven phase model which they would use with any other group. The team which is debriefing the debriefers must be flexible and allow a broad range of questions to be inserted. The whole style of this type of debriefing is more relaxed and conversational. It often helps to allow team members to retell the entire story in chronological order so that everyone can discuss when and to what extent they got involved in the debriefing. Somewhere in the discussion they need to discuss the point at which they felt the greatest emotion for the participants in the debriefing. The debriefing for the debriefers, unlike the formal debriefing with its seven phases, allows a bit more direct questioning of the CISD team. The debriefers of debriefers are more concerned to make sure no important issues are left untouched. They are, however, aware that they are working with their colleagues. Sometimes, the debriefers will insert clarifying statements or educational information for the benefit of all. The debriefing of the debriefers ends when everyone feels that the incident and the teams response has been sufficiently "worked over."

# TIME OUT FOR OVEREXTENDED TEAM MEMBERS

It was mentioned in the section above that some team members might recognize their own needs to take a break from the CISM team and to stop doing debriefings for a period of time. Other team members will not be aware that they have become overextended. They often tend to forget their own pain. They begin to take on more and more CISM responsibility. Little by little, lifting someone else's pain drains their own resources. It happens subtly, almost imperceptibly. Everyone around them gets the idea that they are getting in too deep. They are becoming overextended. Only the overextended person is unaware of the problem.

Here are some warning signs of an overextended CISM team member:

- Excessive worry about the people one has debriefed. This worry goes far beyond that necessary to provide adequate follow-up.

- Intense irritability when a fellow CISM team member attempts to advise a debriefer about something they believe they already know.

- Obsessive thinking about the CISD experience.

- Constant replays of the incident described in the debriefing even though the debriefed was not present at the actual incident.

- Unfounded anger at one's fellow workers or one's loved ones after doing a debriefing.

- Loss of interest in one's own work after debriefings.

- Chronic feelings of fatigue for long periods after debriefings.

- Doing far more for individuals from a particular debriefing than one would do for any other person under similar circumstances.

- Maintaining a high degree of follow-up contacts when they are not necessary.

- Attempts to work independently of the team without appropriate supervision from team professional support staff.

- Frequent, unexplained loss of emotional control after debriefings.

- Sleeplessness after debriefings.

- Agitation, restlessness after debriefings.

- Excessive withdrawal from contact with others after going through a debriefing.

- Excessive volunteering to take on more and more debriefings.

- Feeling upset and jealous whenever others are doing debriefings in which the overextended person is not involved.

- Excessive belief that no one else could provide the "proper" debriefing within the area served by the team.

Peers on a team are the more likely candidates for overextension. This is so because of their more frequent contact with distressed fellow workers. But mental health professionals and clergy personnel may also be subject to the distressing condition. Overextended CISM team members jeopardize their own health and the smooth operation of a CISM team. They need to be helped to regain control of themselves before they begin to do harm. Their fellow team members may be able to point out the problem, or the team coordinator could address it with them. If necessary, the team's clinical director might need to be brought into the situation. Every effort needs to be made to help the person come to their own conclusions that they are getting out of control in the debriefing environment. They will generally be far more cooperative if they can see the problem themselves. The issue should be addressed in a direct and up-front manner which leaves no room for doubt about the dangers of the situation. The person should be given whatever help and guidance may be necessary and some reasonable monitored time frame in which to correct the problem. If no improvement is demonstrated in a reasonable time, the person will eventually need to be removed from the team. Although this is a difficult action to take when the team has such a "dedicated" worker, it is the only choice available for the protection of the individual and the team.

## FOLLOW-UP SERVICES

No community or organization should begin to develop a CISM team without recognizing the fact that follow-up services are an integral part of the CISM services. This should be known from the beginning and not appear as a surprise once the team has been developed.

Follow-up services help to keep team members interested in their work. They feel that they have a genuine purpose between debriefings. They often get the greatest satisfaction from the feedback they receive after providing follow-up services.

Good follow-up services must be planned into the development of the team. They should be an integral part of the team's operating policies and procedures.

## FUND-RAISING

Since the majority of teams operate without paying their team members, the overall operating expenses of the team is generally quite low. There are some direct and hidden costs to operating a CISM team and team organizers must keep that point in mind. The direct costs of team development and operation are usually associated with the initial set up of the team. In most cases the costs are about $6,000 to $10,000. This includes the cost of bringing in a trainer, his or her fees, the costs of air fare or travel to the training site, lodging for the presenter, food and miscellaneous expenses. Other direct costs may be the telephone services, postage, travel to provide team services, office supplies and other items of that nature.

Indirect costs include such things as releasing individuals from their normal duties and replacing them with substitutes during a debriefing. Overtime for fill-in personnel is frequently the biggest hidden cost of operating a team. Other hidden costs include the emergency phone service which is managed by the communications center and billed to the team, the time the coordinators spend deploying teams and keeping team activities going, and the time spent in continuing education for the CISM programs.

Although the costs, outside of the direct developmental costs associated with establishing the team, are not always clear, the team's benefits may far outweigh the direct and indirect costs. Teams are designed to keep good people on their jobs. The costs of replacing those people is far higher than that of maintaining good people who are well trained and experienced.

If identifying the costs of operating a team is difficult, the funding sources to support team operating is even more nebulous. It ranges from the most efficient and effective source of funds -- a line item on the budget of the emergency services, to the interesting -- bake sales and raffles. Some sell T-shirts, caps and pins. Most teams try to gain some support from community business. Many have the benefit of presenting educational services for which they charge fees. Some have received limited grants from the International Critical Incident Stress Foundation, Inc. to help get their team up and running.

Whatever method of funding is chosen to support a team, involving the team members in the process is important to maintaining active membership. People who have a hand in creating or maintaining an organization stay its most loyal supporters. They feel that they have a real role to play in maintaining the health of the organization.

## RAISING SUPPORT FROM EMERGENCY PERSONNEL

There are two main ways the emergency services personnel come to believe in the value of the CISM team. The first method of gaining support is for the CISM team members to teach stress related information frequently to all of the emergency service providers. The simple fact that there is frequent contact from peers who have become knowledgeable about stress and its effects and that these peers are willing to teach others some of what they have learned is a tremendous boost to the credibility of the team.

The second method for the team to gain support is to do an excellent job in debriefings and other direct support functions. When team members respond quickly to requests for help and when they provide efficient and effective services to those who need their help, the team's reputation quickly builds a positive foundation. Team members must also maintain a low profile and not lead people to believe that they are forcing their services upon anyone. It is also necessary that a team quickly correct any mistakes which might occur. Ignoring mistakes is a disruptive way to manage the team affairs and may turn out to be an error which can, under certain circumstances, turn out to be fatal for the team.

## GAINING FURTHER SUPPORT FROM SUPERVISORS AND ADMINISTRATORS

Supervisors and the organization's administrators deserve to know what the team is all about. There is no need for them to know the details of information and reactions discussed during the debriefings or other interventions made by the CISM team members on behalf of distressed emergency personnel. But they must have knowledge about the team, its functions, the types of events it responds to and the manner in which it is called. They cannot use the team properly nor can they support it if they know nothing about it.

Team members would be wise to bring the leaders of the various organizations together in the early stages of the team's development and periodically once it has been established. Information about the team's functions and limitations is essential for the administration and supervisors. Sometimes it is helpful, after the general familiarization sessions, to arrange meetings between key team personnel and the administrators and highest ranking supervisors in each organization. The individual attention paid to the key people in the various organizations ensures use and support of the team. Since teams may be a very new addition in some areas, the leadership of the organizations may have many concerns and questions. Administrators and supervisory personnel must be reassured of the following items:

- The CISM team is run by operations personnel who depend on mental health professionals and clergy personnel for guidance and professional consultations.

- The CISM team encourages recovery from stress. It does not encourage disability claims, workers compensation and litigation against the organization and its leadership.

- The CISM is a prevention program far more than it is a treatment program.

- The cost of team operation are minimal, but the benefits are maximal (difficult to quantify, however). Although some research is currently underway and numerous studies have already been published with very positive results, CISM is a relatively new field. It is only twenty-five years old. It would be unwise to discount the thousands of anecdotal records which have been collected over the past two decades. The experiences of 700 CISM teams in more the 40,000 debriefings cannot be simply ignored. This is especially so when the overwhelming majority of the reports of debriefing services are extremely positive.

- The CISM team cannot overrule a commanding officer, especially when the team is working at the scene of an incident. Any decision which affects the staffing of the operation or the operational procedures must be cleared in advance by the team members. If the decision interferes with the operation, the CISM team member may express his or her concerns but the ultimate decision-making in emergency services falls to the supervisor or administrator.

- The CISM team will assist the supervisors and administrators directly whenever necessary and will make whatever efforts are necessary to advise the command level personnel of situations which may need supervisor direction and leadership.

- The CISM team will keep the administration and leaders of an organization informed of the general nature of the teams activities.

- The CISM team will actively participate in educational programs for the organizations involved in utilizing the teams services.

- The CISM team will actively participate in disaster drills and other activities which will enhance their performance with each other.

- The CISM team will keep the administration informed of developments in the CISM field, particularly completed research projects which affect the services provided or drive further development of the team.

# DISASTER DRILLS

Another way for the team to enhance the active involvement of team members in CISM functions is to participate actively in disaster drills. It is most important for the team to go through the call out procedures, go to the scene and check in with the command post. Team members should set up their operations under the safety officer at the scene. In the incident command system, the safety officer is in charge of all health and safety issues at the scene. Therefore, the CISM team should report to the safety officer, who can bring special considerations to the incident commander.

It is not advisable for the CISM team to have "mock" distressed victims. It is too difficult to fake emotions. The personnel do not like this type of role playing and the team is often perceived as ludicrous when it attempts such artificial "crisis interventions." The best use of the team in a drill situation is to have them go through the steps of being called out, responding to the scene and setting up with the safety officer. The team members should learn about perimeter control points, command post operations, sectors, rehabilitation of personnel, the morgue set up, the media section and numerous other aspects of a disaster situation. Team members could hand out an informational brochure on the functions of a CISM team at the end of the drill. The handout should contain the names of team contacts and the phone numbers to use for emergency call out of the team.

# TEAM EVALUATION

Evaluating team performance is one of the most difficult aspects of maintaining a CISM team. This is true for many reasons. Emergency personnel resist efforts to look too deeply into their organizations and their own personal inner thoughts and emotions. The emergency services are organizations which are long on tradition and short on introspection. They feel that outsiders looking into their organizations and not fully understanding their jobs, may issue a set of recommendations or mandates which could interfere with their ability to perform their jobs. From the individual perspective, emergency workers do not like efforts requiring them to examine their emotions because too close a realization of how much emotions are a part of their lives may jeopardize their abilities to work effectively under field conditions. Emergency personnel work very hard to suppress their emotions and therefore any study which forces them to bring those emotions to the surface for examination will meet with significant resistance. They believe that they need to suppress their emotions to ensure that they will be able to work through a crisis when they are needed. Emergency workers believe firmly that emotions are only distractions from their peak efficiency in handling a traumatic situation.

Another reason evaluation is difficult is that emergency personnel are constantly on the move. They are most reliable when it comes to the performance of their duties but they do not make good subjects for study because they cannot be held in one place long enough to be studied.

Any study of the effects of debriefing on emergency personnel will have to take into consideration the fact that traumatic events continue to occur after the debriefing. Those new events may keep symptoms of stress higher than if the person was able to rest for a week or two after a traumatic event. Studies which evaluate team performance must always be designed with the idea that the researcher is going to observe real world people in real world situations. No carefully designed laboratory exists in which emergency personnel can be examined under tightly controlled conditions.

Even a combination of all of the above reasons why studying the team performance is difficult does not excuse a team from its responsibility of attempting to determine if its interventions are effective and if its performance is efficient. Teams must search out new methods to examine their work. The task is important because, without appropriate evaluation, changes may not be made in the interventions teams make, or changes will be made when none are necessary simply because some one suggests a new idea. In some circumstances, changes may be made which could be harmful. Without evaluation, those changes might do harm before the error is discovered.

Formal studies of the effectiveness and efficiency of the team are necessary, but some basic guidelines need to be adhered to. They are:

- Research and team evaluation must always be secondary to the provision of services such as debriefings, defusings and other processes.

- Individual confidentiality must always be observed.

- Participants should be involved in the study on a voluntary basis.

- People in a study should have appropriate information on which their decision to participate is based.

- The study should be designed around the real world nature of the personnel involved and their jobs.

- The objectives of the study should be clearly stated.

- The limitations of the study should be clearly stated.

- Feedback should always be given to the participants and their organizations at the completion of the study.

- Conclusions should never be drawn from data known to be faulty or from data which are incomplete or from a sample that is too small.

- The researcher has an obligation not only to present the data to the participants but, more importantly to help the participants to properly interpret the data.

Formal research projects are only one of the mechanism to evaluate team performance. There are several other important methods. Feedback from participants in the debriefings should be encouraged and, when offered, it should be listened to very carefully. The participants in a debriefing are often the best sources of information regarding team performance. They can give good hints about the communications used by team members, the clarity of the teaching segments, the perceived genuineness of the team members and things which the team might have missed during the debriefing.

The team should review its cases at its regular meetings as described in the previous section on "regular team meetings." The case reviews give the team a significant opportunity to analyze a case and gather everyone's opinion about how it was handled. Changes in one's personal style or minor changes in the team performance can be targeted during such discussions.

Another aspect of team performance evaluation can be managed by a Peer Review Board to review complaints (internal or external) about errors or deliberate disregard for commonly accepted CISM or CISD practices. The

Peer Review Board is made up of between three and five members (both professional and peer support personnel) of the CISM team who are in good standing. They are designated by the clinical director and the coordinator. At least two should have served on the previous Peer Review Board. The other members may be assigned as necessary to review the complaint.

The Peer Review Board should gather the facts related to the incident as soon as within three days of the complaint or report of inappropriate activity. The board then meets with the member in question within three days of the complaint. The board will evaluate the information gathered and issue a written report with recommendations to the clinical director and the senior coordinator for the team within two days of the meeting with the team member.

The clinical director and the team coordinator will either act upon the recommendations of the board or resubmit the report for further review.

# REVOCATION / SUSPENSION OF MEMBERSHIP

Any organization which develops a mechanism for bringing in new members must also develop a mechanism for removing any of its members from service if their performance is below minimal standards. This is especially important in a situation in which a poor performance can lead to harm to a person or a group struggling through the stresses associated with a critical incident. Team membership can be revoked by the clinical director, the team coordinator or the Peer Review Board. Usually the decision is made when the team leadership has conferred and has reviewed the facts of the situation which caused them to consider the revocation of team membership of one of their team members. Any of the following could be grounds for dismissal from a CISM team.

- Any breech of confidentiality.

- Failure to follow local policies and procedures.

- Organizing or providing a CISD without notifying the team coordinator.

- Organizing or providing a defusing without notifying the team coordinator.

- Not informing the team coordinator of an on-scene support service, a significant other support program, specialty debriefing, individual consults or any other CISM team activity, intervention strategy or educational endeavor.

- Using one's membership on the team to enhance one's private business concerns.

- Using one's membership on the team to enhance one's personal social life. This would be the case if a team member used team membership to gain access to another person for the purposes of a date.

- Going to a scene or location of a critical incident to function on behalf of the CISM team without the prior knowledge or consent of the team coordinator or a designee.

- Failure to be present at an assigned debriefing when the member has made a commitment to do so.

- Consistent failure to attend team meetings and team education programs.

- Acting against the expressed direction of the clinical director or the team coordinator.

- Misrepresenting oneself concerning the affairs or operations of the CISM program.

- Failure to complete the required team paperwork.

# Appendix C

## FOR ADDITIONAL INFORMATION ON:

A. CISM Team Registry
B. CISM Training
C. CISM Support Services
D. ICISF membership
E. Other CISM Issues

Contact:
### *International Critical Incident Stress Foundation, Inc.*

10176 Baltimore National Pike
Suite 201
Ellicott City, MD  21042

Phone:  410-750-9600
Fax:  410-750-9601
www.icisf.org

Emergency:  410-313-2473

# REFERENCES

Adams, J. D. (Ed.). (1980). *Understanding and managing stress.* San Diego,CA: University Associates.

Aguilera, D.C., Messick, J.M. & Farrell, M.S. (1974). *Crisis intervention: Theory and methodology.*St. Louis: C.V. Mosby.

American College of Sports Medicine. (1980). *Guidelines for graded exercise testing and exercise prescription.* Philadelphia: Lea & Febiger.

American Psychiatric Association. (1964). *First aid for psychological reactions in disasters.* Washington, DC: American Psychiatric Association.

American Psychiatric Association. (1968). *Diagnostic and statistical manual of mental disorders,* Second Edition. Washington DC: Author.

American Psychiatric Association. (1980). *Diagnostic and statisical manual of mental disorders,* Third Edition. Washington DC: Author.

American Psychiatric Association. (1987). *Diagnostic and statistical manual of mental disorders,* Third Edition, Revised . Washington, DC: Author.

American Psychiatric Association (1994). *Diagnostic and statistical manual of mental disorders,* Fourth Edition. Washington DC: Author.

Appel, J.W. (1966). Preventive psychiatry. In A. J. Glass and R. J. Bernucci (Eds.). *Neuropsychiatry in World War II* (pp. 373 - 415). Washington, DC: US Government Printing Office.

Appel, J.W., Beebe, G.W. and Hilger, D.W. (1946). Comparative incidence of neuropsychiatric casualties in World War I and World War II. *American Journal of Psychiatry, 102,* 196-199.

Appelbaum, S. H. (1981). *Stress management for health care professionals.* Rockville, MD: Aspen Systems Corp.

Arnold, M. (1970). *Feelings and emotions.* New York: Academic.

Arnold, M. (1984). *Memory and the brain.* Hillsdale, NJ: Erlbaum.

Back, K. J. (1991). Critical incident stress management for care providers in the pediatric emergency department. *Critical Care Nurse,* 12(1), 78-83.

Bailey, P. (1918). War neuroses, shell shock, and nervousness in soldiers. *Journal of the American Medical Association, 71,* 2148-2153.

Beck, A. (1979). *Cognitive Therapy of Depression.* New York: Basic.

Beck, A. and Emery, G. (1985). *Anxiety disorders and phobias.* New York: Basic Books.

Benson, H. (1975). *The relaxation response.* New York: Morrow.

Benson, H. (1983). The relaxation response. *Trends in Neuroscience, 6,* 281-284.

Benson, H., Alexander, S., and Feldman, C. (1975). Decreased premature ventricular contractions through the use of the relaxation response. *Lancet, 2,* 380-382.

Berg, D. (1970). Crisis intervention concepts for emergency telephone services. *Crisis Intervention, 4,* 11-19.

Bettleheim, B. (1984). Afterword. In C. Vegh, *I didn't say good-bye.* New York: E.P. Dutton.

Bisson, J.I., Jenkins, P., Alexander, J., & Bannister, C. (1997). Randomized controlled trial of psychological debriefings for victims of acute burn trauma. *British Journal of Psychiatry, 171,* 78-81.

Bisson, J.I., McFarlane, A. & Rose, S. (2000). Psychological debriefing. In E. Foa, A. McFarlane, & M. Friedman (Eds). *Effective Treatments for PTSD* (pp.39-59). NY: Guilford.

Blampied, N.M. (2000). Single-case research designs: A neglected alternative. *American Psychologist, 55,* 960.

Blau, T.H. (1994). *Psychological services for law enforcement.* New York: John Wiley & Sons, Inc.

Bohl, N. (1991). The effectiveness of brief psychological interventions in police officers after critical incidents. In J.T. Reese, J. Horn, and C. Dunning (eds). *Critical Incidents in Policing, Revised (pp. 31-38).* Washington, D.C.: Department of Justice.

Bohl, N. (1995). Measuring the effectiveness of CISD. *Fire Engineering,* 125-126.

Bordow, S. & Porritt, D. (1979). An experimental evaluation of crisis intervention. *Social Science and Medicine, 13,* 251-256.

Borkovec, T.D., Wilkenson, L., Folensbee, R., and Lerman, C. (1983). Stimulus control applications to the treatment of worry. *Behavioral Research and Therapy, 21,* 247-251.

Breslau, I.N., Davis, G.C., Andreski, P. and Peterson, E. (1991). Traumatic events and post-traumatic stress disorders in an urban population of young adults. *Archives of General Psychiatry, 48,* 216 - 222.

Brett, E.A. and Ostroff, R. (1985). Imagery and post-traumatic stress disorder. *American Journal of Psychiatry, 142,* 417-424.

Breznitz, S. (1980). Stress in Israel. In Selye, H. (Ed.) *Selye's guide to stress research.* New York: Van Nostrand Reinhold Co.

British Psychological Society (1990). *Psychological Aspects of Disaster.* Leicester: British Psychological Society.

Brown, M.W. and Williams. (1918). *Neuropsychiatry and the war: A bibliography with abstracts.* New York: National Committee for Mental Hygiene.

Bunn, T. & Clarke, A. (1979). Crisis intervention. *British Journal of Medical Psychology, 52,* 191-195.

Burgess, A. W. and Balwin, B.A. (1981). *Crisis intervention theory and practice, a clinical handbook.* Englewood Cliffs, NJ: Prentice Hall, Inc.

Burns, C. and Harm, I. (1993). Emergency nurses' perceptions of critical incidents and stress debriefing. *Journal of Emergency Nursing, 19* (5), 431-436.

Busuttil, A. & Busuttil, W. (1995). Psychological debriefing. *British Journal of Psychiatry,* 166, 676-677.

Busuttil, W., Turnbull, G., Neal, L., Rollins, J., West, A., Blanch, N., & Herepath, R. (1995). Incorporating psychological debriefing techniques within a brief group psychotherapy programme for the treatment of post-traumatic stress disorder. *British Journal of Psychiatry,* 167, 495-502.

Butcher, J. (1980). The role of crisis intervention in an airport disaster plan. *Aviation, Space and Environmental Medicine,* 51, 1260-1262. Cambridge University Press.

Campbell, D.T. & Stanley, J.C. (1963). *Experimental and Quasi-experimental Designs for Research.* Chicago: Rand McNally.

Caplan, G. (1961). *An approach to community mental health.* New York: Grine and Stratton.

Caplan, G. (1964). *Principles of preventive psychiatry.* New York: Basic Books.

Caplan, G. (1976). *Support systems and community mental health.* New York: Behavioral Publications, Inc.

Carkhuff, R. and Truax, C. (1965). Lay mental health counseling. *Journal of Consulting Psychology,* 29, 426-431.

Chemtob, C., Tomas, S, Law, W., & Cremniter, D. (1997). Postdiaster psychosocial intervetion. *American Journal of Psychiatry,* 134, 415-417.

Cherniss, C. (1980). *Staff burnout in human service organizations.* New York: Praeger Publishers.

Cohen, R. E. and Ahearn, F. L. (1980). *Handbook for mental health care of disaster victims.* Baltimore, MD: Johns Hopkins University Press.

Corneil, D. W. (1993). Prevalence of post-traumatic stress disorders in a metropolitan fire department. Unpublished Doctoral Dissertation. The Johns Hopkins University, Baltimore.

Couchaine, K.E. and Dowd, E.T. (1994). Group Approaches. In F. Dattilo and A. Freeman (Eds.). *Cognitive-behavioral strategies in crisis interven tion.* New York: Guilford.

Craren, E. J. (Ed.) (1992). *Nebraska statewide CISD program, rules and regulations* (vol. 1) and *Operational policies and procedures* (vol.2). Lincoln, NE: Nebraska Interagency CISD Council.

Davidson, L. and Baum, A. (1986). Chronic stress and post-traumatic stress disorders. *Journal of Consulting and Clinical Psychology,* 54, 303-308.

de Vries, H. (1981). Tranquilizer effect of exercise. *America's Journal of*

*Physical Medicine, 60,* 57-66.

de Vries, H., and Adams, G. (1972). Electromyagraphic comparison of single dose of exercise and meprobamate as to effects of muscular relaxation. *American Journal of Physical Medicine,* 52, 130-141.

Deahl, M., Srinivasan, M., Jones, N., Thomas, J., Neblett, C., & Jolly, A. (2000). Preventing psychological trauma in soldiers. The role of operational stress training and psychological debriefing. *British Journal of Medical Psychology,* 73, 77-85.

Decker, J. & Stubblebine, J (1972). Crisis intervention and prevention of psychiatric disability: A follow-up. *American Journal of Psychiatry,* 129, 725-729.

Donnovan, D. (1991). Traumatology: A field whose time has come. *Journal of Traumatic Stress,* 4, 433-436.

Duffy, J. (1978). Emergency mental health services during and after a major aircraft accident. *Aviation, Space and Environmental Medicine,* 49, 1004-1008.

Duffy, J. (1979). The role of CMHCs in airport disasters. *Technical Assistance Center Report,* 2(1),  7-9.

Dyregrov, A. (1989). Caring for helpers in disaster situations: Psychologi-cal debriefing. *Disaster Management,* 2, 25-30.

Dyregrov, A. (1997). The process of psychological debriefing. *Journal of traumatic Stress,* 10 589-604.

Dyregrov, A. (1998). Psychological debriefing: An effective method? *TRAUMATOLOGYe,* 4, (2), Article 1.

Dyregrov, A. (1999). Helpful and hurtful aspects of psychological debriefing groups. *International Journal of Emergency Mental Health,* 1, 175-181.

Dyregrov, A. & Reidar T. (1988).  Rescue workers emotional reactions following a disaster. *Scandinavian Journal of Psychology.*

Dyregrov, A. & Mitchell, J. (1992). Work with traumatized children — Psychological effects and coping strategies. *Journal of Traumatic Stress,* 5, 5-17.

Ellis, A. (1973). *Humanistic psychology: The rational-emotive approach.* New York: Julian.

Epperson, M. M.(1977). Families in sudden crisis. *Social Work Health Care,* 2, 3.

Epperson-Sebour, M. M. (1985). Response.  In Green (Ed.) *Role stressors and supports for emergency workers.*  Washington, DC: Center For Mental Health Studies of Emergencies., U.S. Department of Health and Human Services.

Everly, G. S. (1979). A technique for the immediate reduction of psycho-physiologic stress reactivity. *Health Education,* 10, 44.

Everly, G. S. (1989). *A clinical guide to the treatment of the human stress response.* New York: Plenum.

Everly, G. S. (1990). Post-traumatic stress disorder as a "disorder of arousal." *Psychology and Health: An International Journal,* 4, 135 - 145.

Everly, G. S. (1992) "Psychotraumatology: A two-factor theory." Paper presented at the Fourth Montreux Congress on Stress, Montreux, Switzerland.

Everly, G.S. (1993a). Psychotraumatology: A two-factor formulation of post-traumatic stress. *Intergrative Physiological and Behavioral Science.,* 28, 270 - 278.

Everly, G.S. (1993b). Neurophysiological considerations in the treatment of post-traumatic stress disorder. In J. Wilson and B. Raphael (Eds). *Hand book of traumatic stress syndromes* (pp. 795 - 801). NY: Plenum.

Everly, G.S. (1994). Short-term psychotherapy of acute adult onset post-traumatic stress: The role of Weltanschauung. *Stress Medicine,* 10, 191 - 196.

Everly, G.S., Jr. (1995). An integrative two-factor model of posttraumatic stress. In G. Everly, Jr. & J. Lating (Eds.) *Psychotraumatology: Key Papers and Core Concepts in Posttraumatic Stress* (pp.27-48). NY: Plenum.

Everly, G.S., Jr. (1999a). Emergency mental health: An overview. *International Journal of Emergency Mental Health,* 1, 3-7.

Everly, G.S., Jr. (1999b). A primer on Critical Incident Stress Management: What's really in a name? *International Journal of Emergency Mental Health,* 1, 77-80.

Everly, G.S., Jr. (2000a). Crisis Management Briefings (CMB). Large group crisis intervention in response to terrorism, disasters, and violence. *International Journal of Emergency Mental Health,* 2 53- 57.

Everly, G.S., Jr. (2000b). Pastoral crisis intervention: Toward a definition. *International Journal of Emergency Mental Health,* 2, 69-71.

Everly, G.S., Jr. (2000c). The role of pastoral crisis intervention in disasters, terrorism, violence, and other community crises. *International Journal of Emergency Mental Health,* 2, 139-142.

Everly, G. S., Jr. & Benson, H. (1989). Disorders of arousal and the relaxation response. *International Journal of Psychosomatics,* 36, 15 - 22.

Everly, G.S., Jr. & Boyle, S. (1999). Critical Incident Stress Debriefing (CISD): A meta-analysis. *International Journal of Emergency Mental Health,* 1, 165-168.

Everly, G.S., Jr., Flannery, R.B., Jr. & Eyler, V. (in press). Critical Incident Stress Management (CISM): A statistical review of the literature. *Psychiatric Quarterly.*

Everly, G.S. Jr., Flannery, Jr., R. B., Eyler, V. & Mitchell, J.T. (in press). A comprehensive, integrated multicomponent approach to crisis intervention. *Advances in Mind-Body Medicine.*

Everly, G.S., Jr., Flannery, R.B., Jr. & Mitchell, J. (2000). Critical Incident Stress Management: A review of literature. *Aggression and Violent Behavior: A Review Journal,* 5, 23-40.

Everly, G. S. and Horton, A.M. (1989). Neuropsychology of PTSD, *Perceptual and Motor Skills,* 68, 807-810.

Everly, G.S. and Lating, J. (Ed.)(1995). *Psychotraumatology: Key papers and core concepts in post-traumatic stress.* NY: Plenum.

Everly, G. S. and Mitchell, J. T. (1992, Dec.). "CISD and the prevention of work-related PTSD." Paper presented to the Second NIOSH/APA Conference on Work-related Stress, Washington D.C.

Everly, G.S., Jr. & Mitchell, J.T. (1999). *Critical Incident Stress Management (CISM): A new era and standard of care in crisis intervention.* Ellicott City, MD: Chevron.

Everly, G.S., Jr. & Mitchell, J.T. (2000). The "debriefing controversy" and crisis intervention. *International Journal of Emergency Mental Health,* 2, 211-225.

Everly, G.S., Jr. & Piacentini, A. (1999, March). The Effects of CISD on trauma symptoms: A meta-analysis. Paper presented to the *APA-NIOSH Work, Stress and Health '99: Organization of Work in a Global Economy* conference, Baltimore.

Everly, G. S. and Rosenfeld, R. (1981). *The nature and treatment of the stress response.* New York: Plenum Press.

Figley, C. R. (Ed.). (1985). *Trauma and its wake,* (Vol. 1). New York: Brunner / Mazel.

Flannery, R.B., Jr.(1998). *The Assaulted Staff Action Program.* Ellicott City, MD: Chevron.

Flannery, R.B., Jr. (1999a). Treating family survivors of mass casualties: A CISM family crisis intervention approach. *International Journal of Emergency Mental Health,* 1, 243-250.

Flannery, R.B., Jr. (1999b). Critical Incident Stress Management (CISM); The assaultive psychiatric patient. *International Journal of Emergency Mental Health,* 1, 169-174.

Flannery, R.B., Jr. (1999c). Critical Incident Stress Management and the Assaulted Staff Action Program. *International Journal of Emergency Mental Health,* 1, 103-108.

Flannery, R.B., Jr., Anderson, E., Marks, L., & Uzoma, L. (2000). The Assaulted Staff Action Program (ASAP) and declines in rates of assaults: Mixed replicated findings. *Psychiatric Quarterly,* 71, 165-175.

Flannery, R.B., Jr., Everly, G.S., Jr. & Eyler, V. (2000). The Assaulted Staff Action Program (ASAP) and declines in Assaults: A meta-analysis. *International Journal of Emergency Mental Health,* 2, 143-146.

Flannery, R.B., Jr., Hanson, M., Penk, W., Flannery, G. & Gallagher, C.(1995).The Assaulted Staff Action Program: An approach to coping with the aftermath of violence in the workplace. In L. Murphy, J. Hurrell, S. Sauter, and G. Keita (Eds.). *Job Stress Interventions* (pp. 199-212). Washington, D.C.: APA Press.

Flannery, R.B., Jr., Hanson, M., Penk, W., Goldfinger, S., Pastva, G. & Navon, M. (1998). *Psychiatric Services*, 49, 241-243.

Flannery, R.B., Jr., Penk, W. & Corrigan, M. (1999). The Assaulted Staff Action Program (ASAP) and declines in the prevalence of assaults: A community-based replication. *International Journal of Emergency Mental Health*, 1, 19-22.

Foa, E., Keane, T. & Friedman, M. (2000). *Effective Treatments for PTSD*. NY: Guilford.

Fowler, D.E. and McGee, R.K. (1973). Assessing the performance of telephone crisis workers: The development of a technical effectiveness scale. In D. Lester and G.W. Brockoop (Eds.), *Crisis intervention and counseling by telephone*. Springfield, IL: Charles C. Thomas.

Freeman, K. (1979). CMHC responses to the Chicago and San Diego airplane disasters. *Technical Assistance Center Report* 2(1), 10-12.

Freud, S. (1913). Further recommendations on the technique of psychoanalysis. In J. Strachey, translator, *The complete psychological works, vol. 12*, NY: Norton.

Friedman, R., Framer, M. & Shearer, D. (1988). Early response to post-traumatic stress. *EAP Digest*, September - October. pp. 45-49.

Girdano, D., Everly, G. & Dusek, D. (1993). *Controlling stress and tension, (4th ed.)*. Englewood Cliffs, NJ: Prentice-Hall.

Gist, R. & Lubin, B. (Eds.) (1989). *Psychosocial aspects of disaster*. New York: John Wiley & Sons.

Graham, N. K. (1981). Done in, fed up, burned out: Too much attrition in EMS. *Journal of Emergency Medical Services*, 6(1), 24-29.

Graham, N. K. (1981). Part 2: How to avoid a short career. *Journal of Emergency Medical Services*, 6 (2), 25-31.

Greden, J.F. (1974). Anxiety or caffeinism: A diagnostic dilemma. *American Journal of Psychiatry*, 131, 1089 - 1092.

Greenstone, J.C. (1993). *Critical Incident Stress Debriefing and Crisis Management*. Austin, Texas: Texas Department of Health.

Harvey, J.H., Orbuch, T. L., Chwlisz, K.D. & Garwood, G. (1991). Coping with sexual assault: The role of account making and confiding. *Journal of Traumatic Stress*, 4, 515-532.

Heider, J. (1974). Catharsis in human potential encounter. *Journal of Humanistic Psychology*, 14, 27 - 47.

Heinman, M. F. (1975). The police suicide. *Journal of Police Science and Administration*, 3(3), 267-273.

Helzer, J., Robins, L. & McEvoy, L. (1987). Post-traumatic stress disorder in the general population. *New England Journal of Medicine, 317*, 1630-1634.

Herman, J. & van der Kolk, B. (1987). Traumatic antecedents of borderline personality disorder. In B. van der Kolk (Ed.), *Psychological trauma* (pp. 111-126). Washington, DC: American Psychiatric Press.

Herman, J. L. (1992). Complex PTSD. *Journal of Traumatic Stress, 5*, 377-392.

Herman, J.L. (1992). *Trauma and Recovery*. New York: Basic Books.

Hersen, M. & Barlow, D. (1976). *Single-case Experimental Designs*: Oxford, England: Pergamon.

Hiley-Young, B. & Gerrity, E.T. Critical incident stress debriefing (CISD): Value and limitations in disaster response. *NCP Clinical Quarterly, 4*, 17-19.

Hobbs, M., Mayou, R., Harrison, B. & Worlock, P. (1996). A randomized controlled trial of psychological debriefing for victims of road traffic accidents. *British Medical Journal, 313*, 1438-1439.

Hoff, L.A. (1978). *People in Crisis: Understanding and Helping*. Menlow Park, CA: Addison-Wesley Publishing Co.

Holmes, R. (1985) *Acts of War: The behavior of men in battle*. New York: Free Press.

Holmes, T.H. & Rahe, R. (1967). The social readjustment rating scale. *Journal of Psychosomatic Research, 11*, 213-218.

Honig, A. (1991). *Cerritos air disaster: Psychological effects*. Paper presented at the First World Congress on Stress, Trauma, and Coping, Baltimore, MD, May 1991.

Horowitz, M. (1976). *Stress response syndromes*. NY: Jason Aronsom.

Horowitz, M.J. (1976). Diagnosis and treatment of stress response syndromes: General principles. In H.J. Parad, H.L.P. Resnik and L.G. Parad (Eds.). *Emergency and disaster management: A mental health source book*. Bowie, MD: The Charles Press Publishers.

Jasnoski, M., Holmes, D., Solomon, S. & Agular, C. (1981). Exercise changes in aerobic capacity and changes in self-perceptions. *Journal of Research in Personality, 15*, 460-466.

Jenkins, S.R. (1996). Social support and debriefing efficacy among emergency medical workers after a mass shooting incident. *Journal of Social Behavior and Personality,11*, 477 - 492.

Johnston, S.J. (1993). Traumatic stress reactions in the crew of the Herald of Free Enterprise. In J.P.Wilson and B. Raphael (Eds.), *International handbook of traumatic stress syndromes*. New York: Plenum Press.

Jones, D. R. (1985). Secondary disaster victims. *American Journal of Psy-*

chiatry, 142, 303-307.

Kahn, M. (1966). The physiology of catharsis. *Journal of Personality and Social Psychology, 3*, 278 - 286.

Keller, K. L. (1991). Stress management for emergency department personnel. *Topics in Emergency Medicine*, September, 70-76.

Kenardy, J. (2000). The current status of psychological debriefing. *British Medical Journal, 321*, 1032-1033.

Kenardy, J.A., Webster, R.A., Lewin, T.J., Carr, V.J., Hazell, P.L., & Carter, G.L. (1996) Stress debriefing and patterns of recovery following a natural disaster. *Journal of Traumatic Stress, 9*, 37 - 49.

Kennedy-Ewing, L. (1988). *Operational and training guide for the Critical incident stress management program of Delaware County, Pennsylvania.* Media, PA: Department of Human Resources.

Kentsmith, D. (1980). Minimizing the psychological effects of a wartime disaster on an individual. *Aviation, Space, and Environmental Medicine, 51, 409 - 413.*

Kilpatrick, D.G., Saunders, B., Amick-McMullan, A., Best, C., Veronen, L., and Renick, H. (1989). Victim and crime factors associated with the development of crime-related post-traumatic stress disorder. *Behavior Therapy, 20*, 199 - 214.

Kliman, A.S. (1975). The Corning flood project: Psychological first-aid following a natural disaster. In H. J. Parad, H.L.P. Resnik and L.G. Parad (Eds.), *Emergency and disaster management: A mental health sourcebook.* Bowie, MD: Charles Press Publishers.

Kraus, H., and Raab, W. (1961). *Hypokinetic disease.* Springfield, IL: Charles C. Thomas.

Kraus, R.P. (1997). Randomisedcontrolled trial of psychological debriefing for victims of acute burn trauma: Comment. *British Journal of Psychiatry, 171*, 583.

Kroes, W. H. and Hurrell, J. J., Jr. (Eds) (1976) *Job stress and the police officer: Identifying stress reduction techniques.* Washington, DC: U.S Department of Health, Education, and Welfare (Pub. No. NIOSH 76-187).

Lang, P. (1971). The application of psychophysiological methods to the study of psychotherapy and behavior modification. In A. Bergin and S. Garfield (Eds.), *Handbook of psychotherapy and behavior change.* New York: Wiley.

Langsley, D., Machotka, P., & Flomenhaft, K. (1971). Avoiding mental health admission: A follow-up. *American Journal of Psychiatry, 127*, 1391-1394.

Lazarus, R. and Folkman, S. (1984). *Stress Appraisal and Coping.* New York: Springer.

Lee, C., Slade, P., & Lygo, V. (1996). The influence of psychological debriefing on emotional adaptation in women following early miscarriage. *British Journal of Psychiatry, 69*, 47-58.

Leeman-Conley, M. (1990). After a violent robbery. *Criminology Australia,* April / May, 4-6.

Lindemann, E. (1944). Symptomatology and management of acute grief. *American Journal of Psychiatry,* 101,141-148.

Lindy, J.D., Grace, M., and Green, B. (1981). Survivors: Outreach to a reluctant population. *American Journal of Orthopsychiatry,* 51, 465-478.

Lipton, M.I. (1994*). Post-traumatic stress disorder: Additional perspectives.* Springfield IL: Charles C. Thomas Publishers.

Maslow, A. H. (1970). *Motivation and personality.* NY: Harper & Row.

Mayou, R.A., Ehlers, A., & Hobbs, M. (2000). Psychological debriefing for road traffic accident victims: Three-year follow-up of a randomised controlled trial. *British Journal of Psychiatry,* 176, 589-593.

Mc Gee, R.K. (1974). *Crisis intervention in the community.* Baltimore: University Park Press.

McCarthy, M. (1988). Stressed employees look for relief in workers' compensation claims. *Wall Street Journal,* , April 7, pp, 34.

McFarlane, A.C. (1988). The longitudinal course of posttraumatic morbidity. *Journal of Nervous and Mental Disease,* 176, 30 - 39.

McGeer, E. & McGeer, P. (1988). Excitotoxins and animal models of disease. In C. Galli, L. Manzo, and P. Spencer (Eds.), *Recent Advances in Nervous System Toxicology* (pp. 107-131). NY: Plenum.

Meichenbaum, D. (1994). *A clinical handbook /practical therapist manual for assessing and treating adults with post-traumatic stress disorder (PTSD).* Waterloo, Ontario, Canada: Institute Press.

Miller, A., et al. (1988, April 25). Stress on the job. *Newsweek,* pp.40-41.

Miller, L. (1999). Critical incident stress debriefing: Clinical applications and new directions. *International Journal of emergency Mental Health,* 1, 253-265.

Miller, S. (1994). Reaching Out to Our Own. *Marines,* June, 9-10.

Mitchell, J. T. (1976). Rescue crisis intervention. *EMS News.* Baltimore, MD: 4(3), 4.

Mitchell, J. T. (1981, November). "Acute stress reactions and burnout in prehospital emergency medical services personnel". Paper presented at the First National Conference on Burnout. Philadelphia, PA.

Mitchell, J. T. (1982). The psychological impact of the Air Florida 90 disaster on fire-rescue, paramedic and police personnel. In R A. Cowley, S. Edelstein and M. Silerstein (Eds.), *Mass casualties: A lessons learned approach , accidents, civil disorders, natural disasters, terrorism.* Washington, D.C.: Department of Transportation (DOT HS 806302).

Mitchell, J. T. (1983). Guidelines for psychological debriefings. *Emergency management course manual.* Emmitsburg, MD: Federal Emergency Management Agency, Emergency Management Institute.

Mitchell, J. T. (1986) Teaming up against critical incident stress. *Chief Fire Executive*, 1(1), 24; 36; 84.

Mitchell, J. T. (1988, July). "CISD Introductory Remarks". Workshop handout Baltimore MD: University of Maryland Baltimore County.

Mitchell, J. T. (1988). Development and functions of a critical incident stress debriefing team. *Journal of Emergency Medical Services*, 13(12), 43-46.

Mitchell, J. T. (1988). The history, status and future of critical incident stress debriefings. *Journal of Emergency Medical Services*,13(11), 49-52.

Mitchell, J. T. (1991). Demobilizations. *Life Net*, vol. 2, (1).

Mitchell, J. T. (1991). Law enforcement applications of critical incident stress teams. In James T. Reese (Ed.), *Critical incidents in policing revised.* Washington, DC: US Department of Justice: Federal Bureau of Investigation.

Mitchell, J. T. (1992). Protecting your people from critical incident stress. *Fire Chief*, 36(5), 61-64.

Mitchell, J. T. (1992). Comprehensive traumatic stress management in the emergency department. The Emergency Nurses Association: Monograph series. 1(8), 3 - 15.

Mitchell, J. T. and Bray, G. P. (1990). *Emergency services stress, guidelines for preserving the health and careers of emergency services personnel.* Englewood Cliffs, NJ: Brady Publishing.

Mitchell, J. T. and Resnik, H. L. P. (1981). *Emergency response to crisis.* Bowie, MD: Brady Publishing. (republished Ellicott City, MD: Chevron Publishing, 1986).

Mitchell, J.T. (1983). When disaster strikes...The critical incident stress debriefing process. *Journal of Emergency Medical Services*, 8, (1), 36-39.

Mitchell, J.T. (1994). Too much help too fast. *Life Net*, a publication of the International Critical Incident Stresss Foundation, Inc., 5(3), 3-4.

Mitchell, J.T. and Dyregrov, A. (1993). Traumatic stress in disaster and emergency personnel: Prevention and intervention. In J.P.Wilson and Beverly Raphael (Eds.), *International handbook on traumatic stress syndromes.* New York: Plenum Press.

Mitchell, J.T. and Everly, G.S. (1993). *Critical incident stress debriefing (CISD): An operations manual for the prevention of traumatic stress among emergency services and disaster workers,* First Edition. Ellicott City, MD: Chevron Publishing.

Mitchell, J.T., Schiller, G., Eyler, V. & Everly, G.S., Jr. (1999). Community crisis intervention: The Coldenham tragedy revisited. *International Journal of Emergency Mental Health,* 1, 227-238.

Moran, C. and Britton, N.R. (1994). Emergency work experience and reactions to traumatic incidents. *Journal of Traumatic Stress*, 7(4), 575-585.

Nakanomiya, J. (1975). History of war medicine in Japan. *National De-*

*fense Medical Journal, 22,* 67-73.

Newman, E.C. (2000). Group crisis intervention in a school setting following an attempted suicide. *International Journal of Emergency Mental Health, 2,* 97-100.

Norman, E. and Getek, D. (1988). Post-traumatic stress in victims of psysicsl trauma [Abstract]. *Proceedings of the 15th Annual National Teaching Institute of the American Association of Critical Care Nurses,* (p.671). Newport Beach, CA: AACCN, 671.

Noy, S. (1991). Combat stress reactions. In R. Gal and A.D. Mangelsdorff (Eds.), *Handbook of military psychology.* Chichester, U.K.: John Wiley and Sons.

Nurmi, L. (1999). The sinking of the Estonia: The effects of Critical Incident Stess Debriefing on Rescuers. *International Journal of Emergency Mental Health, 1,* 23-32.

Ochberg, F. M. (1991). Post traumaitc therapy. *Psychotheraphy, 28,* 5-15.

Olney, J.W. (1978). Neurotoxicity of excitatory amino acids. In E. McGeer, J. Olney, and P. Mcgeer (Eds.), *Kainic acid as a tool in neurobiology,* (pp. 95-122) NY: Raven.

Orner, R. (1994). *Intervention strategies for emergency response groups: A new conceptual framework.* Paper presented at the NATO conference on Stress, Coping and disaster in Bonos, France.

OSHA. (1996). *Guidelines for Preventing Workplace Violence for Health Care and Social Service Workers - OSHA 3148-1996.* Washington, D.C.: Author.

OSHA. (1998). *Recommendations for Workplace Violence Prevention Programs in Late-Night Retail Establishments. – OSHA 3153-1998.* Washington, D.C.: Author.

Parad, H. (Ed.). (1965). *Crisis intervention: Selected readings.* New York: Family Service Association of America.

Parad, L. & Parad, H. (1968). A study of crisis oriented planned short-term treatment: Part II. *Social Casework, 49,* 418-426.

Patrick, P. K. S. (1981). *Health care worker burnout, what it is, what to do about it.* Chicago, IL: Inquiry Books (Blue Cross/ Blue Shield, Assoc.).

Pennebaker, J.W. (1985). Traumatic experience and psychosomatic disease. *Canadian Psychologist, 26,* 82-95.

Pennebaker, J. W. (1990). *Opening up: The healing power of confiding in others.* New York: Avon.

Pennebaker, J. W. (1999). The effects of traumatic disclosure on physical and mental health: The values of writing and talking about upsetting events. *International Journal of Emergency Mental Health, 1,* 9-18.

Pennebaker, J.W. and Beall, S. (1986). Confronting a traumatic event. *Journal of Abnormal Psychology, 95,* 274 - 281.

Pennebaker, J. and Susman, J. (1988). Disclosure of traumas and psychosomatic processes. *Social Science, and Medicine*, 26, 327-332.

Post, R. (1992). Transduction of psychosocial stress onto the neurobiology of recurrent affective disorder. *American Journal of Psychiatry*, 149, 999-1010.

Pugliese, D. (1988, May). Psychological pressures, media: Israeli Defense Forces confronts soldiers' frustrations. *Armed Forces Journal International*, 28.

Pynoos, R.S, Goeenjian, A. and Steinberg, A.M. (1994). Strategies of disaster intervention for children and adolescents. Paper presented at the NATO conference on stress, coping and disaster in Bonos, France.

Raphael, B. (1986).*When disaster strikes: How individuals and communities cope with catastrophe*. New York: Basic Books, Inc. publishers.

Raphael, B. and Wilson, J.P. (1993). Theoretical and intervention considerations in working with victims of disaster. In J.P. Wilson and B. Raphael (Eds.), *International handbook of traumatic stress studies*. New York: Plenum Press.

Raphael, B. & Wilson, J. (Eds.)(2000). Psychological Debriefing. Cambridge, England:

Rapoport, L. (1965). The state of crisis: Some theoretical considerations. In Howard J. Parad, (Ed.). *Crisis intervention: Selected readings*. New York: Family Service Association of America.

Ravenscroft, T. (1994). *Going critical: GMB/ Apex and T&G Unions 1994 survey of occupational stress factors in accident and emergency staff in the London Ambulance Service*. London: GMB/Apex and T&G Unions.

Reese, J. T. (1987). *A history of police psychological services*. Washington, DC: U.S. Department of Justice, Federal Bureau of Investigation.

Reese, J.T. (Ed.). (1991). *Critical incidents in policing, revised*. Washington, DC: U.S. Department of Justice: Federal Bureau of Investigation.

Reese, J. T., Horn, J. M. and Dunning, C. (Eds.) *Critical incidents in policing - revised*. Washington, DC: US Government Printing Office, 1991.

Richards, D. (1999, April) A field study of CISD vs. CISM. Paper presented to the 5th World Congress on Stress, trauma, and Coping, Baltimore.

Robinson, R. (Ed.). (1986, August). "Proceedings from a conference on dealing with stress and trauma in emergency services", Melbourne, Australia.

Robinson, R. (Ed.). (1991). "Discussion paper, Australian Critical Incident Stress Association, Team accreditation". Melbourne: Victoria, Australia.

Robinson, R. (1994). *Follow-up study of health and stress in ambulance services Victoria, Australia,* Part I. Melbourne, Australia: Victorian Ambulance Crisis Counselling Unit.

Robinson, R. C. and Mitchell, J. T. (1993). Evaluation of psychological debriefings. *Journal of Traumatic Stress*, 6(3), 367 - 382.

Robinson, R.C. & Mitchell, J.T. (1993). Evaluation of psychological debriefings. *Journal of TraumaticStress, 6(3), 367 - 382.*

Robinson, R.C. & Mitchell, J.T. (1995). Getting Some Balance Back into the Debriefing Debate. *The Bulletin of the Australian Psychological Society,* 17 (10), 5 - 10.

Roemer, L. and Borkovec, T. (1994). Effects of suppressing thoughts about emotional material. *Journal of Abnormal Psychology,* 103, 467 - 474.

Rogers, O. (1992). "An examination of critical incident stress debriefing for emergency service providers". Unpublished doctoral dissertation, University or Maryland.

Rose, S. & Bisson, J. (1998). Brief early psychological interventions following trauma: A systematic review of literature. *Journal of Traumatic Stress,* 11, 697-710.

Rosenman, I. (1984). Cognitive determinants of emotion. In P. Shaver (Ed.), *Human Stress* (p. ix-xi). New York: AMS Press.

Roth, S. and Newman, E. (1993). The process of coping with incest for adult survivors. *Journal of Interpersonal Violence,* 8, 363-377.

Rubin, J. G. (1990). Critical incident stress debriefing: Helping the helpers. *Journal of Emergency Nursing,* 16 (4), 255-258.

Rueveni, U. (1979). *Networking families in crisis: Intervention strategies with families and social networks.* New York: Human Sciences Press.

Salmon, T. W. (1919). War neuroses and their lessons. *New York Medical Journal,* 109, 993-994.

Sapolsky, R., Krey, L. and McEwen, B. (1984). Stress down regulates corticosterone receptors in a site specific manner in the brain. *Endocrinology,* 114, 287-292.

Schnitt, J.M. (1993). Traumatic stress studies: What's in a name? *Journal of Traumatic Stress,* 6, 405 - 408.

Scurfield, R. M. (1985). Post trauma stress assessment and treatment: Overview and formulation. In C.R. Figley (Ed.), *Trauma and its wake: The study and treatment of post-traumatic stress disorder.* New York: Brunner Mazel.

Seligman, M.E.P. (1995). The effectiveness of psychotherapy. *American Psychologist,* 109, 993-994.

Seligmann, Jean (1994, September 26). Cops who kill- Themselves. *Newsweek,* 124, 58.

Selye, H. (1956). *The stress of life.* New York: McGraw-Hill.

Selye, H. (1974). *Stress without distress.* Philadelphia: Lippincott.

Selye, H. (1976). *Stress in health and disease.* Boston: Butterworth.

Selye, H. (1980). The stress concept today. In I.L. Kutash and L.B. Schlesinger (Eds.), *Handbook on stress and anxiety: Contemporary knowledge, theory and treatment.* San Francisco: Jossey-Bass Publishers.

Shalev, A.Y. (1994). Debrifing following traumatic exposure. In R.J. Ursano, B.G. McCaughey and C.S. Fullerton (Eds.), *Individual and community responses to trauma and disaster: The structure of human chaos.* Cambridge, UK: Cambridge University Press.

Silver, R.L., Boon, C. and Stones, M.H. (1983). Searching for meaning in misfortune: Making sense of incest. *Journal of social issues,* 39, 81 - 102.

Sinyor, D.S., Schwartz, S., Peronnet, F., Brisson, G., and Seraganian, P. (1983). Aerobic fitness level and reactivity to psychosocial stress. *Psychosomatic Medicine,* 45, 205-217.

Slaikeu, K. A. (1984). *Crisis intervention: A handbook for practice and research.* Boston, MA: Allyn and Bacon, Inc.

Sloan, I.H., Rozensky, R.H. Kaplan, L. and Saunders, S.M. (1994). A shooting incident in an elementary school: Effects of worker stress on public safety, mental health and medical personnel. *Journal of Traumatic Stress,* 7(4), 565 - 574.

Small, R., Lumley, J., Donohue, L., Potter, A., & Waldenstrom, U. (2000). Randomised controlled trial of midwife led debriefing to reduce maternal depression after operative childbirth. *British Medical Journal,* 321, 1043-1047.

Smith, J.R. (1985). Rap groups and group therapy for Vietnam veterans. In A.S. Blank, S.M. Sonnenberg, and J. Talbott (Eds.). *Psychiatric problems in Vietnam veterans.* Washington, DC: American Psychiatric Press.

Smith, K.J. and Everly, G.S. (1992, Dec). "A structural model and configural analysis of the relationship between stressors and disease among accountants." Paper presented to the Second NIOSH/APA Conference on Occupational Stress, , Washington DC.

Solomon, Z. ( 1986). Front line treatment of Israeli combat stress reaction casualties: An evaluation of its effectiveness in the1982 Lebanon War. *Israeli Defense Forces Journal,* 3(4), 53-59.

Staff report. (1984, July). Glenn Srodes, 79 dies, Chief of Staff of Hospital. *Pittsburgh Post Gazette.* Pittsburgh, PA.

Sternbach, R. (1966). *Principles of psychophysiology.* New York: Academic Press.

Swanson, W.C., & Carbon, J.B. (1989). Crisis intervention: Theory and Technique. In Task Force Report of the American Psychiatric Association. *Treatments of Psychiatric Disorders.* Wash. D.C.: APA Press.

Taplin, J.R. (1971). Crisis theory: Critique and reformulation. *Community Mental Health Journal,* 7, 13-23.

Taylor, A.J.W and Frazer, A.G. (1982). The stress of post disaster body handling and victim identification work. *Journal of Human Stress,* 8(12), 4-12.

Thompson, J. and Suzuki, I. (1991). Stress in ambulance workers. *Disaster Management, 3*(4), 193-197.

Tindall, J.A. and Gray, H.D. (1985). *Peer power: Becoming an effective peer helper.* Muncie, IN: Accelerated Development, Inc.

Trimble, M. (1981). Post-truamatic neurosis. New York:Wiley.

Tritt, P. (1984). *Mayflower (Denver, CO) Critical incident stress debriefing team protocols.* Denver Colorado Swedish Hospital System, Paramedic Training Program.

Tritt, P. (1986). *Considerations in developing a critical incident stress debriefing team* (handout material for team training). Denver Colorado: Mayflower CISD Team.

Turnbull, G., Busuttil, W., & Pittman, S. (1997). Psychological debriefing for victims of acute burn trauma. *British Journal of Psychiatry, 171,* 582.

Turner, S.W., Thompson, J., and Rosser, R.M. (1993). The kings cross fire: Early implications for organizaing a "phase - two" response. In J.P. Wilson and B. Raphael (Eds.), *International handbook of traumatic stress syndromes.* New York: Plenum Press.

van der Hart, O., Brown, P. and van der Kolk, B. (1989). Pierre Janet's treatment of post-traumatic stress. *Journal of Traumatic Stress, 2,* 379 - 396.

Viney, L. L. (1976). The concept of crisis: A tool for clinical psychologists. *Bulletin of the British Psychological Society, 29,* 387 - 395.

Wagner, M. (1979). Airline disaster: A stress debriefing program for police. *Police Stress.* 2(1), 16 - 20.

Wagner, M. (1979). Stress debriefing - Flight 191: A department program that worked. *Police Star,* 4 - 8.

Watchorn, J.(2000, August). Role of debriefing in the prevention of PTSD. Paper presented to the Inagural Conference on stress, Trauma, & Coping in the Emergency services and Allied Professions. Melbourne, Australia.

Wee, D.F., Mills, D.M. & Koelher, G. (1999). The effects of Critical Incident Stress Debriefing on emergency medical services personnel following the Los Angeles civil disturbance. *International Journal of Emergency Mental Health, 1,* 33-38.

Weller, D. and Everly, G. (1985). Occupational health through physical fitness programming. In G. Everly and R. Feldmen (Eds.), *Occupational health promotion* (pp.127 - 146). New York: Macmillan.

Wessley, S., Rose, S., & Bisson, J. (1998). A systematic review of brief psychological interventions (debriefing) for the treatment of immediate trauma related symptoms and the prevention of post traumatic stress disorder (Cochrane Review). *Cochrane Library,* Issue 3, Oxford, UK: Update Software.

Western Management Consultants. (1996). *The Medical Services Branch*

*CISM Evaluation Report.* Vancouver, B.C.: Author.

Williams, T. (1993). Trauma in the workplace. In J.P. Wilson and B. Raphael (Eds.), *International handbook of traumatic stress syndromes.* New York: Plenum Press.

Wilson, J.P. and Raphael, B. (Eds.). (1993). *International handbook of traumatic stress syndromes.* New York: Plenum Press.

Wilson, J.P., Harel, Z., and Kahan, B. (Eds.). (1988). *Human adaption to extreme stress: From the holocaust to Vietnam.* New York: Plenum Press.

World Health Organization. (1992). *International classification of diseases, tenth edition.* Geneva: United Nations.

Yalom, I. (1970). *The theory and practice of group psychotherapy.* New York: Basic Books.

Yandrick, R. (1990, January). Critical incidents. *EAPA Exchange,* pp.18 - 23.

# INDEX

Critical Incident Stress Debriefing
15, 45, 51, 52, 54, 55, 70, 84, 101, 135, 137, 138, 139, 233, 251
Critical Incident Stress Management
15, 45, 46, 50, 51, 58, 135, 199, 216, 218, 245, 255, 271, 272, 274, 279, 284
Critical Incident Stress Management team  77, 245, 260, 272, 284
CRT  135, 136, 137, 138, 141, 144, 216, 232, 243, 252, 272, 284, 285
cultural difference  150
cumulative stress  227, 267

**D**

debriefing  15, 41,  45, 46, 5 1, 55, 57, 7 0, 73, 84, 1 01, 130, 135,
    137, 142, 148, 149, 167, 189, 195, 199, 204, 217, 222, 225, 233, 251, 259, 273, 287,
    288, 284,  286,  288,  289,  290,  291,  292,  293,  294,  295,  297, 2
    98, 299, 300
defusing  40, 42, 48, 5 7, 59, 62, 68, 70, 89, 97,  98, 101, 103,
    108, 112,  114, 121,  122, 123, 12 4, 125, 126, 1 27, 128, 129, 130,
    131, 132,  133, 141, 1 45, 146, 1 89, 190, 191,  194, 201, 212,
    219, 220, 233, 255, 256, 267, 273, 282, 297, 299
demobilization  48, 102,  103, 104,  105, 106, 107,  108, 109, 110,
    111, 112, 113, 114, 115, 127, 134, 146, 189, 191, 200, 219, 220
denial  62, 125, 148, 191, 192, 211, 213
disaster  30, 32, 42,  43, 45, 50, 51, 52, 55,  58, 65, 70, 73, 85,
    101, 102, 103, 104, 105,  106, 107, 109, 110, 114, 115,  127,
    134, 136, 138, 139, 146, 148, 149, 190, 191, 192,  195,  216,
    217, 218, 219, 220,  226, 227, 228,  230,  231,  233, 252,  259,
    272, 276, 284, 289, 295, 296
disaster drill  107, 295
disaster worker  42, 51, 55, 103, 110, 136, 192, 216, 230, 231, 272
Disorders of Arousal  25
distress  17, 24, 32, 33, 49, 50, 61, 63, 85, 91,  92,  93,  94, 95,
    96, 97, 98, 9 9, 114,  115, 125,  128, 131,  132, 136,  138,
    139, 144, 145, 154, 158, 159, 161, 162, 16 5, 167,  170,  175,
    177,  178,  181,  182, 184,  199, 209, 215,  217, 219, 222,  224,
    229, 248,  249, 253,  255, 256,  279, 286,  287, 288, 291, 294, 296

**E**

emergency medical
    55, 58, 91, 110, 123, 137, 140, 160, 231, 233, 244, 248, 272, 280
emergency service personnel  42, 43, 71, 113, 115, 170, 227, 288
Emotional Integration 20
endocrine axis  21, 22, 23, 28

*eustress* 17

*excessive stress* 15, 17, 20, 23, 24, 25, 26, 27, 28, 41, 42, 43, 66

*Eye Movement Desensitization and Reprocessing* 222

**F**

*fact phase* 62, 167, 171, 172, 173, 175, 183, 196, 231

*family support services* 43, 256

*fire* 30, 46, 51, 52, 55, 58, 67, 85, 87, 110, 137, 140, 160, 184, 218, 230, 231, 233, 244, 246, 248, 255, 272, 273, 280, 283

*fire department* 55, 67

*fire fighter* 30, 51, 52, 55, 85, 87, 230, 233, 244, 255, 280

*fire service* 58, 272, 273

*follow-up services* 57, 86, 133, 182, 186, 196, 233, 251, 252, 286, 288, 289, 292

*food* 105, 106, 108, 109, 110, 111, 114, 154, 155, 217, 288, 292

**G**

*grief* 61, 63, 176, 211, 213, 214, 215, 267, 280, 287

**H**

*homeostatic failure theory* 24

*hormone* 22, 23

*hospital* 46, 48, 49, 52, 55, 58, 71, 91, 221, 246, 251, 272, 274, 277, 280, 283

*hypersensitivity* 25, 38, 39, 40

*hysterical disorder* 17

**I**

*In-service education* 282

*incident report* 155, 157

*informal discussion* 260

*insurance* 251, 254

*International Critical Incident Stress Foundation* 156, 192, 199, 261, 263, 275, 293

*introductory remark* 130, 161, 163, 170, 196, 277

**L**

*law enforcement* 53, 54, 55, 58, 68, 91, 110, 140, 184, 233, 272, 273

legal action  60, 276
life change theory  24
line of duty death  71, 148, 168, 207, 211, 214, 226, 266, 287, 288, 289
linking mechanism  16

## M

maladaptive coping  27
mass disaster  148, 227, 228, 230, 233
mental health professionals
    51, 97, 98, 141, 144, 244, 245, 248, 250, 251, 252, 269
military  47, 48, 49, 50, 55, 58, 70, 112, 113, 221, 272

## N

neuroanatomy  21
neuromuscular nervous system  22
neurotransmitter  38, 39
nurse  51, 55, 70, 73, 91, 123, 221, 233, 244, 245, 250, 255, 256, 273

## O

occupational stress  20, 249
on scene support  42, 91, 92, 93, 94, 99, 114, 200, 273, 299

## P

paramedic  52, 55, 123, 230, 244, 272
parasympathetic nervous system  21
peer counseling  40, 55, 255, 256, 257
peer support  41, 89, 140, 141, 159, 244, 255, 258, 266
personality change  32
physical illness  38, 41
physician  19, 51, 244, 245, 273
police officer  51, 52, 53, 54, 70, 85, 87, 123, 230, 244, 255
post debriefing  180, 182, 212
posttraumatic stress
    29, 30, 31, 35, 37, 38, 39, 40, 43, 59, 66, 67, 68, 73, 85, 227, 233
Posttraumatic Stress Disorder  29, 31, 36, 43, 67, 85, 203, 254, 266
prevention  40, 43, 57, 60, 65, 68,  85, 102, 139, 194,  233, 284,  286,
    294
primary victim  68, 93, 137, 200
primary victims  68, 93, 137, 200
professional support personnel  244, 245, 251, 254
protective barrier  60, 203

stress reaction  28, 29, 30, 47, 49, 52, 70, 73, 85, 91,  102, 104,  110,
    136, 137, 138, 177, 219, 244, 263, 283, 288
stress response  16, 18, 19, 20, 21, 22, 23, 25, 27, 28, 67, 73, 138
stressor  15, 16, 19, 20, 21, 26, 28, 32, 34, 46, 47, 59, 145
suicide  53, 68, 71, 139, 145, 267
supervision  125, 291
sympathetic nervous system  21, 26
symptom phase  62, 130, 176, 177, 193

**T**

Target Organ Arousal  23
teaching phase  161, 163, 177, 178, 179, 208, 209, 213, 226
team development  261, 262, 292
team evaluation  297
team leader  128, 141, 154, 159, 160, 161, 164,  166, 171,  174, 222,
    247, 299
team liaison  257, 260
tertiary victim  137
thought phase  62, 173, 174, 175, 183, 193, 196, 209, 212, 222
transducer  21
trauma  15, 26, 27, 29, 30, 31, 32, 33,  34, 35, 36, 37,  38, 39,  40,
    41, 42, 43, 45, 46, 47, 49, 50, 54,  55, 56,  57, 59, 60,  61, 62,
    63, 65, 66,  67, 68, 70, 71, 73, 77, 78, 85, 86,  89, 101, 102,
    103, 122, 123,  126, 127, 128, 129, 131, 132,  133, 135,  136,
    137, 138, 139,  144,  148, 149, 159, 169, 189, 190,  191, 192,
    193, 194,  195, 203,  212,  216,  221, 222, 225, 227, 229, 230,
    231, 232, 233, 244,  252, 253,  255, 257, 269,  271, 272, 273,
    284, 296, 297
trauma membrane  60
traumatic event  26, 30, 31, 32, 33, 34, 35, 49, 60, 61, 62, 65, 77, 85,
    86, 89, 122, 123, 126, 129, 133, 135, 137, 138, 148,  159, 169,
    190, 194, 203, 221, 225, 229, 252, 253, 255, 272, 273, 297
traumatic stress  26, 29, 30, 31, 32, 35, 36, 37, 38, 39, 40, 42, 43,
    46, 47, 50, 55, 57, 59, 65, 66, 67, 70, 73, 85, 86, 123,  133,
    136, 137, 227, 232, 233, 244, 257, 269, 271, 272, 284
traumatologist  40, 61

# V

*Ventilating the Stress Response* 26, 27
*victim* 29, 30, 35, 37, 39, 47, 50, 51, 59, 60, 65, 67, 68, 70, 85, 88, 93, 137, 138, 139, 145, 191, 200, 217, 219, 220, 252, 272, 296
*volunteer* 41, 92, 291

# W

*weak organ theory* 24
*Wild Land Fire Fighter* 245
*world view* 203